101
GREAT IDEAS
for
Introducing
Key Concepts
in
Mathematics

Author's Note

How often does a world-class mathematician lend his superior intelligence to support the knowledge base of high school mathematics teachers?

Dr. Herbert A. Hauptman, the first mathematician to win the Nobel Prize (1985 Chemistry Prize for a mathematical solution to a problem in crystallography), is an extraordinarily busy man, administering a major research institute and invited to lecture all over the world. Nevertheless, he took the time to coauthor this book—and claimed to enjoy every minute of it. He mentioned how rewarding it was to look at mathematics through a different lens—for the purpose of making the subject interesting for young people. It was fun for him!

As a team, we came up with some unique ideas (Dr. Hauptman claims some may even be entirely original—a rarity in mathematics at this level). For me, working with this brilliant, kind, and gentle man was one of the most exhilarating experiences of my professional career. The challenging discussions, aimed at selecting and refining our ideas to offer teachers the best possible material, were enjoyable and professionally rewarding. I hope the fruit of this most delightful project will enlighten secondary school mathematics teachers for many years to come.

Alfred S. Posamentier
October 18, 2000

101 GREAT IDEAS

for
Introducing
Key Concepts

in
Mathematics

A Resource for Secondary School Teachers

Alfred S. Posamentier
Herbert A. Hauptman

CORWIN PRESS, INC.
A Sage Publications Company
Thousand Oaks, California

Copyright © 2001 by Corwin Press, Inc.

For information:

Corwin Press, Inc.
A Sage Publications Company
2455 Teller Road
Thousand Oaks, California 91320
E-mail: order@corwinpress.com

Sage Publications Ltd.
6 Bonhill Street
London EC2A 4PU
United Kingdom

Sage Publications India Pvt. Ltd.
M-32 Market
Greater Kailash I
New Delhi 110 048 India

Printed in the United States of America

Library of Congress Cataloging-in-Publication Data

Posamentier, Alfred S.
      101 great ideas for introducing key concepts in mathematics: A resource for secondary school teachers / by Alfred S. Posamentier and Herbert A. Hauptman
          p. cm.
   ISBN 0–7619–7512–8 (cloth: acid-free paper)
   ISBN 0–7619–7513–6 (pbk.: acid-free paper)
      1. Mathematics—Study and teaching (Secondary) I. Title: One hundred one great ideas for introducing key concepts in mathematics. II. Title: One hundred and one great ideas for introducing key concepts in mathematics. III. Hauptman, Herbert A. (Herbert Aaron), 1917- IV. Title.

QA11.P617 2000
510.71'2—dc21

                                            00–034558

01   02   03   04   05   06   07   10 9 8 7 6 5 4 3 2 1

Production Editor:	Nevair Kabakian
Editorial Assistant:	Candice Crosetti
Typesetter/Designer:	Technical Typesetting Inc.
Cover Designer:	Michelle Lee

CONTENTS

Preface

One of the most difficult tasks a mathematics teacher faces in the teaching process is finding interesting ways to introduce new topics or developing new concepts for a class. If the textbook does not present clever developments, the teacher must search for alternatives. Obviously, it is easier simply to follow the textbook's approach, which may be dull and uninspiring for the students. As a result, the students may see mathematics as a meaningless jumble of rules presented by the teacher and imitated by the students. Students are often bored and uninterested, and make little or no attempt to understand the idea being developed. They simply memorize the rule or algorithm as it is given and assume that if they can master these rules, then they will succeed on tests. The extent to which such students understand the concepts for use in later courses or for use in real life applications is questionable.

There are a variety of ways to discover new approaches for teaching specific topics in the mathematics classroom. One might use a historical event to introduce a topic, use a physical model to concretize a new concept, use some form of recreational game or challenge to develop an idea, or simply delve into the riches of mathematics to come up with a clever alternative approach to developing a common topic in the school curriculum. None of these techniques is particularly simple. A combination of these techniques is even more difficult to find. However, new approaches to teaching old favorite topics is an essential part of the continuous growth process that every mathematics teacher should experience throughout a teaching career. It is rejuvenating! We respond to this need with this book, which is designed to provide the mathematics teacher with *101 Great Ideas for Introducing Key Concepts in Mathematics: A Resource for Secondary School Teachers*. A by-product is a desire to stimulate teachers to search for yet other techniques.

English teachers are derelict in their responsibility if they do not read books regularly. A history teacher must keep abreast of continuously changing world events to make the teaching of history relevant to students. The science teacher must be aware of new developments in science. Where does the responsibility of the mathematics teacher lie in this regard? New developments in mathematics (such as the proofs of Fermat's last theorem and the four-color map problem), although they may be of general interest to students if presented properly, have technical aspects far beyond high school students' reach. Thus, new developments in mathematics are not particularly appropriate for the mathematics classroom. However, the mathematics teacher does have a professional responsibility to read mathematics books and journals. Doing so enriches the instructional program, and results in new and more exciting ways to teach the material in the syllabus. This book should begin to motivate such explorations.

This book presents motivational ways to teach many of the key topics in the secondary school curriculum. The suggested teaching approaches are presented as though the teacher is completely unfamiliar with them as well as with their underlying mathematics. Every effort has been made to make the discussions clear and complete. The concepts and topics presented here have been chosen as representative of those most commonly taught in the secondary school curriculum.

Some mathematics teachers feel that students who reach high school should no longer require physical models to comprehend mathematical concepts. Learning theorists have found that this is not always true. Chronological age does not always match mental maturity. Many adolescents still need the comfort of a physical model when they are learning a new concept. Consequently, some of the ideas presented in this book involve a hands-on format with materials or devices used by the students and the teacher. Naturally, there is still a heavy reliance on the chalkboard and overhead projector, the standard "tools of the trade." However, the use of a computer is also included.

The format used in this book will enable the teacher to easily find teaching ideas for the specific topic being taught. We arranged the topics by classical subject matter (algebra, geometry, trigonometry, probability and statistics, and miscellaneous topics), yet the actual location of an individual topic may vary with different state curricula.

The topic of each unit is provided by the identifying title. Then the **objective** to be attained by implementing the unit is stated and the **materials** that may be required are listed. The subsequent discussion of the technique or **procedure** is presented with sufficient detail so that a teacher who is entirely unfamiliar with the mathematics underlying the proposed activity will have enough support to feel comfortable with the procedure.

With the exception of the last five units of this book, the units are all independent of one another. The last five units must be read in sequence.

Teachers should begin by reading the book and noting the topics that may be of special interest. These should be tried in class. Teachers should find a marked increase in the interest and comprehension of the mathematics being presented. Finally, teachers should begin to establish a personal collection of teaching ideas beyond those presented in this book, by getting inspiration from professional journals, reading mathematics books, attending lectures at professional conferences, or simply by observing experienced colleagues. We hope that this book will serve as a springboard for teachers to begin collecting their own great ideas for introducing the key concepts they teach!

Acknowledgments

To select 101 ideas to represent the high school curriculum is a daunting task. We are grateful to some ideas offered by Steven R. Conrad, Dr. Stephen Krulik, and Dr. Stephen E. Moresh. The careful proofreading of the final manuscript is also of paramount importance when preparing such a book. For that task, we thank most sincerely Jacob Cohen and Steven R. Conrad. A word of thanks to Sandra L. Finken for her excellent typing of technical parts of the manuscript, and special thanks to our respective, nonmathematical muses Barbara and Edith.

Alfred S. Posamentier
Herbert A. Hauptman
October 18, 2000

About the Authors

Alfred S. Posamentier is Professor of Mathematics Education and Dean of the School of Education of the City College of the City University of New York. He is the author and coauthor of numerous mathematics books for teachers and secondary school students. As a guest lecturer, he favors topics regarding aspects of mathematics problem solving and the introduction of uncommon topics into the secondary school realm for the purpose of enriching the mathematics experience of those students. The development of this book reflects these penchants and grew out of his desire to bring new ideas into the regular classroom instruction.

After completing his AB degree in mathematics at Hunter College of the City University of New York, he took a position as a teacher of mathematics at Theodore Roosevelt High School in the Bronx (New York), where he focused his attention on improving the students' problem-solving skills. He developed the school's first mathematics teams (both at the junior and senior level). He also established a special mathematics class designed to encourage students to explore familiar topics from an unusual viewpoint, and to study topics that are not part of the secondary school curriculum, but are eminently within the scope of an above average high school student. He is currently involved in working with mathematics teachers, nationally and internationally, to help them discover alternative ways to present common topics of the curriculum—essentially the theme of this book.

Immediately upon joining the faculty of the City College (after having received his master's degree there), he began to develop inservice courses for secondary school mathematics teachers, including such special areas as recreational mathematics and problem solving in mathematics.

Dr. Posamentier received his PhD from Fordham University (New York) in mathematics education and has since extended his favorable reputation in mathematics education to Europe. He has been visiting professor at several Austrian, British, and German Universities, most recently at the University of Vienna and at the Technical University of Vienna. At the former, he was a Fulbright Professor in 1990.

In 1989 he was named an Honorary Fellow at the South Bank University (London, England). In recognition of his outstanding teaching, the City College Alumni Association named him Educator of the Year in 1994, and had the day May 1, 1994, named in his honor by the City Council President of New York City. In 1994, he was also awarded the Grand Medal of Honor from the Austrian government, and in 1999, upon approval of Parliament, the President of the Federal Republic of Austria awarded him the title of University Professor of Austria.

Now after 30 years on the faculty of the City College, he still seeks ways to make mathematics interesting to both teachers and students, and sees this book as another medium to reach this objective.

Herbert A. Hauptman is a world-renowned mathematician who pioneered and developed a mathematical method that has changed the whole field of chemistry and opened a new era in research in determination of molecular structures of crystallized materials. Today, Dr. Hauptman's direct methods, which he has continued to improve and refine, are routinely used to solve complicated structures. It was the application of this mathematical method to a wide variety of chemical structures that led the Royal Swedish Academy of Sciences to name Dr. Hauptman recipient of the 1985 Nobel Prize in chemistry.

Dr. Hauptman's work is concerned with the development of methods for determining molecular structures, that is, the arrangement of the atoms in molecules, using the technique of X-ray diffraction. This work is important because it relates molecular structure with biological activity and, therefore, permits a better understanding of life processes. In this way, better methods for the diagnosis and treatment of disease can be devised.

In addition to the Nobel Prize, other honors awarded to Dr. Hauptman include election to the National Academy of Science in 1988, and honorary degrees from the University of Maryland in 1985, The City College of the City University of New York in 1986, University of Parma, Italy, in 1989, D'Youville College, Buffalo, in 1989, Bar-Ilan University, Israel, in 1990, Columbia University in 1990, Technical University of Lodz, Poland, in 1992, Queen's University, Kingston, Canada, in 1993, and Niagara University, New York, in 1996. Additional honors include the City of Buffalo 1995 Citizen of Distinction, 1995; President's Award, Annual Health Care Industries Association Award for Excellence in Western New York Health Care, 1994; Dirac Medal for the Advancement of Theoretical Physics, University of New South Wales, Australia, 1991; Cooke Award, SUNY, 1987; establishment of the Eccles–Hauptman Student Award, SUNY, in 1987; Western New York Man of the Year Award, Buffalo Chamber of Commerce, 1986; Citizen of the Year Award, Buffalo Evening News, 1986; Norton Medal, SUNY, 1986; Induction into Nobel Hall of Science, Museum of Science and Industry, Chicago, Illinois, 1986; Schoellkopf Award, American Chemical Society, (Western NY Chapter) 1986; Gold Plate Award, American Academy of Achievement, 1986; the Patterson Award in 1984 given by the American Crystallographic Association; Scientific Research Society of America, Pure Science Award, Naval Research Laboratory, 1959; Belden Prize in Mathematics, City College of New York, 1936; President, Philosophical Society of Washington, 1969–1970; and President of the Association of Independent Research Institutes, 1979–1980. He has authored over 350 publications, including journal articles, research papers, chapters and books. Dr. Hauptman received his BS from the City College of New York, MS from Columbia University, and PhD from the University of Maryland. From 1947 to 1970, he worked as a mathematician and supervisor in various departments at the Naval Research Laboratory. In 1970, Dr. Hauptman joined the crystallographic group of the Medical Foundation of Buffalo (currently the Hauptman–Woodward Medical Research Institute), of which he became Research Director in 1972. He currently serves as President of the Hauptman–Woodward Medical Research Institute.

With this book, Dr. Hauptman has been able to bring his highly sophisticated knowledge of mathematics and his many years of exploration in the realm of higher mathematics to the advantage of the secondary school audience. His genuine love for mathematics and his desire to motivate America's youth toward an affection and true understanding of mathematics guided Dr. Hauptman through the development of this book.

Introductory Idea

Coming to Terms With Mathematical Terms

Objective: To motivate students throughout their studies to inspect mathematical terms with respect to their roots or common English usage (outside of their mathematical context)

Materials: A good unabridged dictionary and other books on word origins and etymologies

Procedure: Many mathematical terms are seen by students as words whose definitions must be memorized. Students rarely see applications of these words outside their mathematical context. This is akin to having someone learn words from another language simply for use in that language and avoiding tying the words back to their mother tongue, even when possible. To learn the meanings of frequently used mathematical terms without connecting them back to common English usage deprives students of a genuine understanding of the terms involved and keeps them from appreciating the richness and logical use of the English language.

It is advisable to point out to students the use of mathematical terms outside of mathematics. For example, from where does the term **acute angle** come? It comes from the fact that an angle whose measure is less than 90° may be considered a "sharp" point if it is used as an arrowhead. Acute means sharp, as in "an acute pain." Similarly, an **obtuse angle** used in this way would be seen as "dull" or "blunt." A person described as obtuse is not a particularly sharp or bright person.

The term **perpendicular**, which everyone immediately associates with geometry, is also used in common English to mean "moral virtue, uprightness, rectitude."* The **rays** that emanate from the center of a circle to its circumference take on a closely related name, **radius**.

The **rectangle** is a parallelogram that stands erect, and the **right angle**, whose German translation is *rechter Winkel*, shows us the connection to the word "rectangle." Yet, by itself, the word "right" is commonly used in the word "righteous," meaning "upright or virtuous."*

The word **isosceles** typically is used in connection with a triangle or a trapezoid, as in isosceles triangle and isosceles trapezoid. The prefix "isos," which comes from the Greek and means "equal," is also used in many other applications, as in **isomorphism** (meaning equal form or appearance and, in mathematics, two sets in a one-to-one onto relationship that preserves the relationship between

---

* *Webster's Encyclopedic Unabridged Dictionary*, Random House, New York, 1996.

elements in the domain), **isometric** (meaning equal measure), and **isotonic** (in mathematics, sometimes used as isotonic mapping, referring to a monotonic mapping, and in music, meaning that which is characterized by equal tones), just to name a few.

The word "rational" used in the term **rational number** (one that can be expressed as a **ratio** of two integers) means "reasonable" in our common usage. In a historical sense, a rational number was a "reasonable number." Such numbers as $\sqrt{2}$ or π were not considered as "reasonable" in the very early days of our civilization, hence the name **irrational**. The term **ratio** comes directly from the Latin and means "a reckoning, an account, a calculation," whence the word **rate** seems to emanate.

It is clear, and ought to be emphasized, that **natural numbers** got their name because they were the basis for our counting system and were "nature's way" to begin in a study or buildup of mathematics. **Real numbers** and **imaginary numbers** also take their mathematical meanings from their regular English usage.

Even the properties called associative, commutative, and distributive have meanings that describe them. The **associative property** "associates" the first pair (of three elements) of elements together and then the second pair of elements. The **commutative property** changes the position of the first element of two to the second position, much as one "commutes" from the first position (at home) to the second position (at work). The **distributive property** "distributes" the first element between two other elements.

It is clear that when we speak of **ordinal numbers** we speak of the position or order of a number, as in first, second, third and so forth. The **cardinal numbers** refer to the size or magnitude of a number, that is, its importance. In this sense, one might say that the larger the number is, the more "important" it is. In English, we refer to something of "cardinal importance."

From the word "complete," we get the term **complementary**, because it completes something. In its most common usage, an angle is the complement of another if it "completes" a right angle with it.

Once the prefix "con," meaning "with," is understood, such terms as **concentric** (circles that have the same center), **coplanar** (in the same plane), and **concyclic** (points that lie on the same circle) are easily defined. So just pointing out these small hints to students gives the mathematics terms more meaning.

The word "cave," a hollow in a mountain, is related to the term **concave**; both words "paint" similar mental pictures. The term **convex**, stemming from the Latin *convexus*, whith means "vaulted, arched,...drawn together to a point,"* refers to the opposite of concave.

---

* *Webster's Encyclopedic Unabridged Dictionary*, Random House, New York, 1996.

Some words speak for themselves, such as a **bisector**, which sections something into two (equal) parts. The use of the prefix "bi" in mathematics is usually clear. For example, we have **biconditional** (conditional in two directions), **binomial** (having two names or terms), and **bilateral** (two sided). The word **triangle** also is self-descriptive, "three-angled polygon."

When we consider the definition of "factor" in its common English usage (i.e. "one of the elements contributing to a particular result or situation"*), the mathematical definition of **factor** becomes clear (i.e., one of the numbers multiplied to get a product).

If we stretch the imagination just a bit, the term **fraction** also makes sense. It comes from the Latin *fractio*, meaning "a breaking in pieces," which is what a fraction represents: a piece. In some languages, such as German, a language with roots similar to those of English, the word for "fraction" is *Bruch*, which also means "a break or piece," just as the Latin derivation of fraction does. When we *fracture* a bone, we *break* the bone.

It goes without saying that to make students aware of the words used in mathematics, they must know the prefixes that indicate magnitude, such as poly, bi, semi, tri, quad, pent, hex, sept, oct, non, dec and dodec. Combined with suffixes, such as gon and hedron, these prefixes allow students to determine meanings easily.

Not to be overlooked is the term **prime number**, because it stems from the true definition of the word prime. As the word "primitive," which refers to basic elements, in a mathematical sense, a prime number is one of the basic numbers from which, through multiplication, we build the other numbers.

Whenever a new word or term is introduced in mathematics, its relationship to common English usage should be cited. This may require having a good dictionary at ready reference. The time it takes to tie mathematical terms back to ordinary English helps strengthen mathematical understanding as well as enlarge students' regular vocabulary. It is time well spent!

Algebra Ideas

Introducing the Product of Two Negatives

Objective: To have students understand intuitively and abstractly why the product of two negatives is positive

Materials: A video camera and a video tape player

Procedure: Typically a discussion of the product of two negative numbers follows a discussion of the product of a negative number and a positive number (which may be shown as the multiple addition of a negative number or by some other convenient method). This product generally poses no great difficulty for the teacher to demonstrate or for the students to understand.

It is more difficult to develop an analogue for the product of two negative numbers. We can show that the product of two negatives evolves from the pattern

$$(-1)(+3) = -3$$
$$(-1)(+2) = -2$$
$$(-1)(+1) = -1$$
$$(-1)(0) = 0$$

Continuing the pattern seen by successive entries in the second and third numbers of each line gives the following:

$$(-1)(-1) = +1$$
$$(-1)(-2) = +2$$
$$(-1)(-3) = +3$$

How can students get a more genuine intuitive feel for this concept? Perhaps a "real-life" illustration will do.

Consider making a video tape recording of a clear plastic water tank that has a transparent drain tube that we know can empty (*negative*) the tank at the rate of 3 gallons per minute. We tape this event for several minutes, allowing the tank contents to lower. If we run the tape for 2 minutes, the tank will show a decrease of 6 gallons. For 3 minutes, the tank will have emptied 9 gallons.

Suppose we run the tape in reverse (*negative*) for 1 minute. The tank will have refilled by 3 gallons. At twice the normal rate in reverse (*negative*) the tank will gain (*positive*) in content at the rate of 6 gallons per minute. Here a student can see that the product of two negatives (emptying a tank and running a film in reverse) results in a positive.

9

If this is not sufficiently convincing, then perhaps tell students to consider **good guys** (positive) or **bad guys** (negative) who are **entering** (positive) or **leaving** (negative) a town:

1. If the **good guys** (+) **enter** (+) the town,
   that is **good** (+) for the town $(+)(+) = +$
2. If the **good guys** (+) **leave** (−) the town,
   that is **bad** (−) for the town $(+)(-) = -$
3. If the **bad guys** (−) **enter** (+) the town,
   that is **bad** (−) for the town $(-)(+) = -$
4. If the **bad guys** (−) **leave** (−) the town,
   that is **good** (+) for the town $(-)(-) = +$

This example gives students an intuitive feel for the product of two negatives. You, the teacher, should choose the approach most likely to succeed with a particular class.

For the more curious or gifted students, a proof of this concept might be in order. They should know that $(-1) + 1 = 0$. By multiplying both sides of this equation by -1, we get

$$(-1)[(-1) + 1] = (-1)[0]$$

Using the distributive property, we get

$$(-1)(-1) + (-1)1 = (-1)0$$

Because we know that

$$(-1)1 = -1 \quad \text{and} \quad (-1)0 = 0$$

we then have

$$(-1)(-1) + (-1) = 0$$

By adding 1 to both sides of this equation (or by asking "What must be added to (-1) to get 0?"), we get

$$(-1)(-1) = 1$$

which "proves" the relationship.

We might also like to reach back to another topic to validate further that the product of two negatives is a positive. Recall that $(a^x)^y = a^{xy}$, which holds true for $a = 2$, $x = y = -1$.

Therefore,

$$(2^{-1})^{-1} = 2^{(-1)(-1)}$$

By the definition of a negative exponent, we get

$$(2^{-1})^{-1} = \left(\frac{1}{2}\right)^{-1} = 2$$

We can then conclude that

$$2^1 = 2^{(-1)(-1)} \quad \text{or} \quad 1 = (-1)(-1)$$

because, if the bases are equal, so must the exponents be equal.

ALGEBRA IDEA 2

Multiplying Polynomials by Monomials
(Introducing Algebra Tiles)

Objective: To examine the multiplication of polynomials by monomials geometrically

Materials: Algebra tiles

Procedure: In recent years, the use of algebra tiles has enhanced the teaching of abstract concepts and has helped to make working with polynomials more concrete. Depending on the abilities of your students, you may need an entire lesson to introduce the different algebra tiles and to familiarize your students with them. There are commercially made algebra tiles; however, you can make your own by duplicating the following diagrams, on colored paper and cutting them out. Each student should have 10 of each type of tile. Here the nonshaded tiles represent positive numbers and the shaded tiles represent negative numbers

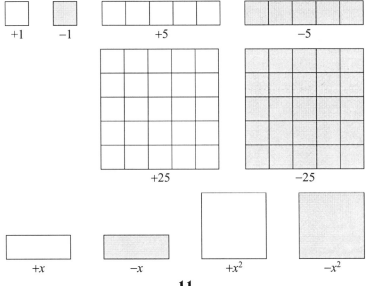

11

The number associated with a rectangular tile represents its area and color. For example, the $+5$ tile has dimensions 5 by 1 and thus its area is 5. Whereas it is unshaded (clear), we use the number $+5$ to identify it. The -5 tile has a similar situation, except that it is shaded and we, therefore, use the number -5 to identify it. Likewise, the $+x$ tile has dimensions x by 1 and its area is, therefore, x. Note that because we are *not* given the length of this tile, we denote it with an x. Note also that an integral number of units do not fit the length.

Pose the question, "How we can multiply $(x + 1)$ by 5 using algebra tiles." If a rectangle is to be created with area $(x + 1) \cdot 5$, it should have length $(x + 1)$ and width 5. Have the students build such a rectangle with their tiles as follows:

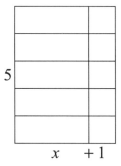

After building such a rectangle, have the students count the algebra tiles to find that the area associated with the rectangle is $5x + 5$. This shows that

$$(x + 1) \cdot 5 = 5x + 5$$

This is equivalent to the distributive law.

Now consider the product $(2x - 1) \cdot x$. The resulting rectangle is

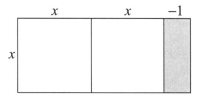

Note that the tile on the right must be a $-x$ tile because of the -1 is one side length. Adding the results represented by the three tiles gives

$$x^2 + x^2 + (-x) \quad \text{or} \quad 2x^2 - x$$

It may be appropriate to show how the distributive law applies here as well.

Before expanding the demonstration to the product of binomials, have the students practice using the technique, especially with respect to signed numbers. Have students use algebra tiles to multiply

1. $(x - 3) \cdot 4$
2. $(2x - 2) \cdot (-1)$
3. $(3 - 2x) \cdot (3)$
4. $(-x + 5) \cdot (-5)$
5. $(x^2 - 3) \cdot (-4)$
6. $(x^2 + 2x - 3)(3)$

Ask students which extra tiles are needed to consider products that involve the variables x and y.

Multiplying Binomials (Using Algebra Tiles)

Objective: To examine the multiplication of binomials by binomials geometrically

Materials: Algebra tiles

Procedure: The basis for this unit is to use the previous work on algebra tiles (see Algebra Idea 2) to multiply binomials. Students should be able to represent algebraically the area of a rectangle, whose sides represent binomials.

Consider the product $(x + 3)^2$. Some students may incorrectly give the answer $x^2 + 9$. To see the correct answer, suggest that students use their algebra tiles to construct a square, each of whose sides has length $x + 3$. The resulting square should look like

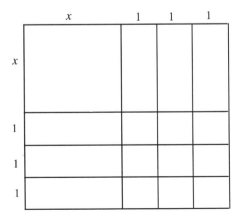

13

Counting the tiles in the resulting square gives one x^2 tile, six x tiles, and nine unit tiles for a total area of $x^2 + 6x + 9$.

This example clarifies the existence of a middle term, $6x$, and its geometric interpretation in the expansion of $(x + 3)^2$.

Now consider the product $(x + 3) \cdot (x - 2)$. Using the previous unit and the preceding model, students should realize that they must construct a rectangle with length $(x + 3)$ and width $(x - 2)$.

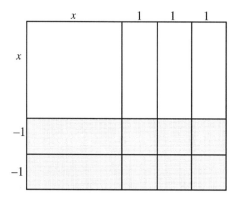

Make sure that the students are careful in multiplying $(-1) \cdot (x) = -x$ to get shaded x tiles.

Likewise, $(-1) \cdot (1) = -1$ means that the six units tiles on the bottom must be shaded.

When combining the tiles, students must consider the idea of a zero sum. For example, adding a $+1$ tile and a -1 tile gives a zero. Likewise, adding a $-x$ tile and a $+x$ tile gives a zero. Thus, we have the sum $x^2 + x - 6$.

The second exercise illustrates that students must take special care to use the correct signs when multiplying with algebra tiles. This is especially apparent in the next example.

Multiply $(x - 3) \cdot (x - 2)$.

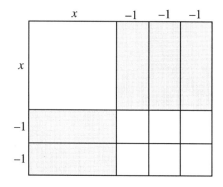

Although this looks like the previous example, extra care must be taken to use the correct signs. Each product of $(-1) \cdot (-1)$ gives an answer of $+1$, which means the six unit squares on the bottom must *not* be shaded.

Once the correct tiles are laid out, the product is easy to read, $x^2 - 5x + 6$.

Eventually students will begin to visualize the tile arrangements and thereby calculate the product mentally.

The preceding process might be extended to finding such products as

1. $(2x + 3) \cdot (x + 4)$
2. $(3x - 5) \cdot (2x + 5)$
3. $(2x - 4) \cdot (2x + 4)$
4. $(3x - 1) \cdot (3x - 5)$

If tiles with dimensions of y units are introduced, students can find products like $(x + y + 1) \cdot (x + 2y - 1)$.

After some practice, students ought to be able to do these products on paper without relying on the tiles; however, the geometric interpretation should be remembered and can be useful later on in the unit on factoring.

$$\boxed{\text{ALGEBRA IDEA } \mathbf{4}}$$

Factoring Trinomials (Using Algebra Tiles)

Objective: To examine the factoring of trinomials geometrically

Materials: Algebra tiles (follows the two previous units using tiles)

Procedure: The basis for this unit is to use students' experience multiplying binomials using algebra tiles and to reverse the process, that is, to represent a trinomial as the area of a rectangle and to find the lengths of its sides. By doing this, students should get a more solid understanding of what is meant by "breaking up" a trinomial so that it can be written as the product of two binomials.

Consider the following problem: What two binomials have the product $x^2 + 6x + 9$? This is the *reverse* of the question we considered when we multiplied binomials. To solve this problem, we will use algebra tiles.

We need to construct a rectangle with area $x^2 + 6x + 9$ and find its length and width. Students should take one x^2 tile, 6 x tiles, and 9 unit tiles. When they form a rectangle, they will probably get the square

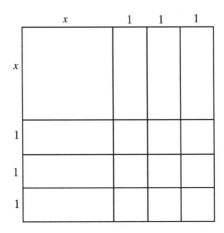

Inspecting the dimensions yields the factors $x + 3$ and $x + 3$. Thus,

$$x^2 + 6x + 9 = (x + 3) \cdot (x + 3) = (x + 3)^2$$

Introduce the term "factoring" and explain that we have "factored" the polynomial $x^2 + 6x + 9$ into a product of binomials.

Now consider factoring $x^2 + 8x + 15$. In this case, a little experimentation will give the rectangle

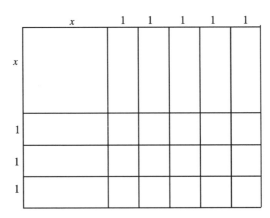

which yields the factors $(x + 5) \cdot (x + 3)$.

Stress the need to form a rectangle with *area* $x^2 + 8x + 15$.

Students should realize that they must arrange the 15 unit tiles (on the bottom) into a small rectangle, before dealing with the eight x tiles. Once they do this, the rectangle falls into place.

Some students may get a slightly different rectangle than shown in the diagram

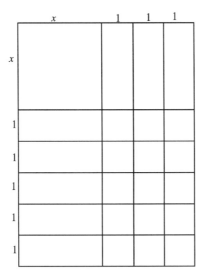

Although the rectangle appears to be different, it has the same area as the previous one. The only difference is that the length and width have been interchanged. This gives the factoring

$$x^2 + 8x + 15 = (x + 3) \cdot (x + 5)$$

This result is, of course, equivalent to the previous one by the commutative law of multiplication. Usually, when factoring using algebra tiles, two possible rectangles arise, with the length and width interchanged.

We are now ready to consider a problem where special care must be taken with respect to the signs of the numbers involved.

Factor $x^2 + x - 6$.

Students should start with one x^2 and six shaded (negative) unit tiles:

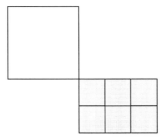

To proceed, they should realize that the two factors of -6 have opposite signs. The diagram suggests that on the top right, we need three x tiles and on the bottom left, we need two x tiles.

Students should experiment with different possibilities. Use two clear x tiles and three shaded ones, or three clear x tiles and two shaded ones. Only the second case yields a middle term of $+x$, as shown in the diagram

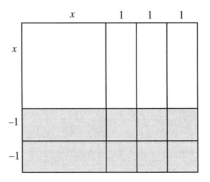

Factor $x^2 - 5x + 6$.

Although this problem is similar to the previous one, the major difference is that students should realize that the missing region must be filled in with shaded (negative) x tiles.

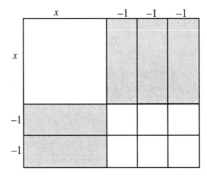

The results agree because each of the unit squares on the bottom is the result of multiplying $(-1) \cdot (-1) = +1$. Thus our result is $x^2 - 5x + 6 = (x - 3) \cdot (x - 2)$.

We consider another problem: factor $x^2 - 1$.

Students should begin with two tiles as follows:

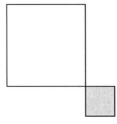

By completing a square using one positive x tile and one negative x tile, we are virtually adding a zero. Thus the factoring becomes $x^2 - 1 = (x - 1) \cdot (x + 1)$.

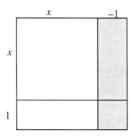

After a while, students can easily progress from this concrete stage of factoring algebraic expressions using algebra tiles to the more abstract stage of factoring using pencil and paper. A major strength of this approach is that it forces students to start with the first and last terms, and then experiment until the middle term comes out correctly. Another advantage to this sort of introduction to factoring is that students continue to identify algebraic concepts with geometric concepts; that is, a trinomial can be considered to be the area of some rectangle whose length and width are binomials.

ALGEBRA IDEA 5

Multiplying Binomials (Geometrically)

Objective: To examine the multiplication of binomials geometrically

Materials: Chalkboard

Procedure: The basis for this unit is to represent algebraically the area of a rectangle whose sides represent binomials. By doing this, students should get a more solid understanding of what is meant by the product of two binomials. It is best to show this procedure by giving a variety of examples.

Consider the product $(x + 3)^2$:

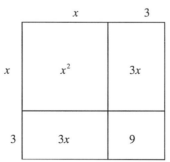

The area we seek is that of the preceding entire square, which is the sum of the four inner regions:

$$x^2 + 3x + 3x + 9 = x^2 + 6x + 9$$

We now consider the product $(x + 5)(x + 3)$:

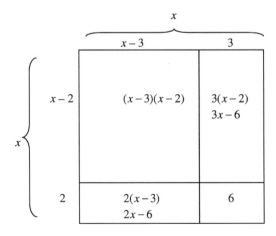

We seek the area of the entire rectangle that comprises the sum of the four inner regions:

$$x^2 + 5x + 3x + 15 = x^2 + 8x + 15$$

A further variation in multiplying binomials is the product $(x + 3)(x - 2)$:

We seek the area of the entire rectangle that comprises the sum of the four inner regions:

The area we seek here is the sum of the areas of the top two rectangles:

$$x^2 - 2x + 3x - 6 = x^2 + x - 6$$

The remaining variation of the two binomial product is $(x - 3)(x - 2)$:

To find the area of the upper left rectangle, we must find the area of the large square and subtract the areas of the other three rectangles from it:

$$x^2 - [(3x - 6) + (2x - 6) + 6] = x^2 - 3x + 6 - 2x + 6 - 6 = x^2 - 5x + 6$$

This activity can be extended to trinomials and other combinations of multiplying two polynomials.

Although the foregoing treatment suggests that the chalkboard be used, cardboard rectangles also can be used to achieve the same effect. It is important to stress that in each case we sought to represent the area of the rectangle that represented the desired product: sometimes it was the entire rectangle and other times it was a part of the larger rectangle. In any case, we have the opportunity to represent the algebraic computation geometrically.

ALGEBRA IDEA 6

Factoring Trinomials (Geometrically)

Objective: To examine the factoring of trinomials geometrically to get a better understanding of the algebraic process

Materials: Chalkboard

Procedure: The basis for this unit is to relate algebraically the representation of the area of a rectangle and the lengths of its sides. By doing this, students should get a more solid understanding of what is meant by "breaking up" a trinomial so that it can be written as the product of two binomials. It is best to show this procedure by giving a variety of examples.

Consider the trinomial $x^2 + 6x + 9$:

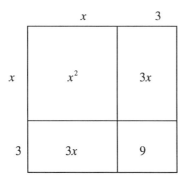

We must partition this trinomial into pieces that can fit a representation of the areas of the smaller rectangles in the diagram. This is like a puzzle, where pieces have to be placed to "fit." We then merely represent the area of the preceding entire square, which is the sum of the four inner regions:

$$x^2 + 6x + 9 = x^2 + 3x + 3x + 9 = (x + 3)^2$$

We now consider the trinomial $x^2 + 8x + 15$, which we wish to factor:

	x	5
x	x^2	$5x$
3	$3x$	15

In a puzzle-solving manner, we must place the components of this trinomial into the rectangles whose areas they are to represent. This requires partitioning the middle term, $8x$. The area of the larger rectangle can be expressed in two ways: the sum of the areas of the four smaller rectangles,

$$x^2 + 8x + 15 = x^2 + 5x + 3x + 15$$

or the area of the entire large rectangle in one multiplication,

$$(x + 5)(x + 3)$$

A further variation in factoring trinomials is seen by deconstructing the trinomial

$$x^2 + x - 6 = x^2 - 2x + 3x - 6$$

		x	3
	$x - 2$	$x(x-2)$ $x^2 - 2x$	$3(x-2)$ $3x-6$
x	2	$2x$	6

This puzzle solution is somewhat more difficult to set up. The sum of the areas of the top two rectangles is represented by the preceding deconstructed trinomial. Its area can be found by taking the product of its length and width: $(x+3)(x-2)$.

The remaining variation of trinomial factoring is $x^2 - 5x + 6$:

The deconstruction of this trinomial is much more complicated and requires a fair amount of insight (and, of course, experience).

Here we will represent the area of the upper left rectangle as the difference between the area of the large square and the sum of the areas of the other three rectangles,

$$x^2 - 5x + 6 = x^2 - 3x + 6 - 2x + 6 - 6 = x^2 - [(3x - 6) + (2x - 6) + 6]$$

which is then equal to the remaining rectangle at the upper left, $(x - 3)(x - 2)$.

This activity is the direct reverse of the preceding unit, but is far more complicated and somewhat more contrived. It is provided to show that multiplication and factoring geometrically can be viewed as reverse operations of each other. Multiplication is the easier one to "see" and do, just as it is so also in arithmetic.

Although the foregoing treatment suggests that the chalkboard be used, cardboard rectangles also can be used to achieve the same effect. It is important to stress that in each case we sought to represent the area of the rectangle that represented the desired product: sometimes it was the entire rectangle and other times it was a part of the larger rectangle. In any case, we have the opportunity to represent the algebraic computation geometrically.

Trinomial Factoring

Objective: To present a simpler method for factoring trinomials

Materials: Chalkboard

Procedure: Factoring simple trinomials is usually a skill that can be easily acquired. However, when there is a coefficient other than 1 for the x^2 term, the factoring process becomes a bit more difficult. We visit this procedure by factoring the example $6x^2 - 7x - 24$.

We follow a series of steps that should lead "automatically" to the factors.

1. Multiply the leading coefficient by the constant and replace the first coefficient with 1

$$x^2 - 7x - (6)(24)$$
$$x^2 - 7x - 144$$

2. Factor the resulting trinomial

$$(x - 16)(x + 9)$$

3. Place the original leading coefficient (here, 6) as the coefficient of x in each term

$$(6x - 16)(6x + 9)$$

4. Factor out and delete common factors from each binomial

$$(3x - 8)(2x + 3)$$

Although this procedure seems a bit convoluted, it does provide an alternative to slower students. For the gifted students, it provides an illustration of algebraic manipulations, which can be justified by inspecting a general situation.

Consider the general problem for the preceding situation:

$$(ax + b)(cx + d) = (ac)x^2 + (ad + bc)x + bd$$

We follow the steps to arrive at the factored form:

1. $(ac)x^2 + (ad + bc)x + bd = x^2 + (ad + bc)x + abcd$
2. $\qquad\qquad\qquad\qquad = (x + ad)(x + bc)$
3. $\qquad\qquad\qquad\qquad = (acx + ad)(acx + bc)$
4. $\qquad\qquad\qquad\qquad = (cx + d)(ax + b)$

Incidentally, this scheme can help you (the teacher) to search for other factorable trinomials to provide as exercises for the students. By letting a and c take on factors of 144, other factorable trinomials can be constructed.

How Algebra Can Be Helpful

Objective: To present a simple problem whose algebraic solution makes it even simpler

Materials: Chalkboard

Procedure: We are inclined to revert to an algebraic solution to a problem that resembles those we have had as exercises in an algebra class. Such a strategy is very common with students. However, presented with a simple arithmetic problem, most students will try trial and error methods in the hope of stumbling onto the correct answer. Intelligent guessing and testing, a more enlightened form of "guess and check," reduces the margin of error. However, sometimes an algebraic solution can be superior. Consider the following example:

Find five pairs of (rational) numbers whose product equals their sum.

Using the intelligent guessing and testing method should yield 2 and 2 as a pair of numbers that satisfies the condition of having the same sum and product. From there on out it gets tougher, because the rest of the numbers that satisfy the required condition are fractions. This is where the usefulness of algebra sets in.

Let a and b represent the sought-after pair of numbers, such that $ab = a + b$. Then $a = \frac{b}{b-1}$. We can see how $a = 2, b = 2$ satisfies this equation. To find other pairs of numbers merely requires us to substitute values for b into the equation to get corresponding values for a. This can be seen in the following table.

b	3	4	5	6	-1	-2	-3
$a = \frac{b}{b-1}$	$\frac{3}{2}$	$\frac{4}{3}$	$\frac{5}{4}$	$\frac{6}{5}$	$\frac{1}{2}$	$\frac{2}{3}$	$\frac{3}{4}$

The algebraic equation can be used to generate many other such pairs of numbers, a matter not so simple without algebra.

Automatic Factoring of a Trinomial

Objective: To provide a method for factoring trinomials that is algorithmic in nature

Materials: Chalkboard

Procedure: The skill of factoring a trinomial usually requires practice and then a feeling for or insight into selection of the right combination of terms to make the correct two binomials. We present here a "system" for factoring a trinomial into two binomials using an automatic procedure.

It is wise to begin this discussion by presenting the product of two binomials and relating the resulting trinomial to these factors. Consider

$$(3x - 2)(2x + 5)$$

which can be multiplied by distributing the first binomial over the terms of the second binomial as

$$(3x - 2)(2x) + (3x - 2)(5) = 6x^2 - 4x + 15x - 10$$

Notice that the product of the first and fourth terms equals the product of the second and third terms (i.e., $-60x^2$). The resulting trinomial is $6x^2 + 11x - 10$.

Look at this in reverse: to factor $6x^2 + 11x - 10$, we break up the middle term into two terms whose sum is $11x$ and whose product equals that of the first and third terms ($-60x^2$); that is, $-4x$ and $+15x$. Then merely factor the common binomial factor as before.

We provide an example of this procedure here. Factor $3x^2 + x - 10$.

Step 1. To split the middle term (x) into two terms whose sum is x and whose product is $(3x^2)(-10) = -30x^2$, we come up with $-5x$ and $6x$.

Step 2. We now factor the common binomial factor from the first two terms and then from the third and fourth terms:

$$3x^2 + 6x - 5x - 10 = 3x(x + 2) - 5(x + 2)$$

Step 3. Factor the binomial again

$$(3x - 5)(x + 2)$$

26

Thus, if a trinomial is factorable into binomials, then it will be possible to split the middle term to yield a product equal to that of the first and third terms of the trinomial. This procedure for introducing factoring may be a bit cumbersome (especially to anyone who is already adept at factoring), but it shows the essence of factoring trinomials. To further convince students of the merit of this procedure, a general case can easily be demonstrated.

Consider the two binomials as factors and generate the trinomial

$$(ax + b)(cx + d) = ax(cx + d) + b(cx + d)$$
$$= acx^2 + adx + bcx + bd$$

Notice that the product of the first and fourth terms equals that of the second and third terms (i.e., $abcdx^2$).

This is the basis for this method of factoring.

Reasoning Through Algebra

Objective: To provide an opportunity to use algebra and some reasoning ability to solve a simple problem

Materials: Chalkboard or Geometer's Sketchpad program

Procedure: Begin by presenting the following problem: Each of the two curved lines (m and n) divides the ellipse in half and partitions the ellipse into the four regions P, Q, R, and S. The vertical line k also divides the ellipse in half, cutting through regions Q and S. How does the area of region P compare to the lightly shaded region of Q?

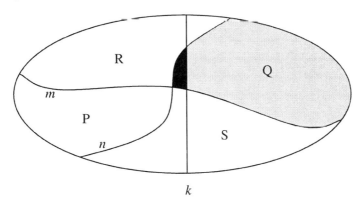

Because each of the lines separates the ellipse into two equal parts, $P + R = Q + S$. Also $P + S = R + Q$. By subtracting these two equations we get $R - S = S - R$. Then $2R = 2S$. Therefore, $R = S$ and $P = Q$. Alternatively, by addition, $2P + R + S = 2Q + S + R$, so $P = Q$ immediately. Whereas the vertical line segment cuts a piece off region Q, the lightly shaded region of Q must be smaller in area than region P. This reasoning and algebraic application is paramount for a good understanding of algebra.

ALGEBRA IDEA 11

Pattern Recognition Cautions

Objective: To show that hasty pattern recognition may or may not be correct

Materials: Chalkboard

Procedure: Present the following sequence and ask for the next number in the sequence:

$$2, 3, 5, 8, \underline{\hspace{1cm}}$$

The expected response from most students is 12. This is obtained by recognizing the pattern as an increasing difference between consecutive terms. The first difference is 1, then 2, then 3, so one might assume that the fourth difference must be 4, hence $8 + 4 = 12$.

One might have recognized another pattern: beginning with 5, each term is the sum of the two predecessor terms. Therefore, $5 + 8 = 13$, which would then be the next number.

It is also possible to see this sequence as one which repeats the four given elements.

2, 3, 5, 8, 2, 3, 5, 8, 2, 3, 5, 8. Therefore, the next number in the sequence (after the 8) is 2.

We can ask the questions, "What pattern did you observe here?" and "How did this pattern help you get the next number?" This activity might go a long way to convince students that mere guessing does not necessarily reveal the desired pattern. The time is here when students get motivated and want to pursue a further study of mathematics, "albeit carefully!"

Caution With Patterns

Objective: To use a deceptive pattern as a way to encourage caution

Materials: Chalkboard

Procedure: Present a very common sequence, such as 1, 2, 4, 8, 16, with the request to find the next member of the sequence. When the next number is given as 31 (instead of the expected 32), cries of "Wrong!" are usually heard. However, 1, 2, 4, 8, 16, 31 can be a legitimate sequence.

To show this, we need to further establish the sequence and then justify its existence in some mathematical way. It would be nice to do this geometrically, because that would provide evidence of a physical nature.

We set up a table of differences (i.e., a chart that shows the differences between terms of a sequence), beginning with the given sequence up to 31, and then work backward once a pattern is established (here at the third difference).

Original sequence	**1**		**2**		**4**		**8**		**16**		**31**
First difference		1		2		4		8		15	
Second difference			1		2		4		7		
Third difference				1		2		3			
Fourth difference					**1**		**1**				

With the fourth differences that form a sequence of constants, we can reverse the process (turn the table upside down) and extend the third differences a few more steps to 4 and 5:

Fourth difference						1		1		1		1	
Third difference				1		2		3		**4**		**5**	
Second difference			1		2		4		7		**11**		**16**
First difference		1		2		4		8		**15**		**26**	
Original sequence	1		2		4		8		16		**31**		**57**

The boldface numbers were obtained by working backward from the third difference sequence. Thus the next numbers of the given sequence are 57 and 99.

The general term is a fourth power expression because we had to go to the third differences to get a constant. The general term (n) is

$$\frac{n^4 - 6n^3 + 23n^2 - 18n + 24}{24}$$

Do not think that this sequence is independent of other parts of mathematics. Consider the Pascal triangle:

```
                1
              1   1
            1   2   1
          1   3   3   1
         \ 1   4   6   4   1
        1 \ 5  10  10   5   1
      1   6 \15  20  15   6   1
    1   7  21 \35  35  21   7   1
  1   8  28  56 \70  56  28   8   1
```

The horizontal sums of the rows of the Pascal triangle to the right of the bold line are 1, 2, 4, 8, 16, 31, 57, 99, 163, which is again our newly developed sequence.

A geometric interpretation can help convince students of the beauty and consistency inherent in mathematics. To do this, we make a chart of the number of regions into which a circle can be partitioned by joining points on the circle.

Number of points on the circle	Number of regions into which the circle is partitioned
1	1
2	2
3	4
4	8
5	16
6	31
7	57
8	99

Now that students can see that this unusual sequence appears in various other fields, a degree of satisfaction may be setting in.

Using a Parabola as a Calculator

Objective: To have students graph the parabola $y = x^2$, perform multiplication and division with it, and justify why it works

Materials: Graph paper and straightedge, or Geometer's Sketchpad program

Procedure: On a large sheet of graph paper (or on Geometer's Sketchpad), have students draw the parabola $y = x^2$. This must be done very accurately. Students are now ready to perform calculations. For example, if they want to multiply $3 \cdot 5$, they would locate the points on the parabola whose abscissas are 3 and -5 (-3 and 5 would also be acceptable.) These points are $(-5, 25)$ and $(3, 9)$. Joining these points with a line segment $(\overline{QR})$ determines a point on the y axis, whose ordinate, 15, is the product of the absolute values of the abscissas of the first two points. See Figure 1.

For further practice, find the product of 2.5 and 3.5. This time, students must draw the line joining points $(2.5, 6.25)$ and $(-3.5, 12.25)$. These are the points on the parabola whose abscissas are 2.5 and -3.5. The ordinate of the point where this line segment, $\overline{GT}$, intersects the y axis is the product of 2.5 and 3.5, that is, 8.75. Naturally, the size of the graph paper determines the degree of accuracy. Noting that division is the inverse operation of multiplication, we can see that $\overline{GT}$ could have been used to find the quotient of $8.75 \div 3.5$.

To determine why this works, consider that $\overline{PQ}$ intersects $y = x^2$ at points (x_1, y_1) and (x_2, y_2), and intersects the y axis at $(0, y_3)$. The proof must conclude that $y_3 = |x_1 x_2|$. See Figure 2.

The proof is as follows:

The slope

$$\overline{PQ} = \frac{y_2 - y_1}{x_2 - x_1} = \frac{x_2^2 - x_1^2}{x_2 - x_1} = x_2 + x_1$$

(since $y_2 = x_2^2$ and $y_1 = x_1^2$).

The slope of $\overline{PQ}$ expressed with any point (x, y) is $\frac{y - y_1}{x - x_1}$. Therefore,

$$\frac{y - y_1}{x - x_1} = x_1 + x_2$$

is the equation of $\overline{PQ}$.

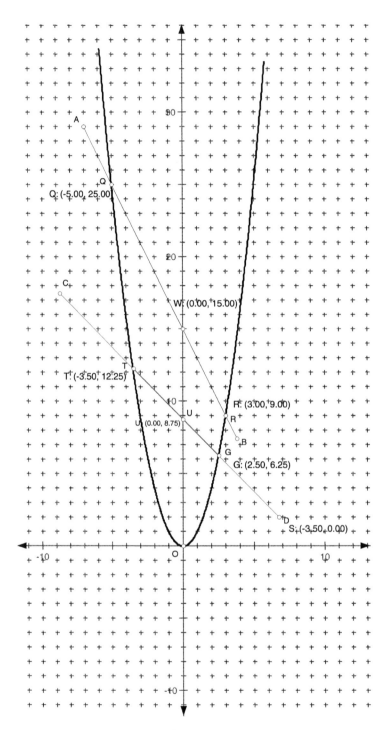

Figure 1

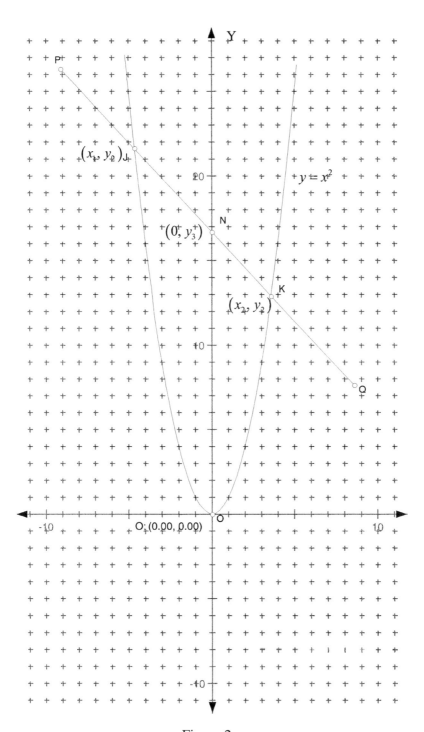

Figure 2

33

At point $(0, y_3)$,

$$\frac{y_3 - y_1}{0 - x_1} = x_1 + x_2 \quad \text{and} \quad y_3 = -x_1^2 - x_1 x_2 + y_1$$

However, $y_1 = x_1^2$; thus, $y_3 = -x_1 x_2$, but this is positive, so $y_3 = |x_1 x_2|$.

Students may wish to experiment with other parabolas to see if there is a more convenient parabola to use for multiplication.

There is another interesting application of this newly established relationship. To construct a segment of length $\sqrt{a}$, we construct a line parallel to the x axis and intersecting the y axis at point $(0, a)$. The segment of that line determined by the y axis and the parabola has length $\sqrt{a}$.

ALGEBRA IDEA **14**

Introducing Literal Equations—Simple Algebra to Investigate an Arithmetic Phenomenon

Objective: To investigate with elementary algebra an incorrect cancellation in fraction reduction that led to a correct result

Materials: Chalkboard

Procedure: Students have been known to do rather strange things when it comes to arithmetic. Some of these strange techniques may lead to a correct answer. Sometimes building on these errors can be quite useful as a motivator or application of an important topic. Here we investigate a rather absurd cancellation scheme in the reduction of fractions that sometimes leads to a correct answer. Under which circumstances does this work and why? This entire demonstration is done with simple algebra. Lots of useful applications of elementary algebra are used.

In his book, *Fallacies in Mathematics*, E. A. Maxwell referred to the following cancellations as howlers:

$$\frac{1\!\!\!/6}{\,\!\!\!/64} = \frac{1}{4} \qquad \frac{2\!\!\!/6}{\,\!\!\!/65} = \frac{2}{5}$$

Begin your presentation by asking students to reduce the following fractions to the lowest terms:

$$\frac{16}{64} \qquad \frac{19}{95} \qquad \frac{26}{65} \qquad \frac{49}{98}$$

After they have reduced each of the fractions to the lowest terms in the usual manner, ask why they didn't simply do it in the following way:

$$\frac{1\!\!\!/6}{6\!\!\!/4} = \frac{1}{4} \qquad \frac{1\!\!\!/9}{9\!\!\!/5} = \frac{1}{5} \qquad \frac{2\!\!\!/6}{6\!\!\!/5} = \frac{2}{5} \qquad \frac{4\!\!\!/9}{9\!\!\!/8} = \frac{4}{8} = \frac{1}{2}$$

At this point your students will be somewhat amazed. Their first reaction is probably to ask if this can be done to any fraction composed of two-digit numbers of this sort. Challenge your students to find another fraction (composed of two-digit numbers) where this type of cancellation works. Students might cite $\frac{55}{55} = \frac{5}{5} = 1$ as an illustration of this type of cancellation. Indicate to them that although this hold trues for all multiples of 11 that yield two-digit results, it is trivial, and our concern is only with proper fractions (i.e., those whose value is less than 1).

After they are thoroughly frustrated, you may begin a discussion about why the preceding four fractions are the only ones (composed of two-digit numbers) where this type of cancellation holds true.

Have students consider the fraction

$$\frac{10x + a}{10a + y}$$

The previous four cancellations were such that when cancelling the as, the fraction was equal to $\frac{x}{y}$. Therefore,

$$\frac{10x + a}{10a + y} = \frac{x}{y}$$

This yields

$$y(10x + a) = x(10a + y)$$
$$10xy + ay = 10ax + xy$$
$$9xy + ay = 10ax$$

and so

$$y = \frac{10ax}{9x + a}$$

At this point have students inspect this equation. They should realize that it is necessary for x, y, and a to be integers, because they were digits in the numerator and denominator of a fraction. It is now their task to find the values of a and x for which y also is an integral.

To avoid a lot of algebraic manipulation, you can have students set up a chart that will generate values of y from $y = \frac{10ax}{9x+a}$. Remind them that x, y, and a must be single digit integers. A portion of the table they will construct follows. Notice that the cases where $x = a$ are excluded, because $\frac{x}{a} = 1$.

x \ a	1	2	3	4	5	6	...	9
1		$\frac{20}{11}$	$\frac{30}{12}$	$\frac{40}{13}$	$\frac{50}{14}$	$\frac{60}{15} = 4$		
2	$\frac{20}{19}$		$\frac{60}{21}$	$\frac{80}{22}$	$\frac{100}{23}$	$\frac{120}{24} = 5$		
3	$\frac{30}{28}$	$\frac{60}{29}$		$\frac{120}{31}$	$\frac{150}{32}$	$\frac{180}{33}$		
$\vdots$								
9								

The portion of the chart that is completed has already generated two of the four integral values of y; that is, when $x = 1$, $a = 6$, then $y = 4$, and when $x = 2$, $a = 6$, then $y = 5$. These values yield the fractions $\frac{16}{64}$ and $\frac{26}{65}$, respectively. The remaining two integral values of y are obtained when $x = 1$, $a = 9$ and when $x = 4$, $a = 9$, yielding $y = 5$, $y = 8$, which in turn yield the fractions $\frac{x}{y} = \frac{19}{95}$ and $\frac{49}{98}$, respectively. This exercise should convince students that there are only four such fractions composed of two-digit numbers.

Students may now wonder whether there are fractions composed of numerators and denominators of more than two digits, where this strange type of cancellation holds true. Have students try this type of cancellation with $\frac{499}{998}$. They should find that

$$\frac{499}{998} = \frac{4}{8} = \frac{1}{2}$$

Soon they will realize that

$$\frac{49}{98} = \frac{499}{998} = \frac{4999}{9998} = \frac{49999}{99998} = \cdots$$

$$\frac{16}{64} = \frac{166}{664} = \frac{1666}{6664} = \frac{16666}{66664} = \frac{166666}{666664} = \cdots$$

$$\frac{19}{95} = \frac{199}{995} = \frac{1999}{9995} = \frac{19999}{99995} = \frac{199999}{999995} = \cdots$$

$$\frac{26}{65} = \frac{266}{665} = \frac{2666}{6665} = \frac{26666}{66665} = \frac{266666}{666665} = \cdots$$

Enthusiastic students may wish to justify these extensions of the original howlers. At this point, students who have a desire to seek out additional fractions that permit this strange cancellation should be shown the fractions

$$\frac{3\!\!\!/32}{8\!\!\!/30} = \frac{32}{80} = \frac{2}{5}$$

$$\frac{3\cancel{8}5}{\cancel{8}80} = \frac{35}{80} = \frac{7}{16}$$

$$\frac{1\cancel{3}8}{\cancel{3}45} = \frac{18}{45} = \frac{2}{5}$$

$$\frac{2\cancel{7}5}{\cancel{7}70} = \frac{25}{70} = \frac{5}{14}$$

$$\frac{1\cancel{6}\cancel{3}}{\cancel{3}2\cancel{6}} = \frac{1}{2}$$

They should verify the legitimacy of this strange cancellation and then set out to discover more such fractions.

Aside from providing an algebraic application that can be used to introduce a number of important topics in a motivational way, this topic can also provide some recreational activities. Here are some more "howlers":

$$\frac{4\cancel{8}\cancel{4}}{\cancel{8}\cancel{4}7} = \frac{4}{7} \qquad \frac{\cancel{5}4\cancel{5}}{6\cancel{5}\cancel{4}} = \frac{5}{6} \qquad \frac{\cancel{4}2\cancel{4}}{7\cancel{4}\cancel{2}} = \frac{4}{7} \qquad \frac{24\cancel{9}}{\cancel{9}96} = \frac{24}{96} = \frac{1}{4}$$

$$\frac{4\cancel{8}4\cancel{8}4}{\cancel{8}4\cancel{8}47} = \frac{4}{7} \qquad \frac{\cancel{5}4\cancel{5}4\cancel{5}}{6\cancel{5}4\cancel{5}4} = \frac{5}{6} \qquad \frac{\cancel{4}2\cancel{4}24}{7\cancel{4}2\cancel{4}2} = \frac{4}{7}$$

$$\frac{\cancel{3}2\cancel{4}3}{4\cancel{3}2\cancel{4}} = \frac{3}{4} \qquad \frac{\cancel{6}4\cancel{8}6}{8\cancel{6}4\cancel{8}} = \frac{6}{8} = \frac{3}{4}$$

$$\frac{14\cancel{7}\cancel{1}\cancel{4}}{\cancel{7}\cancel{1}\cancel{4}68} = \frac{14}{68} = \frac{7}{34} \qquad \frac{\cancel{8}\cancel{7}\cancel{8}\cancel{0}48}{9\cancel{8}\cancel{7}\cancel{8}\cancel{0}4} = \frac{8}{9}$$

$$\frac{1\cancel{4}\cancel{2}\cancel{8}\cancel{5}\cancel{7}\cancel{1}}{\cancel{4}\cancel{2}\cancel{8}\cancel{5}\cancel{7}\cancel{1}3} = \frac{1}{3} \qquad \frac{2\cancel{8}\cancel{5}\cancel{7}\cancel{1}\cancel{4}2}{\cancel{8}\cancel{5}\cancel{7}\cancel{1}\cancel{4}26} = \frac{2}{6} = \frac{1}{3} \qquad \frac{3\cancel{4}\cancel{6}\cancel{1}\cancel{5}\cancel{3}8}{\cancel{4}\cancel{6}\cancel{1}\cancel{5}\cancel{3}84} = \frac{3}{4}$$

$$\frac{7\cancel{6}\cancel{7}\cancel{1}\cancel{2}\cancel{3}\cancel{2}87}{8\cancel{7}\cancel{6}\cancel{7}\cancel{1}\cancel{2}\cancel{3}28} = \frac{7}{8} \qquad \frac{3\cancel{2}\cancel{4}\cancel{3}\cancel{2}\cancel{4}\cancel{3}\cancel{2}\cancel{4}3}{4\cancel{3}\cancel{2}\cancel{4}\cancel{3}\cancel{2}\cancel{4}\cancel{3}\cancel{2}\cancel{4}} = \frac{3}{4}$$

$$\frac{\cancel{1}\cancel{0}\cancel{2}\cancel{5}\cancel{6}\cancel{4}1}{4\cancel{1}\cancel{0}\cancel{2}\cancel{5}\cancel{6}\cancel{4}} = \frac{1}{4} \qquad \frac{\cancel{3}\cancel{2}\cancel{4}\cancel{3}\cancel{2}\cancel{4}3}{4\cancel{3}\cancel{2}\cancel{4}\cancel{3}\cancel{2}\cancel{4}} = \frac{3}{4} \qquad \frac{4\cancel{5}\cancel{7}\cancel{1}\cancel{4}\cancel{2}8}{\cancel{5}\cancel{7}\cancel{1}\cancel{4}\cancel{2}85} = \frac{4}{5}$$

$$\frac{4\cancel{8}4\cancel{8}4\cancel{8}4}{\cancel{8}4\cancel{8}4\cancel{8}47} = \frac{4}{7} \qquad \frac{5\cancel{9}52\cancel{3}8\cancel{0}}{\cancel{9}52\cancel{3}80\cancel{8}} = \frac{5}{8} \qquad \frac{\cancel{4}2\cancel{8}\cancel{5}\cancel{7}14}{6\cancel{4}2\cancel{8}\cancel{5}\cancel{7}1} = \frac{4}{6} = \frac{2}{3}$$

$$\frac{\cancel{5}4\cancel{5}4\cancel{5}4\cancel{5}}{6\cancel{5}4\cancel{5}4\cancel{5}4} = \frac{5}{6} \qquad \frac{6\cancel{9}2\cancel{3}0\cancel{7}6}{\cancel{9}2\cancel{3}0\cancel{7}68} = \frac{6}{8} = \frac{3}{4} \qquad \frac{\cancel{4}2\cancel{4}2\cancel{4}24}{7\cancel{4}2\cancel{4}2\cancel{4}2} = \frac{4}{7}$$

$$\frac{5\cancel{3}8\cancel{4}6\cancel{1}5}{7\cancel{5}\cancel{3}8\cancel{4}6\cancel{1}} = \frac{5}{7} \qquad \frac{2\cancel{0}5\cancel{1}2\cancel{8}2}{8\cancel{2}\cancel{0}5\cancel{1}2\cancel{8}} = \frac{2}{8} = \frac{1}{4} \qquad \frac{3\cancel{1}\cancel{1}6\cancel{8}8\cancel{3}}{8\cancel{3}\cancel{1}\cancel{1}6\cancel{8}8} = \frac{3}{8}$$

$$\frac{\cancel{6}4\cancel{8}\cancel{6}4\cancel{8}6}{8\cancel{6}4\cancel{8}\cancel{6}4\cancel{8}} = \frac{6}{8} = \frac{3}{4} \qquad \frac{4\cancel{8}4\cancel{8}4\cancel{8}4\cancel{8}4}{\cancel{8}4\cancel{8}4\cancel{8}4\cancel{8}47} = \frac{4}{7}$$

This unit provides a motivating application of elementary algebra to investigate an algebraic situation. It is a good use of "literal equations."

37

Introducing Nonpositive Integer Exponents

Objective: To provide students with an understanding of nonpositive integer exponents

Materials: Chalkboard

Procedure: Students who have just begun to understand the nature of positive integer exponents will probably respond to the question, "What does 5^n mean?," with a response such as, "The product of n factors of 5." When asked what the nature of n is, they will probably say it is a positive integer. Try motivating them to consider the nonpositive integers: 0 and the negative integers.

First, if $x \neq 0$ and $m > n$ are positive integers, then clearly $\frac{x^m}{x^n} = x^{m-n}$. If we assume the relationship to be true for arbitrary integers m and n, in particular when $m = n$, it follows that $1 = \frac{x^m}{x^m} = x^{m-m} = x^0$. Therefore, $x^0 = 1$. However, the statement, "x used as a factor 0 times is 1," is meaningless, so to be consistent with the rules of exponents, we *define* $x^0 = 1$; then it has meaning.

In a similar way, a student cannot verbally explain what x^{-4} means. What does it mean to have "x used as a factor -4 times"? Therefore, using the rules of exponents, we can establish a meaning for negative exponents. Since, for example, using our rules of operations with exponents, $x^3 \cdot \frac{x^5}{x^8} = \frac{x^3 \cdot x^5}{x^8} = \frac{x^{3+5}}{x^8} = \frac{x^8}{x^8} = 1$, it follows then that $\frac{x^5}{x^8} = x^{5-8} = x^{-3} = \frac{1}{x^3}$. Therefore, it would be nice for $x^{-3} = \frac{1}{x^3}$, and so we can *define* it this way and our system remains consistent.

You might also show that these definitions enable an observed pattern to continue. Consider

$$3^4 = 81$$
$$3^3 = 27$$
$$3^2 = 9$$
$$3^1 = 3$$

By continuing this pattern of dividing by 3, we find

$$3^0 = 1$$
$$3^{-1} = \frac{1}{3}$$
$$3^{-2} = \frac{1}{9}$$
$$3^{-3} = \frac{1}{27}$$

When we got $\frac{x^k}{x^k} = x^{k-k} = x^0$, we can now consider what value 0^0 should have. Using the same idea, we get $0^0 = 0^{k-k} = \frac{0^k}{0^k}$, which is meaningless, because division by $0^k = 0$ is undefined. Similarly, we cannot define 0^{-k}, because this yields $\frac{1}{0^k}$, which is undefined.

Thus, students can conclude that the base cannot be 0 when the exponent is 0 or negative.

Therefore, the definitions $x^0 = 1$, $x \neq 0$, and $x^{-k} = \frac{1}{x^k}$, $x \neq 0$, become meaningful.

ALGEBRA IDEA **16**

Importance of Definitions in Mathematics (Algebra)

Objective: To demonstrate what can happen when definitions are not heeded in mathematics

Materials: Chalkboard

Procedure: Begin by presenting the following "proof" to the class and then elicit comments:

1. Let $\qquad\qquad\qquad\qquad\qquad\qquad\qquad a = b$
2. Multiply both sides by a $\qquad\qquad\qquad a^2 = ab$
3. Subtract b^2 from both sides $\qquad\quad a^2 - b^2 = ab - b^2$
4. Factor $\qquad\qquad\qquad (a+b)(a-b) = b(a-b)$
5. Divide both sides by $(a-b)$ $\qquad\quad (a+b) = b$
6. Since $a = b$, then $\qquad\qquad\qquad 2b - b$
7. Divide both sides by b $\qquad\qquad\qquad 2 = 1$

An astute student will notice that in step 5 we divided by $a - b$, which is zero, because $a = b$. This violates the definition of division, which prohibits division by 0. The students may ask why division by 0 is not defined. The obvious answer is that if it were permissible, then the dilemma found in the preceding "proof" would hold true and $2 = 1$. You can also appeal to their elementary sense of arithmetic. If $\frac{x}{0} = y$ ($x \neq 0$), then $y \cdot 0 = x$, but there is no value y for which this can be true. Thus division by zero leads to "inconsistencies" and must remain undefined.

There are a number of other demonstrations of weird results where definitions are not heeded. They can be instructive as well as entertaining for students.

1. "Prove" that any two unequal numbers are equal. Assume that $x > y$ and $x = y + z$ when x, y, z are positive numbers. Multiply both sides by $x - y$. Then $x^2 - xy = xy + xz - y^2 - yz$. Subtract xz from both sides:

$$x^2 - xy - xz = xy - y^2 - yz$$

Factoring, we get

$$x(x - y - z) = y(x - y - z)$$

Dividing both sides by $(x - y - z)$ yields $x = y$. Thus x, which was assumed to be greater than y, has been shown to be equal to y. The fallacy occurs in the division by $(x - y - z)$, which is equal to zero.

2. "Prove" that all positive whole numbers are equal. By doing long division, we have, for any value of x,

$$\frac{x - 1}{x - 1} = 1$$

$$\frac{x^2 - 1}{x - 1} = x + 1$$

$$\frac{x^3 - 1}{x - 1} = x^2 + x + 1$$

$$\frac{x^4 - 1}{x - 1} = x^3 + x^2 + x + 1$$

$$\vdots$$

$$\frac{x^n - 1}{x - 1} = x^{n-1} + x^{n-2} + \cdots + x^2 + x + 1$$

Letting $x = 1$ in all of these identities, the right side then assumes the values $1, 2, 3, 4, \ldots, n$. The left side of each of the identities assumes the value $\frac{0}{0}$ when $x = 1$. This problem serves as evidence that $\frac{0}{0}$ can be any number, and is therefore best left undefined.

3. Consider the equation

$$6 + \frac{8x - 40}{4 - x} = \frac{2x - 16}{12 - x} \tag{1}$$

and ask your students if they agree with the statement, "If two fractions are equal and have equal numerators, then they also have equal denominators." Let the students give illustrations using any fractions they choose. Then have them solve Equation 1. Adding the terms on the left-hand side to get

$$\frac{6(4 - x) + 8x - 40}{4 - x} = \frac{2x - 16}{12 - x} \tag{2}$$

However, the left side of Equation 2 is simply $\frac{2x-16}{4-x}$. Hence

$$\frac{2x - 16}{4 - x} = \frac{2x - 16}{12 - x}$$

Because the numerators are equal, this implies $4 - x = 12 - x$. Adding x to both sides, we get $4 = 12$. Again, as in some of the previous examples, division by zero is disguised. Have students find the error. Point out that axioms cannot be blindly applied to equations without considering the values of the variables for which the equations are true. Thus, Equation 1 is not an identity that is true for all values of x; it is satisfied only by $x = 8$. Have students solve $(12 - x)(2x - 16) = (4 - x)(2x - 16)$ to verify this. Thus, $x = 8$ implies that the numerators are zero. You may also have the students prove the general case for $\frac{a}{b} = \frac{a}{c}$, to show that a cannot be zero.

4. Another violated definition also brings us to a dilemma. This example involves neglecting to consider that a quantity has two square roots of equal absolute value: one is positive and the other is negative. As an example, take the equation $16 - 48 = 64 - 96$. Adding 36 to both sides gives $16 - 48 + 36 = 64 - 96 + 36$. Each member of the equation is now a perfect square, so that $(4 - 6)^2 = (8 - 6)^2$. By taking the square root of both sides, we get $4 - 6 = 8 - 6$. Adding 6 to both sides implies $4 = 8$. The fallacy in this example lies in equating the unequal square roots. The correct answer should be $(4 - 6) = -(8 - 6)$.

5. Another often overlooked definition is dramatized by the following demonstration: Students may have "learned" that $\sqrt{a}\sqrt{b} = \sqrt{ab}$; for example, $\sqrt{2} \cdot \sqrt{5} = \sqrt{2 \cdot 5} = \sqrt{10}$. However, this can also cause a dilemma when we consider $\sqrt{-1}\sqrt{-1} = \sqrt{(-1)(-1)} = \sqrt{1} = 1$, because $\sqrt{-1}\sqrt{-1} = (\sqrt{-1})^2 = -1$. Clearly we have incorrectly concluded that $1 = -1$, because both equal $\sqrt{-1}\sqrt{-1}$. Students should try to explain the error. They should realize that we cannot apply the ordinary rules for multiplication of radicals to imaginary numbers. $\sqrt{a}\sqrt{b} = \sqrt{ab}$ is only defined when at least one of the values of a, b is not negative.

6. This can be seen further with the following demonstration: Consider the "proof" that can be used to show $-1 = +1$ is

$$\sqrt{-1} = \sqrt{-1}$$
$$\sqrt{\frac{1}{-1}} = \sqrt{\frac{-1}{1}}$$
$$\frac{\sqrt{1}}{\sqrt{-1}} = \frac{\sqrt{-1}}{\sqrt{1}}$$
$$\sqrt{1}\sqrt{1} = \sqrt{-1}\sqrt{-1}$$
$$1 = -1$$

Have students substitute i for $\sqrt{-1}$ and -1 for i^2 to see where the flaw occurs. With each definition violation, awkward or weird results appear. This in itself justifies the definitions.

Introduction to Functions

Objective: To introduce the concept of a function

Materials: A chalkboard would suffice; however, a toy bow and arrow set might be helpful for demonstration purposes

Procedure: In mathematics, finding concrete analogues to represent abstract concepts is not always easy. One example where a physical model can be used to explain an abstract concept is in development of the notion of a function.

We use the model of a bow shooting arrows at a target. The arrows represent the *domain* and the target represents the *range*. The bow (and its aiming) is the *function*. We will accept that an arrow can be used only once.* We know that the elements in the domain can be used only once and are therefore distinct. The arrows can hit the same point on the target more than once. Therefore, points in the range can be used more than once. This is the definition of a function: a *mapping* of all elements of one set onto another, with the elements of the first set used exactly once. Some points on the target may never be hit by an arrow, but all the arrows must be used. Stated somewhat differently, some elements in the range may not be used, but all elements in the domain must be used.

When all points on the target (the range) are hit,[†] the function (or mapping) is called an *onto function*.

When each point on the target is used only once, the function is called a *one-to-one function*.

When each point on the target is used exactly once (i.e., once and only once), the function is called a *one-to-one onto function* or may be called a *one-to-one correspondence*.

Using the analogy of a bow shooting arrows to a target to represent the concept of a function enables the students to conceptualize this abstract notion in a way that should instill permanent understanding of the concept of a function.

---

* Actually a gun and bullets would be a better analogue than the bow and arrow, because each bullet *really* can be used only once. For this illustration, make it clear that the arrow, once shot, cannot be used again.

[†] Obviously, in reality, an infinite number of arrows would be required, so it must be appropriately simulated.

When Algebra Explains Arithmetic

Objective: To show how some simple arithmetic relationships can be explained algebraically

Materials: Chalkboard

Procedure: Begin by showing students the pattern

$$25 \cdot 25 = 625$$
$$35 \cdot 35 = 1225$$
$$45 \cdot 45 = 2025$$
$$55 \cdot 55 = 3025$$
$$65 \cdot 65 = 4225$$

In each of these cases, the product seems to end with "25" and the remaining two digits form a number that is the product of the tens digit and the tens digit increased by 1; that is,

$$625 = (2)(3) \text{ and } 25$$
$$1225 = (3)(4) \text{ and } 25$$
$$2025 = (4)(5) \text{ and } 25$$

and so on.

Algebra enables us to establish that this pattern holds for all such squarings. The original numbers for squaring are of the form $10n + 5$. By squaring, we get

$$(10n + 5)(10n + 5) = 100n^2 + 100n + 25 = 100(n)(n + 1) + 25$$

We can readily see where the different components come from.

A second and slightly more exciting illustration is as follows. Select any three-digit number with all digits different from one another. Write all six possible two-digit numbers that can be formed from the three digits selected earlier. Then divide their sum by the sum of the digits in the original three-digit number. Students should all get the same answer, 22.

For example, consider the three-digit number 365. Take the sum of all the possible two-digit numbers that can be formed from these three digits:

$$36 + 35 + 63 + 53 + 65 + 56 = 308$$

The sum of the digits of the original three-digit number is $3 + 6 + 5 = 14$, and $\frac{308}{14} = 22$.

Again we begin with a general representation of the number: $100x + 10y + z$. We now take the sum of all the two-digit numbers taken from the three digits:

$$(10x + y) + (10y + x) + (10x + z) + (10z + x) + (10y + z) + (10z + y)$$
$$= 10(2x + 2y + 2z) + (2x + 2y + 2z)$$
$$= 11(2x + 2y + 2z)$$
$$= 22(x + y + z)$$

which, when divided by $(x + y + z)$, is 22.

These illustrations show the value of algebra in explaining simple arithmetic phenomena. There are lots of other similar examples to exhibit the power of algebra. However, there are times when an algebraic solution to a problem is not an advantage. Consider the following problem: Find four consecutive numbers whose product is 120. Algebraically this requires solving an equation such as

$$x(x + 1)(x + 2)(x + 3) = 120$$

Rather than to try to solve this quartic equation, a nonalgebraic solution might be preferable. Simply guess intelligently and check to get the solution $2 \cdot 3 \cdot 4 \cdot 5 = 120$. We tried to show here that algebra can be very useful to introduce or explain some arithmetic relationships, but is not always the method of choice.

ALGEBRA IDEA 19

Sum of an Arithmetic Progression

Objective: To develop formulas for the sum of an arithmetic progression

Materials: Chalkboard or overhead projector

Procedure: Many formulas are often just given to the students, and neither rationale nor derivation is presented. This activity derives a formula for the sum of an arithmetic progression in two different ways.

Carl Friedrich Gauss was perhaps one of the most gifted mathematicians of all time. Part of his success in mathematics can be attributed to his uncanny ability to "number crunch," that is, to do arithmetic calculations with incredible speed and accuracy. Many of his theorems evolved from this ability to do what most others could not. It gave him a much greater insight into quantitative relationships, and enabled him to make the many breakthroughs for which he is still so famous today. The often told story* about his days in elementary school can be used as an excellent lead-in to the topic of adding an arithmetic sequence of numbers.

As the story goes, young Gauss's teacher, Mr. Büttner, wanted to keep the class occupied, so he asked the class to add the numbers from 1 to 100. He had barely finished giving the assignment, when young Gauss put his slate down with simply one number on it, the correct answer! Of course, Mr. Büttner assumed Gauss had the wrong answer or cheated. In any case, he ignored this response and waited for the appropriate time to ask the students for their answers. No one, other than Gauss, had the right answer. What did Gauss do to get the answer mentally? Gauss explained his method:

Rather than to add the numbers in the order in which they appear,

$$1 + 2 + 3 + 4 + \cdots + 97 + 98 + 99 + 100$$

he felt it made more sense to add the first and the last, then add the second and the next-to-last, then the third and the third-from-the-last, and so on. This led to a much simpler addition:

$$1 + 100 = 101 \qquad 2 + 99 = 101 \qquad 3 + 98 = 101 \qquad 4 + 97 = 101$$

Simply put, there are 50 pairs of numbers, each of which totals 101. Therefore the desired sum is $50 \cdot 101 = 5050$.

Although many textbooks may mention this cute story, they fail to use Gauss's technique to derive a formula for the sum of an arithmetic progression.

We generalize Gauss's method of addition. Consider the arithmetic progression sum

$$S = a + [a+d] + [a+2d] + [a+3d] + \cdots + [a+(n-2)d] + [a+(n-1)d]$$

where a is the first term, d is the common difference between terms, and n is the number of terms assumed at first to be even. Following Gauss's method of adding the first and nth terms gives:

$$a + [a + (n-1)d] = 2a + (n-1)d$$

Adding the second and $(n-1)^{\text{th}}$ term gives

$$[a+d] + [a+(n-2)d] = 2a + (n-1)d$$

---

* According to E. T. Bell in his famous book, *Men of Mathematics* (Simon and Schuster, New York, 1937), Gauss, in his adult years, told this story, but explained that the situation was far more complicated than the simple one we currently tell. He told of his teacher, Mr. Büttner, giving the class a five-digit number, such as 81,297, asking them to add a three digit number, such as 198, to it 100 times successively, and then find the sum of that series. We can only speculate about which version is true!

Adding the third and $(n-2)^{\text{th}}$ term gives

$$[a + 2d] + [a + (n-3)d] = 2a + (n-1)d$$

If we continue in this same manner until all the pairs have been added, we obtain $\frac{n}{2}$ such pairs, which gives the formula

$$S = \left(\frac{n}{2}\right)[2a + (n-1)d]$$

Students should now derive the same formula when n is odd. Students may be shown another derivation of this same formula by considering the arithmetic progression written in the expected order and then in the reverse order.

First, the "proper" order,

$$S = a + [a+d] + [a+2d] + [a+3d] + \cdots + [a+(n-2)d] + [a+(n-1)d]$$

where a is the first term, d is the common difference between terms, and n is the number of terms. Then, the reverse order,

$$S = [a+(n-1)d] + [a+(n-2)d] + [a+(n-3)d] + \cdots + [a+2d] + [a+d] + a$$

We then add the two preceding equations:

$$2S = [2a+(n-1)d] + [2a+(n-1)d] + [2a+(n-1)d] + \cdots + [2a+(n-1)d]$$

$$S = \left(\frac{n}{2}\right)[2a + (n-1)d]$$

Now that the formula has been derived, first in the Gaussian way and then in the more traditional way, students ought to practice using the formula to find the sums of given arithmetic progressions.

ALGEBRA IDEA 20

Averaging Rates

Objective: To have students realize that the average rate is not simply the arithmetic mean

Materials: Chalkboard

Procedure: Begin by posing the following problem: On Monday, a plane makes a round trip flight (with no wind) from New York City to Washington at an average speed of 300 miles per hour. The next day, Tuesday, there is a wind of constant speed (50 miles per hour) and direction (blowing from New York City to Washington). With the same speed setting as on Monday, this same plane makes the same round trip on Tuesday. Will the Tuesday trip require more time, less time, or the same amount of time as the Monday trip?

This problem should be slowly and carefully posed so that students notice that the only thing that has changed is the "help and hindrance of the wind." All other controllable factors are the same: distance, speed regulation, airplane conditions, and so forth. An expected response is that the two round trip flights ought to be the same, especially because the same wind is helping and hindering two equal legs of a round trip flight.

We let this problem lie unresolved for a while and digress to an entirely different situation. Closer to "home," we pose a question about the earned grade for a student who scored 100% on nine of ten tests in a semester and on the other test scored only 50%. Would it be fair to assume that this student's performance for the term was 75% (i.e., $\frac{100+50}{2}$)? The reaction to this suggestion tends toward applying appropriate weight to the two scores under consideration. The 100% was achieved nine times as often as the 50% and, therefore, ought to get the appropriate weight. Thus, a proper calculation of the student's average ought to be $\frac{9(100)+50}{10} = 95$. This clearly appears more just!

Now, how might this relate to the airplane trip? Realization that the two legs of the "wind trip" require different amounts of time should lead to the notion that the two speeds of this trip cannot be weighted equally because they were done for different lengths of time. Therefore, the time for each leg should be calculated and appropriately apportioned to the related speed.

We first find the times of the two legs of the round trip in the wind:

$$t_1 = \frac{d}{350} \quad \text{and} \quad t_2 = \frac{d}{250}. \quad \text{So that } t = t_1 + t_2 \approx 0.006857d \text{ hours.}$$

Denoting by t' the time for the round trip on Monday (when there is no wind), we find

$$t' = \frac{2d}{300} \approx 0.006667d < 0.006857d = t$$

Hence it takes longer for the round trip on Tuesday than it does on Monday.

The total time for the wind round trip is

$$t = \frac{d}{350} + \frac{d}{250}$$

The "total rate" or rate for the wind round trip (which is really the average rate) is

$$r = \frac{2d}{\frac{d}{250} + \frac{d}{350}} = \frac{2(350)(250)}{250 + 350} \approx 291.67$$

The "total rate," or rate for the round trip on Monday is

$$r' = \frac{2d}{0.006667d} \approx 299.98 > 291.67 \approx r$$

Hence the average rate on Monday is greater than the average rate on Tuesday. This average of rates is called the *harmonic mean* between the two speeds of 350 and 250 miles per hour. It might prove fruitful to digress to a discussion of the harmonic mean and its related series, the harmonic sequence.*

The harmonic mean for a and b is $\frac{2ab}{a+b}$, and for three numbers, a, b, and c, the harmonic mean is

$$\frac{3abc}{ab + bc + ac}$$

As part of any good mathematics instruction program, it is most important to include the warning that the averaging of rates cannot be handled as though they were ordinary numbers, because they exist over varying amounts of time.

ALGEBRA IDEA 21

Using Triangular Numbers to Generate Interesting Relationships

Objective: To derive some interesting properties of triangular numbers

Materials: Chalkboard

Procedure: Begin by introducing triangular numbers as numbers that can be represented as points arranged in the form of an equilateral triangle:

We use the notation T_n to represent the nth triangular number. We notice that

$$T_1 = 1 \qquad T_2 = 1 + 2 = 3 \qquad T_3 = 1 + 2 + 3 = 6$$

* For further work with the harmonic sequence, see *Probability and Statistics Ideas 8 and 9*. Additional information can be found in A. S. Posamentier and J. Stepelman, *Teaching Secondary School Mathematics: Techniques and Enrichment Units*, 5th edn. pp. 384–386 and 456–457 (Merrill/Prentice–Hall, Englewood Cliffs, NJ, 1999).

$$T_4 = 1 + 2 + 3 + 4 = 10 \quad \text{and} \quad T_n = 1 + 2 + 3 + 4 + 5 + \cdots + n$$

Through some experimentation, we can see that

$$T_0 = 0 \quad \text{(Definition)}$$
$$T_0 + T_1 = 0 + 1 = 1$$
$$T_1 + T_2 = 1 + 3 = 4$$
$$T_2 + T_3 = 3 + 6 = 9$$
$$T_3 + T_4 = 6 + 10 = 16$$

which can be generalized to

$$T_{n-1} + T_n = n^2 \tag{1}$$

Similar experimentation yields

$$T_0 = 0$$
$$T_1 - T_0 = 1$$
$$T_2 - T_1 = 2$$
$$T_3 - T_2 = 3$$
$$T_4 - T_3 = 4$$
$$\vdots$$
$$T_n - T_{n-1} = n \tag{2}$$

If we add Equations 1 and 2, we get a familiar result,

$$2T_n = n^2 + n = n(n+1)$$
$$T_n = \frac{1}{2}n(n+1)$$

which is the sum of the first n natural numbers. (In Algebra Idea 19, we approached this in a different way.)

Consider now the product of Equations 1 and 2:

$$(T_{n-1} + T_n)(T_n - T_{n-1}) = n^2 \cdot n = n^3$$
$$T_n^2 - T_{n-1}^2 = n^3$$

Each of the preceding equalities can be justified inductively, but for the purposes of introducing some order in the number system to a secondary school class, this treatment suffices.

The current representation of powers of n should be extended as we have in the preceding equation. So far we have

$$T_n - T_{n-1} = n$$
$$T_n + T_{n-1} = n^2$$
$$T_n^2 - T_{n-1}^2 = n^3$$

Further representations are left as a challenge for the class!

Introducing the Solution of Quadratic Equations Through Factoring

Objective: To show the solution of a quadratic equation as an extension of the solution of a linear equation, which then leads to the method of factoring a trinomial

Materials: A chalkboard or overhead projector

Procedure: Once students have gained familiarity with the solution of linear equations, let them try to extend this to the solution of quadratic equations. They should be encouraged to try to set up an analogous situation. With linear equations, students are accustomed to collecting the variable terms on the left side of the equation and the constants on the right side.

Let students try this procedure with the equation $x^2 + 5x + 6 = 0$. They will then rearrange the equation to read $x^2 + 5x = -6$. Although it may be possible for some clever youngsters to think of factoring $x^2 + 5x$ (motivating the later use of factoring) and then reach the brilliant insight that $x = -2$ or $x = -3$ yield solutions, it will be impossible for any student to guarantee that those are the only solutions.

Now ask the students what number on the right side of the equation might be easier to work with than the -6. With coaxing from you, the students should now be able to experience the advantage of having a 0 on the right side as opposed to the -6 or, for that matter, any other number. With a 0 on the right side, they again have the task of factoring the left side (if possible). Factoring the original quadratic $(x + 2)(x + 3) = 0$, leads to the deduction that $(x + 2) = 0$ or $(x + 3) = 0$ are the *only* two possibilities to obtain a product of zero.

Students' understanding that the method of solution for a quadratic equation as an extension of the already familiar method of solving linear equations is not particularly fruitful will provide a more solid appreciation for the factoring technique. Once this concept has been grasped, students should be ready to apply this technique to trinomials that are not immediately factorable. After learning and applying the technique of "completing the square" to nonfactorable quadratics, they can apply it to the general form $ax^2 + bx + c = 0$, $a \neq 0$, which will produce a general formula for solving all quadratic equations.

This development builds on the students' prior knowledge. It allows the students to attempt a normal extension and then provides the proper stimulus for modifying the development in a fruitful direction.

Rationalizing the Denominator

Objective: To demonstrate the usefulness of rationalizing the denominator of a fraction

Materials: Chalkboard

Procedure: Begin by presenting the following problem. Evaluate the series sum

$$\frac{1}{1+\sqrt{2}} + \frac{1}{\sqrt{2}+\sqrt{3}} + \frac{1}{\sqrt{3}+\sqrt{4}} + \cdots + \frac{1}{\sqrt{1999}+\sqrt{2000}}$$

Starting the solution of this problem can be quite difficult if one is not accustomed to expressing denominators in terms of rational numbers. This procedure should be discussed and taught at this point before the foregoing problem is revisited.

When the process of rationalizing the denominator of a fraction has been mastered, the problem can be approached by considering the general term $\frac{1}{\sqrt{k}+\sqrt{k+1}}$.

Rationalizing this denominator yields

$$\frac{1}{\sqrt{k}+\sqrt{k+1}} \cdot \frac{\sqrt{k}-\sqrt{k+1}}{\sqrt{k}-\sqrt{k+1}} = \sqrt{k+1}-\sqrt{k}$$

This allows us to rewrite the series as

$$\left(\sqrt{2}-\sqrt{1}\right) + \left(\sqrt{3}-\sqrt{2}\right) + \left(\sqrt{4}-\sqrt{3}\right) + \cdots$$
$$+ \left(\sqrt{1999}-\sqrt{1998}\right) + \left(\sqrt{2000}-\sqrt{1999}\right)$$

which equals

$$\sqrt{2000} - \sqrt{1} = 20\sqrt{5} - 1 \approx 43.7213596$$

By showing how the process of rationalizing the denominator of a fraction makes the fraction much more workable, the procedure will become a useful tool in the arsenal of techniques taught in algebra.

Paper Folding to Generate a Parabola

Objective: To construct an envelope of tangents for a parabola by folding paper

Materials: Waxed paper and a pen that can write on it

Procedure: A revealing approach to understanding the properties of a parabola is to have students generate or construct it by means of the envelope of tangents to the curve. The basic idea used here is that a parabola is the locus of points equidistant from a fixed line (called the directrix) and a fixed point (called the focus) not on that line. We shall generate each tangent by applying this locus rule. This is done by folding a sheet of paper and noting the pattern of the creases that result. Although any thin piece of paper may be used, a piece of waxed paper, which shows its creases very clearly, probably is the best paper to use for this activity.

Folding paper to generate a parabola

Select a line segment, $\overline{AB}$, as the *directrix*. Choose a point, P, not on $\overline{AB}$, to serve as the *focus*. Fold the paper so that point P coincides with any point on $\overline{AB}$. Make a careful and distinct crease. You now have "constructed" the perpendicular bisector of a segment joining P and the chosen point on $\overline{AB}$. Repeat this procedure by "placing" point P at a different position on $\overline{AB}$. Make another crease. Continue this process until P has been made to coincide with many different points on $\overline{AB}$. The more creases made, the clearer the parabola that will emerge from the tangent lines. It will not be necessary to actually draw

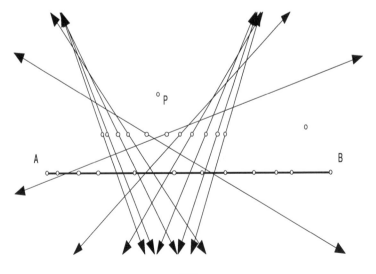

the parabola, merely to observe how the many lines appear to be tangent to this (not drawn) parabola. The drawing on page 52 which indicates the result of folding the waxed paper, was done with the Geometer's Sketchpad computer program. By doing the construction on the computer, we have the ability to distort the diagram and inspect what aspects of the construction remain constant under various positions. Here we can see that the midpoints of the segments joining P with its various images on $\overline{AB}$ are collinear and that line is parallel to $\overline{AB}$.

The finished product makes an excellent bulletin board display, as well as a model suitable for discussing this conic section. Concepts such as the focus and directrix of a parabola are easily brought out in the process of construction which reveals the foldings, more clearly seen to be tangents to the parabola, as the envelopes of the curve.

Here are some difficult questions for the exceptional student:

1. Is it really obvious that the collection of folds coincides with the tangents to the curve and is therefore the envelope of the parabola? How would you go about knowing this?

2. Denote by Q an arbitrary point in the plane, and by p, the distance from Q to the focus P, and by d; the distance from Q to the directrix $\overleftrightarrow{AB}$. Show that Q is "inside" of, on, or "outside" of the parabola, according as $p < d$, $p = d$, $p > d$ respectively.

3. Employ "difficult question 2" to answer "difficult question 1."

ALGEBRA IDEA 25

Paper Folding to Generate an Ellipse

Objective: To construct the envelope of the ellipse by folding paper in such a way that the foldings constitute the tangents to the curve

Materials: Waxed paper and a pen that can write on it

Procedure: A revealing approach to understanding the properties of an ellipse is to have students generate or construct it by means of the envelope of tangents to the curve. This is done by folding a sheet of paper and noting the pattern of the creases that results. Although any thin piece of paper may be used, a piece of waxed paper, which shows its creases very clearly, is probably the best paper to use for this activity.

Folding paper to generate an ellipse

Draw a circle with center at O. Select a point other than O, but also *inside* the circular region. Call this point P. The foci of the ellipse to be constructed will be seen to be O and P. Fold the paper in such a way that the point P, coincides with a point, P' on the circumference of the circle. Make a distinctive crease. Fold the paper again so that P coincides with another point, P'', on the circumference. Crease again. Repeat the process until P has been made to coincide with many points along the circumference of the circle. The resulting creases will form the envelope, which consists of the foldings, now seen to be the tangents to the ellipse.

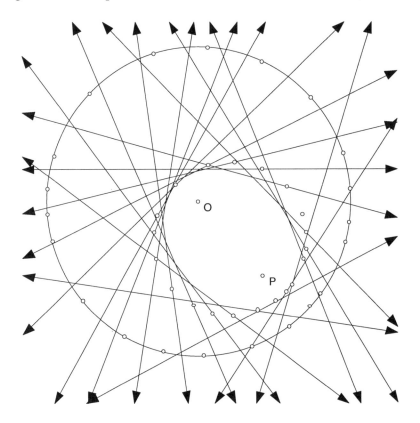

The finished product makes an excellent bulletin board display, as well as a model suitable for discussing this conic section. Concepts such as the foci of the ellipse are easily brought out in the process of the construction which reveals the foldings, now clearly seen to be tangents of the ellipse, as the envelope of the curves.

To understand why the curve so constructed is an ellipse, we consider the figure

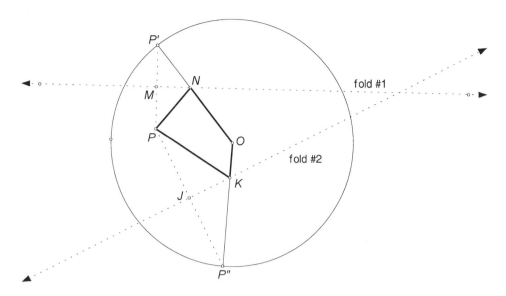

The ellipse is the locus points, the sum of whose distances to two fixed points (foci) is a constant. We show that N (the intersection of fold #1 with $\overleftrightarrow{P'O}$) and K (the intersection of fold #2 with $\overleftrightarrow{P''O}$) in the figure are two points on the ellipse (points of tangency of folds). Since fold #1 is the perpendicular bisector of $\overline{PP'}$, $P'N = PN$, $PN + NO = P'N + NO = P'O$. Similarly for fold #2, (the perpendicular bisector of $\overline{PP''}$) $PK = P''K$, and $PK + KO = P''K + KO = P''O$. However, $P'0 = P''O$ because they are radii of the same circle, O. Thus, $PN + NO = PK + KO$ or the points K and N must be points on the same ellipse.

Difficult questions for the exceptional student:

1. Denote by Q an arbitrary point in the plane, by QP, the distance between Q and the focus P, QO, the distance between Q and the focus O, and by r the radius of the circle. Show that Q is inside of, on, or outside of the ellipse accordingly $QP + QO < r$, $QP + QO = r$, or $QP + QO > r$, respectively.

2. Employ "difficult questions 1" to show that the collection of folds coincides with the collection of tangents to the ellipse and therefore is the envelope of the ellipse.

Paper Folding to Generate a Hyperbola

Objective: To construct an envelope of tangents for a hyperbola by folding paper

Materials: Waxed paper and a pen that can write on it

Procedure: A revealing approach to understand the properties of a hyperbola is to have students generate or construct it by means of the envelope of tangents to the curve. This is done by folding a sheet of paper and noting the pattern of the creases that results. Although any thin piece of paper may be used, a piece of waxed paper, which shows its creases very clearly, is probably the best paper to use for this activity.

Folding paper to generate a hyperbola

Draw a circle with center at O. Select a point, P, *outside* the circle. These points, O and P, will turn out to be the foci of the hyperbola. Fold the sheet of paper in such a way that the point P coincides with a point on the circumference of the circle. Make a distinctive crease. Repeat this procedure so that point P coincides with another point on the circumference. Crease again. Repeat this process until P has been made to coincide with many points along the circumference of the circle. The resulting creases form the envelope of tangents that describe the hyperbola. Again, the more creases made, the more clearly defined the hyperbola will be.

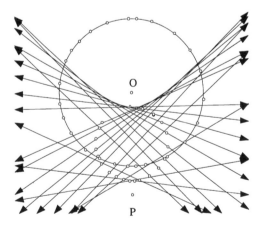

It may take some experimentation to select the best positions for P to map onto along the circle. The two branches of the hyperbola ought to become visible shortly. This will depend on the size of the radius of the circle, as well as on

how close to the circle we place point P. Several attempts may be required to obtain a satisfactory hyperbola.

The finished product makes an excellent bulletin board display, as well as a model suitable for discussing this conic section. Concepts such as the foci of the hyperbola are easily brought out in the process of the actual foldings of the envelopes of the tangents to the curves.

The justification for this construction may be of interest to some classes. Here we consider the definition of the hyperbola as the locus of points, the difference of whose distances to two fixed points (loci) is a constant. Consider the following figure.

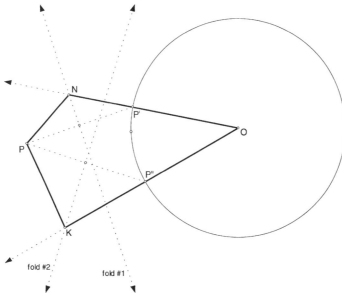

The line, fold #1, is obtained by folding the fixed point P onto the point P' on the circumference of the circle. The point N is the intersection of $\overleftrightarrow{OP'}$ and the fold. The folding itself forms the perpendicular bisector of $\overline{PP'}$. Similarly, fold #2 is obtained by folding P onto the point P'' on the circumference. The point K is the intersection of $\overrightarrow{OP''}$ and fold #2. The folding itself creates the perpendicular bisector of $\overline{PP''}$. The point N is on the perpendicular bisector of $\overline{PP'}$, $PN = P'N$, so that $NO - PN = NO - P'N = P'O$, the radius of the fixed circle. Similarly, since K is on the perpendicular bisector of $\overline{PP''}$, $PK = P''K$, so that $KO - PK = KO - P''K = P''O$, the radius of the fixed circle. Thus, $NO - PN = KO - PK$. Hence the difference of the distances of each of the points N and K form the fixed points P and O is a constant (the radius of the circle). It follows that the points N and K lie on the hyperbola having P and O as foci.

A difficult question for the exceptional student: In analogy with the "difficult questions" of the preceding section on the ellipse, show that the collection of folds coincides with the collection of tangents to the hyperbola and therefore is the envelope of the hyperbola.

Using Concentric Circles to Generate a Parabola

Objective: To enable students to see the locus definition of a parabola through simple geometry

Materials: Geometer's Sketchpad program or ruled paper and a pair of compasses

Procedure: Students who are familiar with the Geometer's Sketchpad program can follow along with the instructions that we present here for use with a ruled sheet of paper and a pair of compasses.

Begin by selecting a center point conveniently chosen on the sheet of ruled paper (on one of the lines). As shown in the accompanying figure, we make successive concentric circles with a common center and with the initial radius equal to the distance between two consecutive lines on the paper. Each successive circle has a radius one such unit larger than its predecessor. The resulting drawing should look like this:

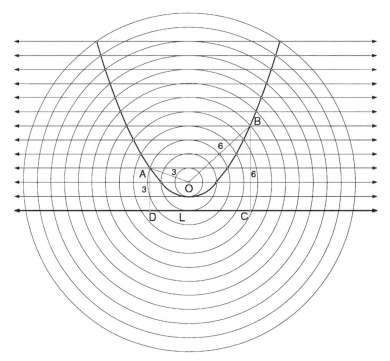

We have selected the points of intersection of the circles and the ruled lines that represent points that are the same distance from point O as they are from line L (the bold line). For example, point A is 3 units from point O and 3 units from line L. Similarly, point B is 6 units from point O and 6 units from line L.

The resulting points all lie on the indicated parabola, because the definition of a parabola is the locus of points equidistant from a given point, the focus, and a given line (not on the point), the directrix. Students should experiment to determine how another shape of parabola can be formed with this scheme.

Using Concentric Circles to Generate an Ellipse

Objective: To enable students to see the locus definition of an ellipse through simple geometry

Materials: Geometer's Sketchpad program or plain paper and a pair of compasses

Procedure: Students who are familiar with the Geometer's Sketchpad program can follow along with the instructions that we present here for use with a plain sheet of paper and a pair of compasses.

Begin by selecting two center points conveniently chosen on the sheet of plain paper. As shown in the accompanying figure, we make successive concentric circles with common centers and with radii consecutively increasing by the amount of the length of the initial radius (i.e., of the inner circle). The resulting drawing should look like this:

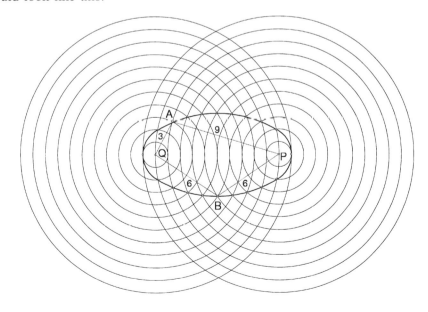

We have selected the points of intersection of the circles that represent points, the sum of whose distances from the two circle centers is the same. That is, point A is 3 units from point Q and 9 units from point P. The sum of these distances is the same for all the points on the ellipse drawn. For a further example, point B is 6 units from each of the points P and Q, which fits our requirement (in this case) for having a sum of 12 units. Were we to continue selecting points, the sums of whose distances to the given points are equal, the resulting points will all lie on the indicated ellipse. This is consistent with the definition of an ellipse, which is the locus of points the sum of whose distances from two fixed points (the foci) are constant. Students should experiment to determine how another shape of ellipse can be formed with this scheme.

ALGEBRA IDEA **29**

Using Concentric Circles to Generate a Hyperbola

Objective: To enable students to see the locus definition of a hyperbola through simple geometry

Materials: Geometer's Sketchpad program or plain paper and a pair of compasses

Procedure: Students who are familiar with the Geometer's Sketchpad program can follow along with the instructions that we present here for use with a plain sheet of paper and a pair of compasses.

Begin by selecting two center points conveniently chosen on the sheet of plain paper. As shown in the accompanying figure, we make successive concentric circles with common centers and with radii consecutively increasing by the amount of the length of the initial radius (i.e., of the inner circle). The resulting drawing should look as shown in the page 60.

We have selected the points of intersection of the circles, which represent points, the difference of whose distances from the two circle centers is the same. That is, point A is 4 units from point Q and 10 units from point P. The difference of these distances is the same for all the points on the hyperbola drawn. For a further example, point B is 14 units from point Q and 8 units from point B, which fits our requirement (in this case) for having a difference of 6 units. Were we to continue selecting points, the differences of whose distances to the given points are equal, the resulting points will all lie on the indicated hyperbola. This is consistent with the definition of a hyperbola, which is the locus of points, the difference of whose distances from two fixed points (the foci) are constant.

Students should experiment to determine how another shape hyperbola can be formed with this scheme.

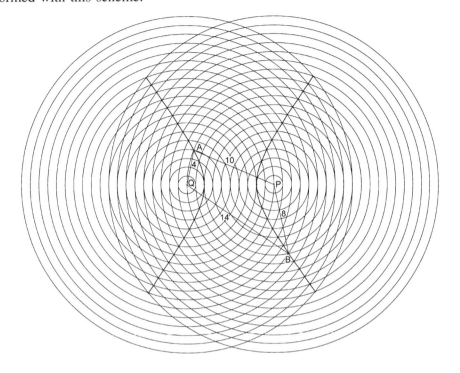

Summing a Series of Powers

Objective: To develop a technique to find the sum of a series of powers as a way to introduce patterns to derive formulas

Materials: Chalkboard

Procedure: Many formulas are often given to students without proper explanation or justification. This unit provides a technique for deriving common formulas for summing a series of powers.

We begin with a familiar request, to find the sum of the natural number arithmetic progression

$$1 + 2 + 3 + \cdots + n$$

Two different ways to find this sum were presented in Algebra Idea 19. We present here an alternative method, which then will be used to find the sum of another series.

61

Repeatedly using the expansion for $(1 + n)^2$ yields

$$(1 + 1)^2 = 1^2 + 2 \cdot 1 + 1^2$$
$$(1 + 2)^2 = 1^2 + 2 \cdot 2 + 2^2$$
$$(1 + 3)^2 = 1^2 + 2 \cdot 3 + 3^2$$
$$(1 + 4)^2 = 1^2 + 2 \cdot 4 + 4^2$$
$$(1 + 5)^2 = 1^2 + 2 \cdot 5 + 5^2$$
$$\vdots \qquad \vdots$$
$$(1 + n)^2 = 1^2 + 2n + n^2$$

Sum both sides to get

$$2^2 + 3^2 + 4^2 + 5^2 + \cdots + (n + 1)^2 = n + 2(1 + 2 + 3 + 4 + 5 + \cdots + n)$$
$$+ 1^2 + 2^2 + 3^2 + 4^2 + 5^2 + \cdots + n^2$$

or

$$(n + 1)^2 = (n + 1) + 2(1 + 2 + 3 + 4 + 5 + \cdots + n)$$

Therefore,

$$1 + 2 + 3 + 4 + 5 + \cdots + n = \frac{(n + 1)^2 - (n + 1)}{2} = \frac{n(n + 1)}{2}$$

Let us now find the sum of the squares of the natural numbers:

$$1^2 + 2^2 + 3^2 + 4^2 + 5^2 + \cdots + n^2$$

Similarly, let us try to use the cubic expansion (the binomial theorem is useful here):

$$(1 + 1)^3 = 1^3 + 3 \cdot 1 + 3 \cdot 1^2 + 1^3$$
$$(1 + 2)^3 = 1^3 + 3 \cdot 2 + 3 \cdot 2^2 + 2^3$$
$$(1 + 3)^3 = 1^3 + 3 \cdot 3 + 3 \cdot 3^2 + 3^3$$
$$(1 + 4)^3 = 1^3 + 3 \cdot 4 + 3 \cdot 4^2 + 4^3$$
$$(1 + 5)^3 = 1^3 + 3 \cdot 5 + 3 \cdot 5^2 + 5^3$$
$$\vdots \qquad \vdots$$
$$(1 + n)^3 = 1^3 + 3n + 3n^2 + n^3$$

Sum both sides to get

$$2^3 + 3^3 + 4^3 + 5^3 + \cdots + (n + 1)^3 = n + 3(1 + 2 + 3 + 4 + 5 + \cdots + n)$$
$$+ 3(1^2 + 2^2 + 3^2 + 4^2 + 5^2 + \cdots + n^2)$$
$$+ (1^3 + 2^3 + 3^3 + 4^3 + 5^3 + \cdots + n^3)$$

or

$$(n+1)^3 = n + 3(1 + 2 + 3 + 4 + 5 + \cdots + n)$$
$$+ 3(1^2 + 2^2 + 3^2 + 4^2 + 5^2 + \cdots + n^2) + 1 \tag{1}$$

Substitute into equation (1)

$$1 + 2 + 3 + 4 + 5 + \cdots + n = \frac{n(n+1)}{2}$$

We should have

$$1^2 + 2^2 + 3^2 + \cdots + n^2 = \frac{(n+1)^3 - (n+1)}{3} - \frac{n(n+1)}{2}$$
$$= \frac{(n+2)n(n+1)}{3} - \frac{n(n+1)}{2}$$
$$= \frac{n(n+1)(2n+1)}{6}$$

We are now ready to find the sum of the cubes of the natural numbers: $1^3 + 2^3 + 3^3 + 4^3 + 5^3 + \cdots + n^3$.

Using a similar method, expand $(1+n)^4$ to find this sum:

$$(1+1)^4 = 1^4 + 4 \cdot 1 + 6 \cdot 1^2 + 4 \cdot 1^3 + 1^4$$
$$(1+2)^4 = 1^4 + 4 \cdot 2 + 6 \cdot 2^2 + 4 \cdot 2^3 + 2^4$$
$$(1+3)^4 = 1^4 + 4 \cdot 3 + 6 \cdot 3^2 + 4 \cdot 3^3 + 3^4$$
$$(1+4)^4 = 1^4 + 4 \cdot 4 + 6 \cdot 4^2 + 4 \cdot 4^3 + 4^4$$
$$(1+5)^4 = 1^4 + 4 \cdot 5 + 6 \cdot 5^2 + 4 \cdot 5^3 + 5^4$$
$$\vdots \qquad \vdots$$
$$(1+n)^4 = 1^4 + 4n + 6n^2 + 4n^3 + n^4$$

Sum both sides of these equations to get

$$2^4 + 3^4 + 4^4 + 5^4 + \cdots + (n+1)^4 = n + 4(1 + 2 + 3 + 4 + 5 + \cdots + n)$$
$$+ 6(1^2 + 2^2 + 3^2 + 4^2 + 5^2 + \cdots + n^2)$$
$$+ 4(1^3 + 2^3 + 3^3 + 4^3 + 5^3 + \cdots + n^3)$$
$$+ 1^4 + 2^4 + 3^4 + 4^4 + 5^4 + \cdots + n^4$$

or

$$(n+1)^4 = n + 1 + 4(1 + 2 + 3 + 4 + 5 + \cdots + n)$$
$$+ 6(1^2 + 2^2 + 3^2 + 4^2 + 5^2 + \cdots + n^2) \tag{2}$$
$$+ 4(1^3 + 2^3 + 3^3 + 4^3 + 5^3 + \cdots + n^3)$$

By substituting the equations

$$1 + 2 + 3 + 4 + 5 + \cdots + n = \frac{n(n+1)}{2}$$

and

$$1^2 + 2^2 + 3^2 + \cdots + n^2 = \frac{n(n+1)(2n+1)}{6}$$

into Equation 2, we get

$$(n+1)^4 = (n+1) + 2n(n+1) + n(n+1)(2n+1)$$
$$+ 4(1^3 + 2^3 + 3^3 + 4^3 + 5^3 + \cdots + n^3)$$

Therefore,

$$1^3 + 2^3 + 3^3 + \cdots + n^3 = \frac{n^2 (n+1)^2}{4}$$

Using a similar method, we should be able to find the formula for the sum of a series in the form

$$1^k + 2^k + 3^k + 4^k + 5^k + \cdots + n^k \quad \text{(where } k \text{ and } n \text{ are integers)}$$

ALGEBRA IDEA 31

Sum of Limits

Objective: To provide students with convincing evidence that care must be taken when inspecting "limits"

Materials: Chalkboard or Geometer's Sketchpad

Procedure: This objective is best demonstrated with two simple illustrations. Consider them separately and then notice their connection.

Illustration 1. It is simple to see that the sum of the lengths of the bold segments (the "stair steps") in the following diagram is equal to $a + b$.

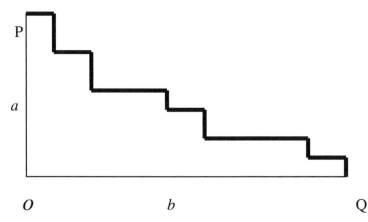

Nothing is wrong! While the set consisting of the stairs does indeed approach closer and closer to the straight line segment PQ, it does *not* therefore follow that the *sum* of the bold (horizontal and vertical) lengths approaches the length of $\overline{PQ}$, contrary to intuition. There is no contradiction here, only a failure on the part of our intuition.

Another way to "explain" this dilemma is to argue the following. As the "stairs" get smaller, they increase in number. In an extreme situation, we have 0-length dimensions (for the stairs) used an infinite number of times, which then leads to considering $0 \cdot \infty$, which is meaningless!

Another interpretation is that in each case the sum of the bold segments (steps) is equal to the constant $a + b$. The limit of a constant must be the constant $(a + b)$ and not $\sqrt{a^2 + b^2}$.

A similar situation arises with the following example.

Illustration 2. In the accompanying figure, the smaller semicircles extend from one end of the diameter of large semicircle to the other.

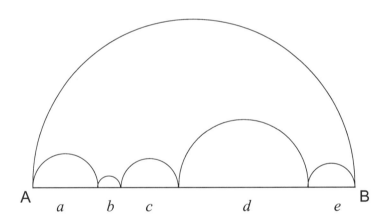

It is easy to show that the sum of the arc lengths of the smaller semicircles is equal to the arc length of the larger semicircle. That is, the sum of the smaller semicircles is

$$\frac{\pi a}{2} + \frac{\pi b}{2} + \frac{\pi c}{2} + \frac{\pi d}{2} + \frac{\pi e}{2} = \frac{\pi}{2}(a + b + c + d + e) = \frac{\pi}{2}(AB)$$

which is the arc length of the larger semicircle. This may not "appear" to be true, but it is! As a matter of fact, as we increase the number of smaller semicircles (where, of course, they get smaller) the sum "appears" to be approaching the length of the segment AB, but, in fact, does not!

Again, the set consisting of the semicircles does indeed approach the length of the straight line segment AB. It does *not* follow, however, that the *sum* of the semicircles approaches the *length* of the limit, in this case AB.

This "apparent limit sum" is be absurd, since the shortest distance between points A and B is the length of segment AB, not the semicircle arc AB (which equals the sum of the smaller semicircles). This is an important concept to present to students, best done with the help of these motivating illustrations, so that future misintetpretations can be avoided.

Linear Equations With Two Variables

Objective: To "solve" one equation with two variables

Materials: Chalkboard

Procedure: Students are trained in secondary school to look for a second equation when they are given one equation (usually linear) with two variables. This is quite normal, because when a unique solution is sought, two equations are usually needed. This should not imply that given one equation with two variables leaves them helpless. Quite to the contrary. They can certainly graph one equation with two variable on the xy plane. This should confirm that there are many (an infinite number) (x, y) values that satisfy this equation—the points on the line. However, suppose the question requires integer solutions. Not an unreasonable request. This leads to some interesting strategies, which can enrich an algebra lesson on linear equations.

Have students solve the following problem: Suppose you are asked by your employer to go to the post office and buy 6-cent and 8-cent stamps. He gives you 5 dollars to spend. From how many combinations of 6-cent and 8-cent stamps could you select to make your purchase?

Most students promptly realize that there are two variables that must be determined, say x and y. Letting x represent the number of 8-cent stamps and y represent the number of 6-cent stamps, the equation $8x + 6y = 500$ should follow. This can then be simplified to $4x + 3y = 250$. At this juncture, the students should realize that although this equation has an infinite number of solutions, it may or may not have an infinite number of *integer* solutions; moreover, it may or may not have an infinite number of *positive* integer solutions (as called for by the original problem of buying stamps). The first issue to consider is whether integer solutions, in fact, exist.

For this determination, a useful theorem may be employed. It states that "if the greatest common factor of a and b is also a factor of k, where a, b, and k are integers, then there exist an infinite number of integer solutions for x and y in $ax + by = k$. Equations of this type, whose solutions must be integers, are known as Diophantine equations in honor of the Greek mathematician, Diophantus, who wrote about them.

Since the greatest common factor of 3 and 4 is 1, which is a factor of 250, there exist an infinite number of integer solutions to the equation $4x + 3y = 250$. The question now facing your students is how many (if any) *positive* integer solutions exist?

One possible method of solution is often referred to as Euler's method (Leonhard Euler, 1707–1783). To begin, students solve for the variable with the coefficient of least absolute value, in this case, y. Thus

$$y = \frac{250 - 4x}{3}$$

This must be rewritten to separate the integer parts as

$$y = 83 + \frac{1}{3} - x - \frac{x}{3} = 83 - x + \frac{1 - x}{3} \tag{1}$$

Now introduce another variable, say t, and let $t = \frac{1-x}{3}$. In view of Equation 1, t must be an integer, since x, y, and 83 are all integers. Solving for x yields $x = 1 - 3t$. Since there is no fractional coefficient in this equality, the process does not have to be repeated as it otherwise would have to be (i.e., each time introducing new variables, as with t). Now, substituting for x in yields Equation 1 yields

$$y = \frac{250 - 4(1 - 3t)}{3} = 82 + 4t$$

For various integer values of t, generate corresponding values for x and y. A table of values such as the following might prove useful:

t	$\cdots$	-2	-1	0	1	2	$\cdots$
x	$\cdots$	7	4	1	-2	-5	$\cdots$
y	$\cdots$	74	78	82	86	90	$\cdots$

Perhaps by generating a more extensive table, students will notice for which values of t positive integer values for x and y may be obtained. However, this

67

procedure for determining the number of positive integer values of x and y is not very elegant. Guide the students to simultaneously solve the inequalities

$$1 - 3t > 0 \quad \text{and} \quad 82 + 4t > 0$$

Thus

$$t < \frac{1}{3} \quad \text{and} \quad t > -20\frac{1}{2} \quad \text{or} \quad -20\frac{1}{2} < t < \frac{1}{3}$$

This indicates that there are 21 possible combinations of 6-cent and 8-cent stamps that can be purchased for 5 dollars.

Students may find it helpful to consider the solution to a more difficult Diophantine equation, such as the following example.

Solve the Diophantine equation $5x - 8y = 39$.

Solve for x, because its coefficient has the lower absolute value of the two coefficients:

$$x = \frac{8y + 39}{5} = y + 7 + \frac{3y + 4}{5}$$

*Let $t = \frac{3y+4}{5}$. Then t must be an integer. Solve for y:

$$y = \frac{5t - 4}{3} = t - 1 + \frac{2t - 1}{3}$$

*Let $u = \frac{2t-1}{3}$. Then u must be an integer. Solve for t:

$$t = \frac{3u + 1}{2} = u + \frac{u + 1}{2}$$

*Let $v = \frac{u+1}{2}$. Then v must be an integer. Solve for u:

$$u = 2v - 1$$

We may now reverse the process because the coefficient of v is an integer. Substituting in the reverse order,

$$t = \frac{3u + 1}{2}$$

Therefore

$$t = \frac{3(2v - 1) + 1}{2} = 3v - 1$$

Also

$$y = \frac{5t - 4}{3}$$

---

* The newly introduced variable represents the fraction on the right side of the equation.

Therefore

$$y = \frac{5(3v - 1) - 4}{3} = 5v - 3$$

Similarly

$$x = \frac{8y + 39}{5}$$

Therefore

$$x = \frac{8(5v - 3) + 39}{5} = 8v + 3$$

Since v must be an integer, the following table indicates how the various solutions of this Diophantine equation may be generated. Students should be urged to inspect the nature of the members of the solution set.

v	$\cdots$	-2	-1	0	1	2	$\cdots$
x	$\cdots$	-13	-5	3	11	19	$\cdots$
y	$\cdots$	-13	-8	-3	2	7	$\cdots$

ALGEBRA IDEA **33**

Introducing Compound Interest Using "The Rule of 72"

Objective: To make the "Rule of 72" meaningful through use of the compound interest formula

Materials: Chalkboard and a scientific calculator

Procedure: The introduction to compound interest is usually presented in textbooks through a challenge question about how money will grow at a certain interest rate over a specified period of time. This has worked well over the years and when it is presented as a "real" problem it has all the necessary motivational attributes of a good lead-in to the topic. However, it might be nice to try to use the "Rule of 72" to generate some interest in the compound interest formula.

Let us first introduce the famous "Rule of 72." It states that roughly speaking *money will double in $\frac{72}{r}$ years when it is invested at an annual compounded interest rate of r%*. So, for example, if we invest money at an 8% compounded annual interest rate, it will double its value in $\frac{72}{8} = 9$ years.

To investigate why or if this really works, we consider the compound interest formula

$$A = P \left(1 + \frac{r}{100}\right)^n$$

where A is the resulting amount of money and P is the principal invested for n interest periods at $r\%$ annually.

We need to investigate what happens when $A = 2P$. The foregoing equation then becomes

$$2 = \left(1 + \frac{r}{100}\right)^n \tag{1}$$

It then follows that

$$n = \frac{\log 2}{\log \left(1 + \frac{r}{100}\right)} \tag{2}$$

Let us make a table of values from Equation 2 with the help of a scientific calculator:

r	n	nr
1	69.66071689	69.66071689
3	23.44977225	70.34931675
5	14.20669908	71.03349541
7	10.24476835	71.71337846
9	8.043231727	72.38908554
11	6.641884618	73.0607308
13	5.671417169	73.72842319
15	4.959484455	74.39226682

If we take the arithmetic mean (the usual average) of the nr values, we get 72.04092314, which is quite close to 72, and so our "Rule of 72" seems to be a very close estimate for doubling money at an annual interest rate of $r\%$ for n interest periods.

An ambitious teacher or a teacher with a strong mathematics class might try to determine a "rule" for tripling and quadrupling money similar to the way we dealt with the doubling of money. The form of Equation 2 for k-tupling would be

$$n = \frac{\log k}{\log \left(1 + \frac{r}{100}\right)}$$

which for $r = 8$, gives the value for $n = 29.91884022(\log k)$.

Thus $nr = 239.3507218 \log k$, which for $k = 3$ (the tripling effect) gives us $nr = 114.1993167$. We could then say that for tripling money, we have a "rule of 114."

However far this topic is explored, the important issue here is that the common "Rule of 72" can be a nice way to make the topic of compound interest appealing.

ALGEBRA IDEA 34

Generating Pythagorean Triples

Objective: To derive a set of parametric equations that can be used to generate Pythagorean triples and use it to investigate some properties of such triples

Materials: Chalkboard or overhead projector

Procedure: Pythagorean triples appear as a normal part of any discussion of the Pythagorean theorem. Other than to mention the "cleanness" of having integers that fit the relationship $a^2 + b^2 = c^2$, little special attention is paid to these important and interesting numbers. Perhaps if students saw some of the nice relationships that can be found through simple explorations, these triples would get the prominence they deserve.

Begin by having students find some of these triples. The most popular triple is $(3, 4, 5)$, which leads directly to others that are multiples of this triple, such as $(6, 8, 10)$, $(9, 12, 15)$, and $(30, 40, 50)$. We limit our discussion here to the primitive triples, namely, those whose elements are relatively prime (that is, whose greatest common factor is 1).

Students should be able to list other primitive Pythagorean triples:

$$(5, 12, 13), \quad (8, 15, 17), \quad (7, 24, 25), \quad (9, 40, 41), \quad (12, 35, 37), \cdots$$

Students should be encouraged to identify some properties of these primitive Pythagorean triples, such as

- Two members are odd and one is even
- Some have members that differ by 1
- The product of the members is divisible by 60
- One element is divisible by 5

Such statements can be investigated best by considering the parametric equations that generate Pythagorean triples. Parametric equations are equations in which an original set of variables is expressed in terms of a second set of variables called the parameters. By assigning values to the parameters, we can obtain a set of values for our original variables. Although students rarely use parametric equations in their early work in algebra, they are often quite important in the later study of mathematics and are worthwhile getting acquainted with early. In the case of Pythagorean triples, they are particularly useful.

Here is a set of parametric equations that are used to generate sets of Pythagorean triples,

$$a = u^2 - v^2$$
$$b = 2uv$$
$$c = u^2 + v^2$$

where a and b are the legs of the right triangle and c is the hypotenuse, that is, $a^2 + b^2 = c^2$.

By setting up a table of values for these parametric equations, students can begin to get an insight into some of the characteristics they noticed before:

u	v	$u^2 - v^2$	$2uv$	$u^2 + v^2$
2	1	3	4	5
3	2	5	12	13
4	1	15	8	17
4	3	7	24	25
5	4	9	40	41
3	1	8	6	10
5	2	21	20	29
6	1	35	12	37
6	5	11	60	61
7	2	45	28	53

Beginning with this table, students will be able to make conjectures about the nature of special Pythagorean triples based on the values of u and v. That is, what must be true of u and v so that the triple is primitive? What must be true about u and v for two of the elements to differ by 1? Students can then ask further questions and the class discussion can take on any direction the teacher chooses. In effect, here you have an extension of the discussion of the Pythagorean theorem that flows naturally from the usual treatment of the topic.

Finding Sums of Finite Series

Objective: To develop formulas for determining the sums of various finite series so that mathematical induction applications can become more meaningful

Materials: A chalkboard

Procedure: Mathematical induction has become thoroughly entrenched in secondary school curricula. Many textbooks provide a variety of applications of this technique of proof. Most popular among these applications is proving that specific series have given formulas as sums. Although most students merely work the proof as required, some may question how the sum of a particular series was actually generated. This topic will provide you with a response to students' requests to derive formulas for certain series summations.

A **finite sequence** is a finite set of ordered elements or terms, each related to one or more of the preceding elements in some specifiable way.

Let us now consider any finite sequence of elements $u_1, u_2, \ldots, u_n$. We can obtain the partial sums

$$S_1 = u_1$$
$$S_2 = u_1 + u_2$$
$$S_3 = u_1 + u_2 + u_3$$
$$\vdots$$
$$S_n = u_1 + u_2 + \cdots + u_n$$

We call this sum $u_1 + u_2 + \cdots + u_n$ a **finite series** of the elements of the sequence $u_1, u_2, \ldots, u_n$. S_n represents the total sum of these elements. For example, if we have the sequence 1, 2, 3, 4, the series is $1 + 2 + 3 + 4$, and the sum S_4 is 10.

This example is simple. However, if instead of considering the four terms 1, 2, 3, and 4, we consider n terms $1, 2, 3, \ldots, n$, it is not as simple to calculate their sum $S_n = 1 + 2 + 3 + \ldots + n$.

Sometimes, there are easy ways to calculate the sum of a specific series, but we cannot apply that particular method to all series.

For example, the previous series $1 + 2 + 3 + \cdots + n$, can be calculated by using the artifice

$$1 = 1 = \frac{1 \cdot 2}{2}$$

$$1 + 2 = 3 = \frac{2 \cdot 3}{2}$$

$$1 + 2 + 3 = 6 = \frac{3 \cdot 4}{2}$$

$$\vdots$$

$$1 + 2 + \cdots + n = \frac{n(n + 1)}{2}$$

which is the total sum of the series.

This means that if we want to calculate the sum of the series $1 + 2 + 3 + \cdots + 10$, we have

$$S_{10} = \frac{10(10 + 1)}{2} = \frac{10 \cdot 11}{2} = 55$$

We cannot apply this artifice to every series. Therefore, we must find a more general method that permits us to calculate the sums of several series. This method is given by the following theorem:

Theorem: Let us consider a finite series $u_1 + u_2 + u_3 + \cdots + u_n$. If we can find a function $F(n)$ such that $u_n = F(n + 1) - F(n)$, then, $u_1 + u_2 + \cdots + u_n = F(n + 1) - F(1)$.

Proof: We have by hypothesis that $u_n = F(n + 1) - F(n)$. Therefore, if we apply it for $n - 1, n - 2, \ldots, 3, 2, 1$, we will get the following relationships:

$$u_n = F(n + 1) - F(n)$$
$$u_{n-1} = F(n) - F(n - 1)$$
$$u_{n-2} = F(n - 1) - F(n - 2)$$
$$\vdots$$
$$u_2 = F(3) - F(2)$$
$$u_1 = F(2) - F(1)$$

If we now add these relationships, we get $u_1 + u_2 + u_3 + \cdots + u_n = F(n+1) - F(1)$, which proves the theorem.

Before students embark on applications, have them consider the following examples:

1. Find the sum of the series $1 + 2 + 3 + \cdots + n$. Because $u_n = n$, we consider $F(n) = An^2 + Bn + C$. (A polynomial one degree higher than u_n should be

74

used.) Therefore, $F(n + 1) = A(n + 1)^2 + B(n + 1) + C$. According to the theorem, we must have

$$u_n = F(n + 1) - F(n)$$
$$n = [A(n + 1)^2 + B(n + 1) + C] - [An^2 + Bn + C]$$
$$= 2An + (A + B)$$

Therefore, by equating coefficients of powers of n we get $2A = 1$ and $A + B = 0$.

By solving these simultaneously, we get $A = \frac{1}{2}$ and $B = -\frac{1}{2}$. Therefore,

$$F(n) = \frac{1}{2}n^2 - \frac{1}{2}n + C,$$
$$F(n + 1) = \frac{1}{2}(n + 1)^2 - \frac{1}{2}(n + 1) + C,$$
$$F(1) = C$$

Thus,

$$1 + 2 + 3 + \cdots + n = F(n + 1) - F(1)$$
$$= \frac{1}{2}(n + 1)^2 - \frac{1}{2}(n + 1)$$
$$= \frac{1}{2}n(n + 1).$$

2. Find the sum of the series $1^2 + 2^2 + 3^2 + \cdots + n^2$. Since $u_n = n^2$, we consider $F(n) = An^3 + Bn^2 + Cn + D$ [One degree higher than u_n, because the highest power of $F(n)$ will be annihilated in $F(n + 1) - F(n)$]. Thus $F(n + 1) = A(n + 1)^3 + B(n + 1)^2 + C(n + 1) + D$. Now

$$u_n = n^2 = F(n + 1) - F(n)$$
$$n^2 = [A(n + 1)^3 + B(n + 1)^2 + C(n + 1) + D]$$
$$- [An^3 + Bn^2 + Cn + D]$$
$$= 3An^2 + (3A + 2B)n + (A + B + C)$$

By equating coefficients of powers of n, we get $3A = 1$, $3A + 2B = 0$, and $A + B + C = 0$, and by solving simultaneously, we get

$$A = \frac{1}{3} \qquad B = -\frac{1}{2} \qquad C = \frac{1}{6}$$

Thus,

$$F(n) = \frac{1}{3}n^3 - \frac{1}{2}n^2 + \frac{1}{6}n + D$$
$$F(n + 1) = \frac{1}{3}(n + 1)^3 - \frac{1}{2}(n + 1)^2 + \frac{1}{6}(n + 1) + D$$
$$F(1) = \frac{1}{3} - \frac{1}{2} + \frac{1}{6} + D = D$$

Hence,

$$1^2 + 2^2 + 3^2 + \cdots + n^2 = F(n+1) - F(1)$$
$$= \frac{1}{3}(n+1)^3 - \frac{1}{2}(n+1)^2 + \frac{1}{6}(n+1)$$
$$= \frac{n(n+1)(2n+1)}{6}$$

3. Find the sum of the series $1^3 + 3^3 + 5^3 + \cdots + (2n-1)^3$. Whereas u_n is of third degree,

$$F(n) = An^4 + Bn^3 + Cn^2 + Dn + E$$

and

$$F(n+1) = A(n+1)^4 + B(n+1)^3 + C(n+1)^2 + D(n+1) + E$$

Thus,

$$u_n = (2n-1)^3 = F(n+1) - F(n)$$

or

$$8n^3 - 12n^2 + 6n - 1 = 4An^3 + (6A+3B)n^2 + (4A+3B+2C)n$$
$$+ (A+B+C+D)$$

By equating coefficients, $4A = 8$ and $A = 2$; $6A + 3B = -12$ and $B = -8$; $4A + 3B + 2C = 6$ and $C = 11$; $A + B + C + D = -1$ and $D = -6$. Therefore,

$$F(n) = 2n^4 - 8n^3 + 11n^2 - 6n + E$$
$$F(n+1) = 2(n+1)^4 - 8(n+1)^3 + 11(n+1)^2 - 6(n+1) + E$$
$$F(1) = -1 + E$$

Thus,

$$1^3 + 3^3 + 5^3 + \cdots + (2n-1)^3 = F(n+1) - F(1)$$
$$= 2(n+1)^4 - 8(n+1)^3 + 11(n+1)^2$$
$$- 6(n+1) + E - (-1 + E)$$
$$= 2n^4 - n^2 = n^2(2n^2 - 1)$$

4. Find the sum of the series $\frac{1}{2} + \frac{1}{4} + \ldots + \frac{1}{2^n}$. Let us consider

$$F(n) = \frac{A}{2^n}$$

and, therefore,

$$F(n+1) = \frac{A}{2^{n+1}}$$

76

Hence, $u_n = F(n+1) - F(n)$. Thus $\frac{1}{2^n} = \frac{A}{2^{n+1}} - \frac{A}{2^n}$, therefore $A = -2$. Hence,

$$F(n+1) = -\frac{1}{2^n} \quad \text{and} \quad F(1) = -1$$

Therefore,

$$\frac{1}{2} + \frac{1}{4} + \cdots + \frac{1}{2^n} = F(n+1) - F(1)$$

$$= -\frac{1}{2^n} + 1 = 1 - \frac{1}{2^n}$$

After sufficient practice, students should be able to find $F(n)$ more easily.

In effect, students should now be able to find the sum of a given series and not just prove by mathematical induction that a given sum is correct. As a further assurance of successful learning, students should be able to do the following exercises:

Find the sum of the series $1 + 8 + 27 + \cdots + n^3$.

Find the sum of the series $\frac{1}{5} + \frac{1}{25} + \frac{1}{125} + \cdots + \frac{1}{5^n}$.

Find the sum of the series $\frac{1}{2} + \frac{2}{2^2} + \frac{3}{2^3} + \frac{4}{2^4} + \cdots + \frac{n}{2^n}$.

Find the sum of the series $1 \cdot 2 + 2 \cdot 3 + 3 \cdot 4 + \cdots + n(n+1)$.

Find the sum of the series $\frac{1}{1 \cdot 2} + \frac{1}{2 \cdot 3} + \frac{1}{3 \cdot 4} + \cdots + \frac{1}{n(n+1)}$.

Find the sum of the series $\frac{1^2}{2} + \frac{2^2}{2^2} + \frac{3^2}{2^3} + \frac{4^2}{2^4} + \cdots + \frac{n^2}{2^n}$.

Find the sum of the series $1 \cdot 2 \cdot 3 + 2 \cdot 3 \cdot 4 + 3 \cdot 4 \cdot 5 + \cdots + n(n+1)(n+2)$.

Find the sum of the series $\frac{1}{1 \cdot 2 \cdot 3} + \frac{1}{2 \cdot 3 \cdot 4} + \frac{1}{3 \cdot 4 \cdot 5} + \cdots + \frac{1}{n(n+1)(n+2)}$.

Find the sum of the infinite series $\frac{1}{2} + \frac{1}{4} + \frac{1}{8} + \frac{1}{16} + \cdots$.

Find the sum of the infinite series $\frac{1}{2} + \frac{2}{2^2} + \frac{3}{2^3} + \frac{4}{2^4} + \cdots$.

Find the sum of the infinite series $\frac{1^2}{2} + \frac{2^2}{2^2} + \frac{3^2}{2^3} + \frac{4^2}{2^4} + \cdots$.

Find the sum of the infinite series $\frac{1}{1 \cdot 2} + \frac{1}{2 \cdot 3} + \frac{1}{3 \cdot 4} + \frac{1}{4 \cdot 5} + \cdots$.

Find the sum of the infinite series $\frac{1}{1 \cdot 2 \cdot 3} + \frac{1}{2 \cdot 3 \cdot 4} + \frac{1}{3 \cdot 4 \cdot 5} + \cdots$.

Geometry Ideas

Sum of the Measures of the Angles of a Triangle

Objective: To discover and prove that the sum of the measures of the angles of a triangle is 180°

Materials: A paper cutout of a scalene triangle

Procedure: Tell students to cut a conveniently large scalene triangle from a piece of paper. They should then fold one vertex so that it touches the opposite side and so that the crease is parallel to that side.

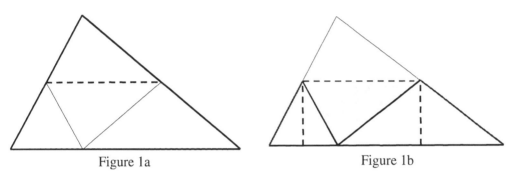

Figure 1a   Figure 1b

They should then fold the remaining two vertices to meet the first vertex at a common point. Students will notice that the three angles of the triangle together form a straight angle (line) and hence have an angle sum of 180°.

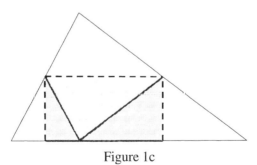

Figure 1c

One could also tear the three vertices from the triangle and place them together to form the straight angle. It is more elegant to use the folding procedure. However, it is also nice to show why this folding procedure has the vertices meet at a point on the side of the triangle. Establishing this phenomenon is tantamount to proving the theorem.

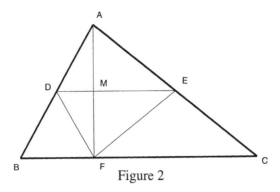

Figure 2

The proof of this theorem follows directly from the paper-folding exercise. By folding the top vertex along a parallel crease (i.e., $\overline{DE} \parallel \overline{BC}$), $\overline{AF} \perp \overline{ED}$ at M. Since $\overline{MF} \cong \overline{AM}$, or M is the midpoint of $\overline{AF}$, D and E are midpoints of $\overline{AB}$ and $\overline{AC}$, respectively, because a line parallel to one side of a triangle (either $\triangle BAF$ or $\triangle CAF$) and bisecting a second side of the triangle also bisects the third side. It is then easy to show that because $\overline{AD} \cong \overline{DF}$, $\overline{DB} \cong \overline{DF}$ and, similarly, $\overline{EF} \cong \overline{EC}$, so the folding over of vertices B and C fits at F to form a straight angle along $\overline{BFC}$. The more formal proof thus follows directly from the exercise.

GEOMETRY IDEA 2

Introducing the Sum of the Measures of the Interior Angles of a Polygon

Objective: To provide alternative ways to convince students of the constant sum of the measures of the interior angles of a (convex) polygon

Materials: Chalkboard, writing materials, or Geometer's Sketchpad

Procedure: Beginning with the notion that the sum of the measures of the angles of a triangle is 180°, students usually conjecture that the sum of the measures of the angles of a quadrilateral may be 360°, because the sum of the measures of the angles of a rectangle (a special type of quadrilateral) is $4 \cdot 90° = 360°$. How can students use this knowledge to find the sum of the measures of the interior angles of *any* polygon?

Here we request that students "triangulate" the area inside the polygon, that is, partition the region inside the polygon into triangular regions with no overlap and no region omitted. We offer three possible triangulations. For each we derive the sum of the measures of the interior angles of the polygon. This is a good way to introduce the concept.

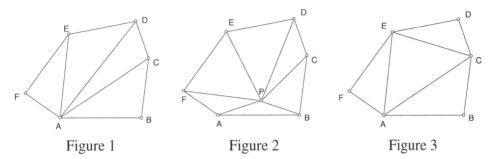

Figure 1   Figure 2   Figure 3

In Figure 1, where a vertex of the given polygon is selected and the diagonals are drawn from there to each of the other vertices, it is clear that the sum of the measures of the interior angles of the polygon is the same as the sum of the measures of the angles of the triangles. Using this drawing scheme, the number of triangles also is 2 less than the number of sides of the polygon. Therefore, the angle sum is 180° times the number of triangles, which for an n-sided polygon is $(n − 2)180°$.

In Figure 2, a point is chosen in the interior of the polygon. From that point segments are drawn to each of the vertices of the polygon. There are n triangles for an n-sided polygon. The sum of the measures of the interior angles of the polygon is the sum of the measures of the angles of the triangles minus the sum of the measures of the angles at point P, which is 360°. Therefore, the sum of the measures of the interior angles of an n-sided polygon is $180n° − 360° = 180(n − 2)°$.

In Figure 3, the region was triangulated in such a way that only diagonals were drawn, yet in such a way that no diagonal intersected any other one (except at an endpoint). Again, the number of triangles needed to triangulate the region is two less than the number of sides of the polygon. Hence, the result is as before.

Encourage students to triangluate the interior region of a polygon in any suitable way and then reach the appropriate interior angle-measure sum.

Sum of the Measures of the Exterior Angles of a Polygon. I

Objective: To discover and prove that the sum of the measures of the exterior angles of a polygon is 360°

Materials: A copy of the following series of drawings, or the ability to show Figure 1 on a screen (e.g. with Geometer's Sketchpad) and then to reduce it in size to an extreme

Procedure: Begin the lesson by showing students figure 1 and ask them to focus on the sum of the measures of the exterior angles. Either have a very large version of this figure redrawn on a large piece of paper or the chalkboard, or have a series of drawings of this figure each significantly smaller than its predecessor. The last figure should be so small that the polygon almost appears as a point. Then have students conjecture about the sum of the measures of the exterior angles, which now may look like they are lines emanating from a point rather than extensions of sides of a polygon.

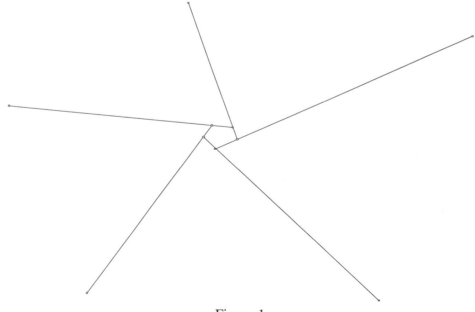

Figure 1

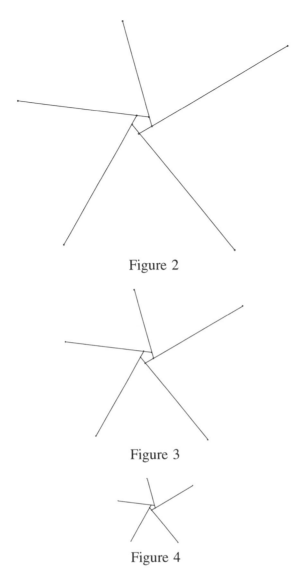

Figure 2

Figure 3

Figure 4

The effect of reducing this figure successively can be achieved either by moving the figure further away from the class or by presenting them with progressively smaller figures. Students should eventually realize that the sum of the measures of the exterior angles appears as a complete revolution about a point (the extreme situation, where the polygon reduces to a point) or 360°.

This concept can also be seen with a physical model by observing a gradually closing camera lens. Many such lenses use a pentagonal opening. By closing the shutter, you can reduce the pentagon to a tiny pentagon that looks almost like a point. Then examine the extensions of the sides that form the exterior angles and it should appear as the sum of the measures of the angles completely around a point (the reduced pentagon). The traditional proof can now be used to establish this angle sum more formally. The lesson can now continue in the usual manner.

Sum of the Measures of the Exterior Angles of a Polygon. II

Objective: To discover the sum of the measures of the exterior angles of a polygon

Materials: Geometer's Sketchpad or a chalkboard

Procedure: We use an inductive approach to help discover the sum of the measures of the exterior angles of a polygon. We, therefore, begin with a polygon with the least number of sides—a triangle.

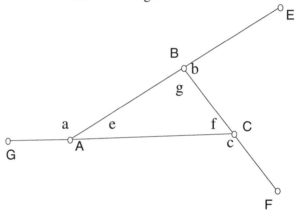

At each vertex of the triangle, there are two supplementary angles, so

$$a + e = 180 \qquad g + b = 180 \qquad f + c = 180$$

Therefore,

$$a + e + g + b + f + c = 3(180) = 540$$

However, $e + g + f = 180$. Thus,

$$a + b + c = 3(180) - 180 = 2(180) = 360$$

A similar argument can then be made for any other polygon. We consider a hexagon as an example.

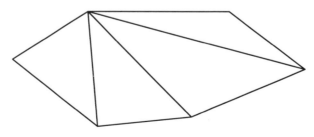

We triangulate the hexagonal region and notice that the sum of the measures of the interior angles of the hexagon is 4(180). As before, we notice that the sum of the measures of the interior and the exterior angles is 6(180); therefore, the sum of the measures of the exterior angles is $6(180) - 4(180) = 2(180) = 360$.

In the general case, for an n-sided polygon,

the sum of the measures of the interior and the exterior angles is $n(180)$

$-$ the sum of the measures of the interior angle of the polygon

$= (n - 2)(180)$

so the sum of the measures of the exterior angles is $2(180) = 360$.

Triangle Inequality

Objective: To discover the triangle inequality and prove it true

Materials: A box of spaghetti and a chalkboard

Procedure: Carefully give each student 10 spaghetti sticks. Tell students to take each spaghetti stick and break it into three parts. Then they are to place the three pieces on their desks and try to form a triangle. They are to keep a log for each attempt with a spaghetti stick. Reviewing their 10 attempts should lead students to conclude that only when the sum of the lengths of any two sides is greater than the length of the third side is a triangle possible.

Students have probably heard that "the shortest distance between two points is a straight line." We can use this fact to arrive at the triangle inequality: *the sum of the lengths of any two sides of a triangle must be greater than the length of the third side*.

In the following figure, the shortest distance between points A and B is segment AB, that is, $AC + CB > AB$.

$C \cdot$

$A \cdot$ $B \cdot$

87

This relationship (or theorem) can be proved rather simply. Consider the triangle ABC and choose the point D on $\overrightarrow{CA}$ so that $AD = AB$.

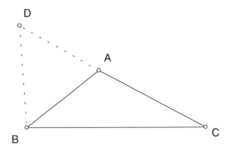

Because $\angle ADB \cong \angle ABD$ in isosceles triangle DAB, then $m\angle DBC > m\angle ADB$. It then follows that (for $\triangle DBC$) $DC > BC$, because in a triangle the greater side is opposite the greater angle. However, because $AD = AB$, $DC = AC + AB$. Therefore, $AC + AB > BC$, which is what we wanted to prove.

GEOMETRY IDEA 6

Don't Necessarily Trust Your Geometric Intuition

Objective: To demonstrate that what seems obvious may not necessarily be so

Materials: Chalkboard, a large cardboard circle, and a piece of string longer than the circumference of the circle

Procedure: Geometry is often referred to as the visual part of mathematics. We tend to believe many things as we see them. Such optical tricks are useful to put geometry students on guard and make them more discriminating learners. There are also notions in geometry that just don't seem to "make sense." For example, when asked to compare the two segments in Figure 1, the one on the right side looks longer. In Figure 2, the bottom segment also looks longer. In actuality the segments have the same length.

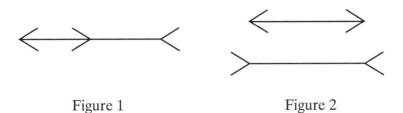

Figure 1   Figure 2

In Figure 3 the crosshatched segment appears to be longer than the solid one, and in Figure 4, the narrower and vertical stick appears to be longer than the other two even though to the left they are shown to be the same length. A further optical illusion can be seen in Figure 5, where $\overline{AB}$ appears to be longer than $\overline{BC}$. This isn't true: $\overline{AB} \cong \overline{BC}$.

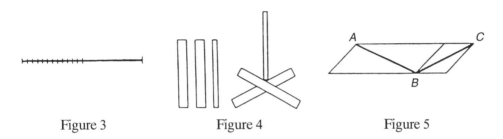

Figure 3   Figure 4   Figure 5

In Figure 6 the vertical segment clearly appears to be longer, but isn't.

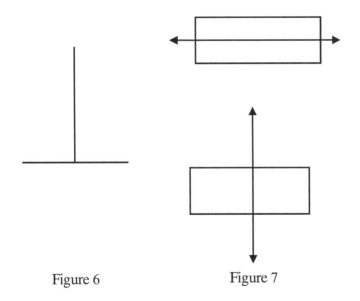

Figure 6   Figure 7

In Figure 7 the horizontal segment appears to be longer, but isn't.

89

The curve lengths and curvature of the diagrams in Figures 8 and 9 are quite deceiving. Such optical tricks are important to point out to students so that they do not rely solely on their visual observations:

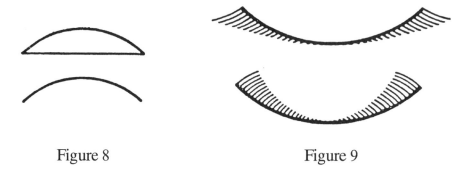

Figure 8   Figure 9

The square between the two semicircles in Figure 10 looks larger than the unencumbered square to the left, and in Figure 11, the white square within the large black box looks smaller than that above it.

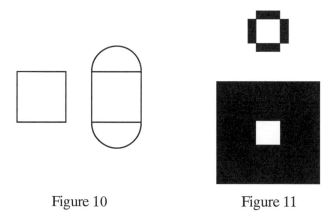

Figure 10   Figure 11

We see further evidence of fooling the senses in Figure 12, where the circle inscribed in the square (on the left) appears to be smaller than the circle circumscribed about the square (on the right).

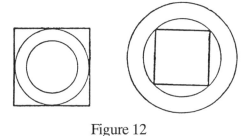

Figure 12

Figures 13, 14, and 15 show how relative placement can affect the appearance of a geometric diagram. In Figure 13, the center square appears to be the largest of the group. In Figure 14, the center circle on the left appears to be larger than the center circle on the right. In Figure 15, the center sector on the left appears to be larger than the center sector on the right. In all of these cases, the two figures that appear not to be the same size are, in fact, the same size!

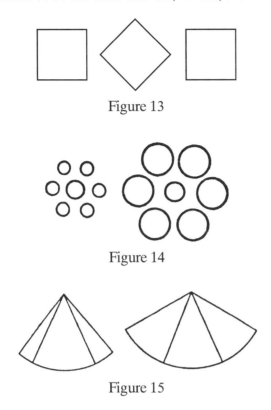

Figure 13

Figure 14

Figure 15

We offer here an illustration. Consider a rope tied along the equator of the Earth, that is, circumscribing the entire Earth sphere. Now lengthen this enormously long rope by 1 meter. It is no longer tightly tied around the Earth. If we lift this loose rope equally around the equator so that it is uniformly spaced above the equator, will a mouse fit beneath the rope?

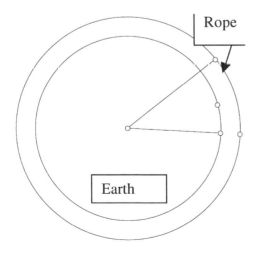

Rope

Earth

We are looking for the distance between the circumferences of these two circles. Whereas the size of neither circle is given, suppose the small (inner) circle is extremely small, so small that it has a radius of length 0 and is thus reduced to a point. Then the distance between the circles is merely the radius of the larger circle. The circumference of this larger circle is $2\pi R = C+1$, or $2\pi R = 0+1 = 1$, where C is the circumference of the earth (now for the sake of this problem reduced to 0) and $C + 1$ is the length of the rope. The distance between the circles is $R = \frac{1}{2\pi} = 0.159$ meters, which would allow a mouse to comfortably fit beneath the rope.

This unit is intended to demonstrate that even in geometry, not everything is "intuitively obvious" and that there are geometric "facts" that not only seem to be wrong, but do not necessarily make sense without careful inspection.

GEOMETRY IDEA 7

Importance of Definitions in Mathematics (Geometry)

Objective: To demonstrate what can happen when definitions are not heeded in mathematics

Materials: Chalkboard

Procedure: It is interesting and impressive to show what happens when definitions in mathematics are not adhered to. We begin by showing some rather absurd results in such cases.

Begin the discussion by challenging your students to draw on the chalkboard any scalene triangle, which you will then "prove" to be isosceles. Consider the scalene $\triangle ABC$ to be isosceles, draw the bisector of $\angle C$ and the perpendicular bisector of $\overline{AB}$. From their point of intersection, G, draw perpendiculars to $\overline{AC}$ and $\overline{CB}$, meeting them at points D and F, respectively.

Note, that there are four possibilities for the preceding description for various scalene triangles:

1. Where $\overline{CG}$ and $\overline{GE}$ meet inside the triangle (Figure 1):

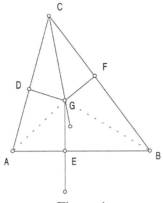

Figure 1

2. Where $\overline{CG}$ and $\overline{GE}$ meet on $\overline{AB}$ (Figure 2):

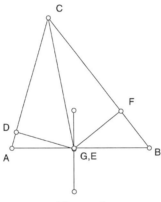

Figure 2

3. Where $\overline{CG}$ and $\overline{GE}$ meet outside the triangle, but the perpendiculars $\overline{GD}$ and $\overline{GF}$ fall on $\overline{AC}$ and $\overline{CB}$ (Figure 3):

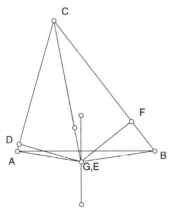

Figure 3

4. Where $\overline{CG}$ and $\overline{GE}$ meet outside the triangle, and the perpendiculars $\overline{GD}$ and $\overline{GF}$ meet $\overrightarrow{CA}$ and $\overrightarrow{CB}$ outside the triangle (Figure 4):

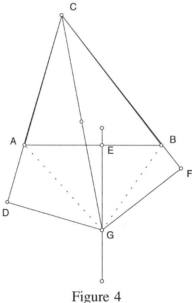

Figure 4

The "proof" of the fallacy can be demonstrated with any of Figures 1–4.

Given: $\triangle ABC$ is scalene
Prove: $AC = BC$ (or $\triangle ABC$ is isosceles)

"*Proof*": Whereas $\angle ACG \cong \angle BCG$ and $rt\angle CDG \cong rt\angle CFG$, $\triangle CDG \cong \triangle CFG$ [side–angle–angle (SAA)]. Therefore, $DG = FG$ and $CD = CF$. Since $AG = BG$ (a point on the perpendicular bisector of a line segment is equidistant from the endpoints of the line segment) and $\angle ADG$ and $\angle BFG$ are right angles, $\triangle DAG \cong \triangle FBG$ (because they have respective hypotenuse and leg congruent). Therefore, $DA = FB$. It then follows that $AC = BC$ (by addition in Figures 1, 2, and 3, and by subtraction in Figure 4).

At this point students will be quite disturbed. They will wonder where the error was committed that permitted this fallacy to occur. Some students will be clever enough to attack the correctness of the figures. By rigorous construction, students will find a subtle error in the figures:

1. The point G *must* be outside the triangle.
2. When perpendiculars meet the sides of the triangle, one will meet a side *between* the vertices, whereas the other will not (Figure 5).

94

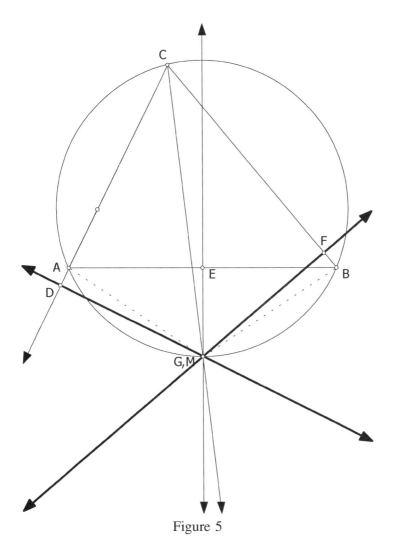

Figure 5

Some discussion of Euclid's neglect of the concept of betweenness should follow. However, the beauty of this particular fallacy is the powerful proof of items 1 and 2, which indicates the *error* of the fallacy.

Begin by considering the circumcircle of $\triangle ABC$. The bisector of $\angle ACB$ must contain the midpoint, M, of $\overgroup{AB}$ (because $\angle ACM$ and $\angle BCM$ are congruent inscribed angles). The perpendicular bisector of $\overline{AB}$ must bisect $\overgroup{AB}$, and, therefore, must pass through M. Thus, the bisector of $\angle ACB$ and the perpendicular bisector of $\overline{AB}$ intersect *outside* the triangle at M (or G). This eliminates the possibilities shown in Figures 1 and 2.

Now have students consider an inscribed quadrilateral $ACBG$. Because the opposite angles of an inscribed (or cyclic) quadrilateral are supplementary, $m\angle CAG + m\angle CBG = 180$. If $\angle CAG$ and $\angle CBG$ are right angles, then $\overline{CG}$ would be a diameter and $\triangle ABC$ would be isosceles. Therefore, since $\triangle ABC$ is scalene,

95

$\angle CAG$ and $\angle CBG$ are not right angles. In this case, one angle must be acute and the other obtuse. Suppose $\angle CBG$ is acute and $\angle CAG$ is obtuse. Then in $\triangle CGB$, the altitude on $\overline{CB}$ must be *inside* the triangle, whereas in obtuse $\triangle CAG$, the altitude on $\overline{AC}$ must be *outside the triangle*, thus eliminating the possibility shown in Figure 3. (This is usually readily accepted by students, but can be easily proved.) The fact that one and *only one* of the perpendiculars intersects a side of the triangle *between* the vertices destroys the fallacious "proof." It is important for you to stress the importance of the concept of betweenness in geometry. This demonstration hinges on the definition of betweenness, a concept not available to Euclid, which ought to be brought to the attention of students. Without defining the concept of betweenness, the preceding fallacy arises.

There are lots of available geometric fallacies or paradoxes, each of which demonstrates the violation of a basic definition. These sources can be found in most libraries. One such book is *Excursions in Advanced Euclidean Geometry* by Alfred S. Posamentier (Addison-Wesley, Reading, MA, 1984).

The reader is also referred to Geometry Unit 27 for other illustrations that meet the objective of this unit.

GEOMETRY IDEA 8

Proving Quadrilaterals to Be Parallelograms

Objective: To review methods of proving quadrilaterals to be parallelograms

Materials: Chalkboard or overhead projector

Procedure: There are many popular methods for proving a quadrilateral to be a parallelogram. Beginning with the definition of a parallelogram (both pairs of opposite sides are parallel), most textbooks include such methods as proving one pair of sides both congruent and parallel, or both pairs of opposite sides congruent, or both pairs of opposite angles congruent. However, the topic begins to take an interesting turn, and also a form of completeness, when students begin to investigate which two pairs of the following options lead to a conclusion that a given quadrilateral is a parallelogram:

> One pair of opposite angles congruent
> One pair of opposite sides congruent
> One pair of opposite sides parallel

To keep track of the various combinations, a table such as follows can be established. You may be surprised to notice that the only "pair of pairs" that does *not* lead to proving a parallelogram is one pair of opposite sides parallel and *another* pair of opposite sides congruent. (This leads to a trapezoid.)

	Pair of opposite sides congruent	Pair of opposite sides parallel	Pair of opposite angles congruent
Pair of opposite sides congruent	Yes	Same pair only	Yes
Pair of opposite sides parallel	Same pair only	Yes (definition)	Yes
Pair of opposite angles congruent	Yes	Yes	Yes

The preceding table, augmented by the notion that diagonals that bisect each other also prove a parallelogram, provides a very fertile area for developing proofs and also gives a certain sense of completeness that is often lacking in the typical textbook treatment of this topic.

GEOMETRY IDEA 9

Demonstrating the Need to Consider All Information Given

Objective: To show how omitting the obvious can be a costly fault

Materials: Geometric construction tools or the Geometer's Sketchpad program

Procedure: A rather simple-to-present problem in geometry can prove to be vexing if the obvious is not considered. This is a dilemma for many inexperienced students. It is up to you (the teacher) to provide students with this experience to use in future endeavors.

Consider the following problem: Three equal circles *A*, *B*, and *C* meet at a common point *P* and intersect each other (pair wise) at points *K*, *L*, and *M*, as shown in Figure 1:

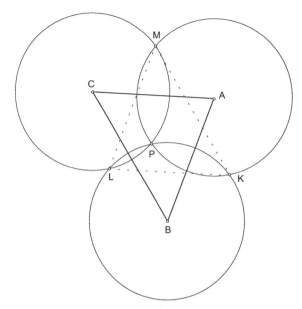

Figure 1

The question is, "Why are triangles *ABC* and *KLM* congruent?" Typically, students exploring the path to proving these two triangles congruent are searching for angles or sides to be proved congruent without using one important fact, which is that the circles are all congruent. (Not just saying they're congruent, but representing it in the diagram.) The logical thing to do is to draw many of the radii of the circles because they are all the same length. This ought to produce something helpful. We draw the radii to each of the points of intersection of the circles and get a rather familiar figure.

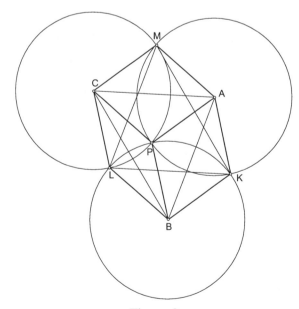

Figure 2

The bold figure in Figure 2 is familiar to us as a parallelepiped. There are also several rhombuses to be seen. These familiar shapes will be helpful to prove the triangles congruent. Using rhombus $CPBL$ (since $CP = PB = BL = LC$) and rhombus $MAPC$, we find $\overline{LB} \parallel \overline{MA}$ and $\overline{LB} \cong \overline{MA}$. Therefore, $MABL$ is a parallelogram and $\overline{ML} \cong \overline{AB}$. In a similar way, we can show that $\overline{MK} \cong \overline{CB}$ and $\overline{LK} \cong \overline{CA}$, making $\triangle ABC \cong \triangle LMK$.

The key to the solution of this problem should make students aware of the need to list all given items, even if they are offshoots of the given statement. Doing so enabled us to "draw" a parallelepiped, which, in turn, led us to the solution of a rather difficult problem.

If we complete the parallelepiped drawing by showing the "background lines" (see Figure 3), then another interesting property emerges: the three points of intersection of the pairs of circles lie on a circle equal in size to the other three circles.

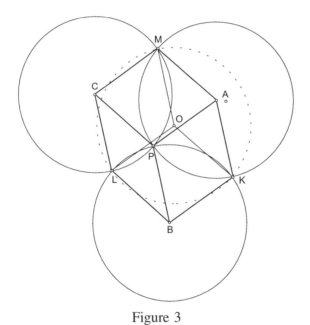

Figure 3

We drew the fourth circle with dashed lines. We can show that the center of this fourth circle is the point O, which is the "background" vertex of the parallelepiped drawn as a projection on the plane. If this is truly a projection of the parallelepiped, then $\overline{OK} \cong \overline{OL} \cong \overline{OM}$, which are also the same lengths as the radii of the other three circles. Thus the circle that contains the intersection points of the pairs of circles is equal to the other three circles.

Had we not noticed the projection of the parallelepiped, we could have done this proof as a plane geometry task, noting that the various rhombuses can be used to establish the same results, albeit strictly as a plane geometry exercise.

This geometric configuration first highlights the important notion of establishing all the given information even if it is directly stated, and then shows how some unusual thinking serves to enrich the students' geometric perceptions.

Midline of a Triangle

Objective: To prove and apply the properties of the midlines of a triangle

Materials: Geometer's Sketchpad

Procedure: Begin by drawing a quadrilateral using Geometer's Sketchpad. This can be easily done by drawing four connected line segments. Successively highlight each segment and instruct the program to construct the midpoint of each side. Then join these midpoints consecutively. With the "arrow" pointer, drag one (or more than one) vertex to assume various positions and observe what shapes the inside quadrilateral takes. It will always be a *parallelogram*.

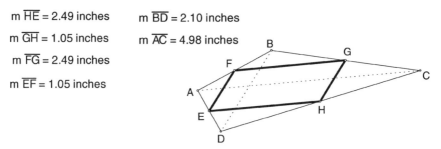

m $\overline{HE}$ = 2.49 inches   m $\overline{BD}$ = 2.10 inches

m $\overline{GH}$ = 1.05 inches   m $\overline{AC}$ = 4.98 inches

m $\overline{FG}$ = 2.49 inches

m $\overline{EF}$ = 1.05 inches

Using the measure monitor, have students drag this vertex to positions that yield a *rhombus* from the inside parallelogram. What must be true about the original quadrilateral for the inside parallelogram to be a rhombus? [congruent diagonals]

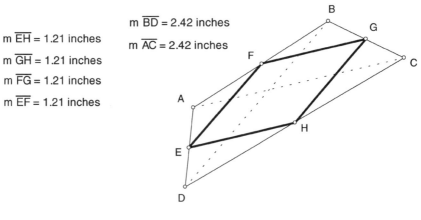

m $\overline{EH}$ = 1.21 inches   m $\overline{BD}$ = 2.42 inches

m $\overline{GH}$ = 1.21 inches   m $\overline{AC}$ = 2.42 inches

m $\overline{FG}$ = 1.21 inches

m $\overline{EF}$ = 1.21 inches

Using the measure monitor, have students drag this vertex to positions that yield a *rectangle* from the inside parallelogram. What must be true about the original quadrilateral for the inside parallelogram to be a rectangle? [perpendicular diagonals]

m $\overline{HE}$ = 2.49 inches   m $\overline{BD}$ = 1.34 inches

m $\overline{GH}$ = 0.67 inches   m $\overline{AC}$ = 4.98 inches

m $\overline{FG}$ = 2.49 inches

m $\overline{EF}$ = 0.67 inches

m∠BLA = 90°

m∠FEH = 90°

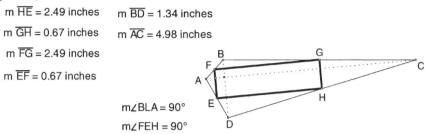

Using the measure monitor, have students drag this vertex to positions that yield a *square* from the inside parallelogram. What must be true about the original quadrilateral for the inside parallelogram to be a square? [congruent and perpendicular diagonals]

m $\overline{BD}$ = 1.50 inches

m $\overline{AC}$ = 1.50 inches

m $\overline{EH}$ = 0.75 inches

m $\overline{GH}$ = 0.75 inches

m $\overline{FG}$ = 0.75 inches

m $\overline{EF}$ = 0.75 inches

m∠BPA = 90°

m∠EFG = 90°

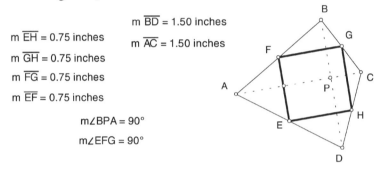

In each of the foregoing cases, $\overline{FG} \parallel \overline{EH}$ and $\overline{FG} \cong \overline{EH}$, because both $\overline{FG}$ and $\overline{EH}$ are half the length of $\overline{AC}$ and parallel to $\overline{AC}$.

Similarly for $\overline{EF}$ and $\overline{GH}$, which are half the length of and parallel to $\overline{BD}$. Students soon realize that the type of parallelogram is dependent on the length and relative position of the diagonals of the original quadrilateral *ABCD*. The various measures are marked (and obtained from Geometer's Sketchpad).

GEOMETRY IDEA **11**

Length of the Median of a Trapezoid

Objective: To prove that the length of the median of a trapezoid is the average of the lengths of the bases

Materials: Chalkboard or Geometer's Sketchpad program

Procedure: Present the students with the following diagram, where $ABCD$ is a trapezoid with median $\overline{MN}$, and instruct them to draw $\overline{BE} \parallel \overline{AD}$ and $\overline{NQ} \parallel \overline{BE} \parallel \overline{AD}$.

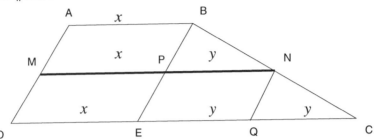

The plan here is to guide students to demonstrate that the length of the median of a trapezoid is one-half the sum of the lengths of the bases. Students already should have defined the median as the segment that joins the midpoints of the nonparallel sides of the trapezoid and established that the median is parallel to the bases. This demonstration is done using the pieces of segments noted in the diagram.

Students should realize that because $\overline{NQ} \parallel \overline{BE}$ and N is the midpoint of $\overline{BC}$, then $\overline{NQ}$ bisects $\overline{EC}$.

For convenience, we let $CQ = QE = y$. By definition, we have a parallelogram $PNQE$ and $PN = y$.

From the various parallelograms, we also have $AB = MP = DE = x$.

Students can now plainly see that $MN = x + y$ and $AB + DC = 2x + 2y$, so $MN = \frac{1}{2}(AB + DC)$.

Another way to establish the length of the median of a trapezoid can be done using a rotation. Consider trapezoid $ABCD$, which is rotated $180°$ through the midpoint, N, of $\overline{BC}$.

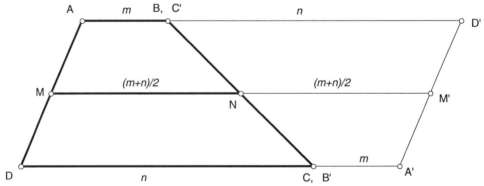

This gives us parallelogram $AD'A'D$, where $\overline{M'M}$, which is parallel and joins the midpoints of $\overline{AD}$, $\overline{BC}$, and $\overline{A'D'}$, has length $m + n$. Since N is the midpoint of $\overline{M'M}$, $MN = \frac{m+n}{2}$.

Pythagorean Theorem

Objective: To have students discover various interesting proofs of the Pythagorean theorem

Materials: Chalkboard, overhead projector, and Geometer's Sketchpad

Procedure: Begin by asking the class the question, "What do Pythagoras, Euclid, and President James A. Garfield have in common?"

In 1876, while still a member of the House of Representatives (and five years before becoming President of the United States), James A. Garfield published an original proof of the Pythagorean theorem in the *New England Journal of Education.* This theorem, believed to have been originally proved by Pythagoras in about 525 BC, was also proved by Euclid in 300 BC. In the discussion that follows, we briefly consider these extraordinarily clever proofs, especially considering the level of development of mathematics at the time.

You may wish to begin the introduction of the Pythagorean theorem by having students prove the theorem using the relationships among the sides of a right triangle, where the altitude is drawn to the hypotenuse. This can be done by simply completing a few exercises.

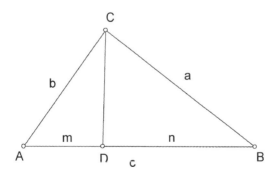

In the preceding figure, $\overline{CD}$ is an altitude of right $\triangle ABC$, with right angle at C, so that $\triangle ADC \sim \triangle CDB \sim \triangle ACB$. The lengths of the segments are marked in the figure. Referring to the figure, complete each of the following statements.

1. AC is a mean proportional between ____ and ____. $[c, m]$

2. Therefore, $\frac{c}{b} = \frac{b}{?}$ or $b^2 =$ ___. Why? $\left[\frac{c}{b} = \frac{b}{m}, \ cm\right]$

3. ___ is the mean proportional between AB and BD. $[a]$

103

4. Therefore, $\frac{-}{a} = \frac{-}{n}$ or $a^2 = \underline{\quad}$. Why? $\left[\frac{c}{a} = \frac{a}{n}, \; cn\right]$

5. Adding the results of Exercises 2 and 4, we get
$a^2 + b^2 = \underline{\quad} + \underline{\quad} = \underline{\quad}(m + n)$ $[cn + cm = c\,(m + n)]$

6. However, $m + n = \underline{\quad}$. $[c]$

7. Therefore, $a^2 + \underline{\quad} = \underline{\quad}$. $\left[a^2 + b^2 = c^2\right]$

This essentially proves the Pythagorean theorem.

Students will enjoy the novelty of the proofs by the three famous people mentioned previously. Begin by showing the demonstration that is believed to have been used by the *Pythagoreans* to show their famous theorem.

The following two squares have the same area.

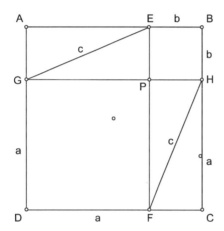 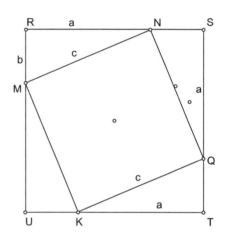

The one on the left is composed of four congruent right triangles and two squares, the total area of which is equal to $4(\frac{1}{2}ab) + a^2 + b^2$.

The one on the right is composed of four congruent right triangles and one square, the total area of which is equal to $4(\frac{1}{2}ab) + c^2$.

After establishing that the quadrilateral inside the square at the right is also a square (with side length c), we may conclude that $a^2 + b^2 = c^2$.

Euclid's proof also uses area, but in a much different way. We are given right $\triangle ABC$ with $m\angle C = 90$; $BAED$, $CAKH$, and $CBFG$ are squares. We are to prove that* $\mathscr{A}$ square $CBFG + \mathscr{A}$ square $CAKH = \mathscr{A}$ square $BAED$ (that is, $a^2 + b^2 = c^2$).

---

* We shall use the symbol $\mathscr{A}$ to represent "area of."

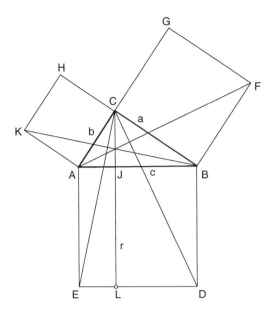

Draw $\overline{FA}$ and $\overline{CD}$. Then we can show that $\triangle FBA \cong \triangle CBD$, so that $\mathscr{A}\triangle FBA = \mathscr{A}\triangle CBD$. Draw $\overline{CL} \parallel \overline{BD}$. Whereas $\triangle CBD$ and rectangle $BJLD$ share the same base and altitude, $\mathscr{A}\triangle CBD = \frac{1}{2}\mathscr{A}$ rectangle $BJLD$; likewise $\mathscr{A}\triangle FBA = \frac{1}{2}\mathscr{A}$ square $CBFG$. Therefore, $\mathscr{A}$ rectangle $BJLD = \mathscr{A}$ square $CBFG$.

We can also show that $\triangle BAK \cong \triangle EAC$. It follows that $\mathscr{A}$ rectangle $JAEL = \mathscr{A}$ square $CHKA$. Therefore, $\mathscr{A}$ square $CHKA + \mathscr{A}$ square $CBFG = \mathscr{A}$ rectangle $BJLD + \mathscr{A}$ rectangle $JAEL$. However, $\mathscr{A}$ rectangle $BJLD + \mathscr{A}$ rectangle $JAEL = \mathscr{A}$ square $BAED$. Thus, $\mathscr{A}$ square $CBFG + \mathscr{A}$ square $CHKA = \mathscr{A}$ square $BAED$, or $a^2 + b^2 = c^2$.

To begin *President James A. Garfield's proof*, we consider right $\triangle ABC$ with $m\angle C = 90$. We let $AC = b$, $BC = a$, and $AB = c$. We need to show that $a^2 + b^2 = c^2$.

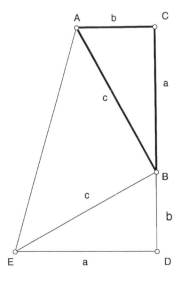

Select D on $\overleftrightarrow{BC}$ so that $BD = AC$ and $\overline{CBD}$. Consider $\overline{DE} \perp \overline{CBD}$ so that $DE = BC$. We can show that quadrilateral $ACDE$ is a trapezoid. Also $\mathscr{A} \triangle ABC = \mathscr{A} \triangle BED$ and $AB = BE$.

$$\mathscr{A} \text{ trapezoid } ACDE = \frac{1}{2}CD(AC + DE) = \frac{1}{2}(a+b) \cdot (a+b) = \frac{1}{2}(a+b)^2$$

$$\mathscr{A} \triangle ABE = \frac{1}{2}AB \cdot BE = \frac{1}{2}c^2$$

Also $\mathscr{A} \triangle ABC = \frac{1}{2}AC \cdot BC = \frac{1}{2}ab$. However, $\mathscr{A}$ trapezoid $ACDE = \mathscr{A} \triangle ABE + 2\mathscr{A} \triangle ABC$. Substituting, we get

$$\frac{1}{2}(a+b)^2 = \frac{1}{2}c^2 + 2\left(\frac{1}{2}ab\right)$$
$$(a+b)^2 = c^2 + 2ab$$

and it follows that $a^2 + b^2 = c^2$.

GEOMETRY IDEA **13**

Angle Measurement With a Circle
by Moving the Circle

Objective: To prove the theorems on measuring angles related to a circle, using a physical model

Materials: Cardboard, string, and a pair of scissors, or use of Geometer's Sketchpad software program

Procedure: This activity is designed to demonstrate all of the measurements of the variations of an angle related to a circle. This activity can be carried out very nicely by cutting out a circle from a piece of cardboard and drawing a convenient inscribed angle on it. The measure of that angle should be the same as that formed by two pieces of string that are affixed to a rectangular piece of cardboard (see Figure 1).

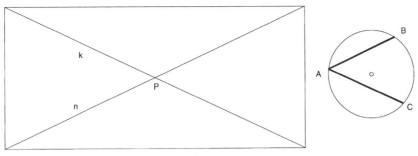

Figure 1

The theorem that establishes that the measure of an inscribed angle of a circle is one-half the measure of the intercepted arc is assumed.

By moving the circle to various positions, we are able to find the measure of an angle formed by

- Two chords intersecting inside the circle (but not at its center)
- Two secants intersecting outside the circle
- Two tangents intersecting outside the circle
- A secant and a tangent intersecting outside the circle
- A chord and a tangent intersecting on the circle

We begin by demonstrating the relationship between the arcs of the circle and the angle formed by *two chords intersecting inside the circle* (but not at its center). Place the cardboard circle into a position so that $\overline{AB} \parallel n$ and $\overline{AC}$ is on k as in Figure 2.

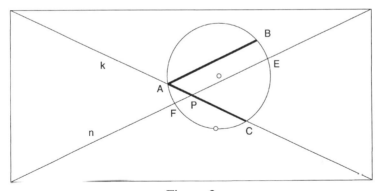

Figure 2

Notice that $m\angle A = \frac{1}{2}m\overset{\frown}{BEC}$ and $m\angle A = m\angle EPC$. Therefore, $m\angle P = \frac{1}{2}m\overset{\frown}{BEC} = \frac{1}{2}(m\overset{\frown}{BE} + m\overset{\frown}{EC})$. However, because parallel lines cut off congruent arcs on a given circle, $m\overset{\frown}{BE} = m\overset{\frown}{AF}$. It then follows that $m\angle P = \frac{1}{2}(m\overset{\frown}{AF} + m\overset{\frown}{EC})$, which shows the relationship of the angle formed by two chords, $\angle P$, and its intercepted arcs, $\overset{\frown}{AF}$ and $\overset{\frown}{EC}$.

107

Consider next the angle formed by *two secants intersecting outside the circle*. Place the cardboard circle into the position shown in Figure 3.

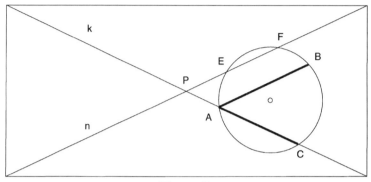

Figure 3

Begin by recalling that $m\angle P = \frac{1}{2}m\overset{\frown}{BC}$ and $m\angle FPC = m\angle A$. Since $m\overset{\frown}{AE} = m\overset{\frown}{BF}$, we can add and subtract it to the same quantity without changing the value of the original quantity. Thus,

$$m\angle P = \frac{1}{2}\left(m\overset{\frown}{BC} + m\overset{\frown}{BF} - m\overset{\frown}{AE}\right)$$
$$= \frac{1}{2}\left(m\overset{\frown}{FBC} - m\overset{\frown}{AE}\right)$$

In a similar way we can demonstrate the relationship between an angle formed by *two tangents intersecting outside the circle* and its intercepted arcs. We move the cardboard circle into the position shown in Figure 4.

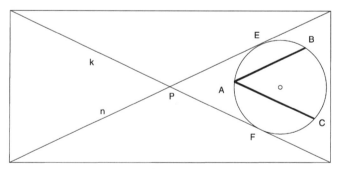

Figure 4

In this case, the equality of arcs $\overset{\frown}{AE}$ and $\overset{\frown}{BE}$ as well as that of arcs $\overset{\frown}{AF}$ and $\overset{\frown}{CF}$ is key to demonstrating the desired relationship.

We have

$$m\angle P = m\angle A = \frac{1}{2}m\overset{\frown}{BC}$$

$$= \frac{1}{2}\left(m\overset{\frown}{BE} + m\overset{\frown}{BC} + m\overset{\frown}{CF} - m\overset{\frown}{AE} - m\overset{\frown}{AF}\right)$$

$$= \frac{1}{2}\left(m\overset{\frown}{EBCF} - m\overset{\frown}{EAF}\right)$$

Again, by sliding the cardboard circle to the position shown in Figure 5, we can find the measure of the angle formed by *a tangent and a secant intersecting outside the circle*.

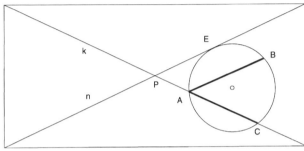

Figure 5

This time we rely on the equality of arcs $\overset{\frown}{AE}$ and $\overset{\frown}{BE}$. By adding and subtracting these equal arcs, we get

$$m\angle P = m\angle A = \frac{1}{2}m\overset{\frown}{BC} = \frac{1}{2}\left(m\overset{\frown}{BC} + m\overset{\frown}{BE} - m\overset{\frown}{AE}\right)$$

$$= \frac{1}{2}\left(m\overset{\frown}{EBC} - m\overset{\frown}{AE}\right)$$

To complete the various possibilities of positions for the cardboard circle, place it so that we can find the relationship between *an angle formed by a chord and a tangent intersecting at the point of tangency* and its intercepted arc (see Figure 6).

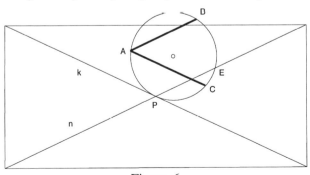

Figure 6

The crucial arc equality this time is $m\widehat{AP} = m\widehat{CP}$, and $m\widehat{AP} = m\widehat{BE}$. We begin as before:

$$m\angle P = m\angle A = \frac{1}{2}m\widehat{BEC}$$

$$= \frac{1}{2}\left(m\widehat{BE} + m\widehat{EC} + m\widehat{PC} - m\widehat{AP}\right)$$

$$= \frac{1}{2}\left(m\widehat{EC} + m\widehat{PC}\right) = \frac{1}{2}m\widehat{PCE}$$

This activity can also be done quite nicely with a computer drawing program such as Geometer's Sketchpad.

GEOMETRY IDEA 14

Angle Measurement With a Circle

Objective: To prove the theorems on measuring angles related to a circle

Materials: Prepare a photocopy of the accompanying diagram

Procedure: In Geometry Idea 13, the class should have learned that the central angle of a circle has a measure equal to the measure of its intercepted arc and the inscribed angle of a circle has a measure equal to one-half of the measure of its intercepted arc. This activity enables students to discover the relationship between the intercepted arc measures of a circle and angles formed by two tangents, by a tangent and a secant, by two secants, by a tangent and a chord meeting at the point of tangency, and by two chords.

Essentially, what the students should be guided to realize is that they are then able to relate an angle formed outside, on, or inside the circle to the intercepted arcs. Completing the following exercises will foster this realization. Have students work independently on these exercises before reviewing them with the class.

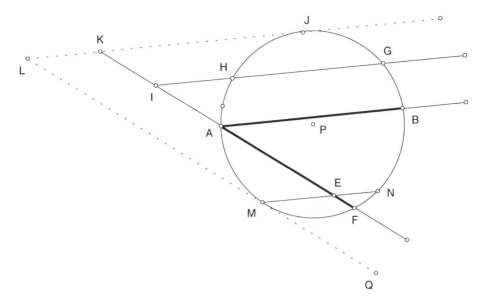

Complete the following exercises, while considering parallel all those lines in the accompanying figure that appear to be parallel. All answers are arcs. Then express each boldface statement in general terms

1. Why are the following angles congruent?
   $\angle JLM$, $\angle JKF$, $\angle GIF$, $\angle BAF$, $\angle NEF$, and $\angle NMQ$

2. $m\angle BAF = \frac{1}{2}m$____

3. $m\overset{\frown}{BN} = m$____ $= m$____

4. $m\angle NMQ = m\angle BAF = \frac{1}{2}\left(m\overset{\frown}{BN} + m\text{\_\_\_\_}\right) = \frac{1}{2}\left(m\overset{\frown}{MF} + m\text{\_\_\_\_}\right)$
   $= \frac{1}{2}m$____

5. $m\angle NEF = m\angle BAF = \frac{1}{2}\left(m\overset{\frown}{BN} + m\text{\_\_\_\_}\right) = \frac{1}{2}\left(m\overset{\frown}{AM} + m\text{\_\_\_\_}\right)$

6. $m\angle GIF = m\angle BAF = \frac{1}{2}m\text{\_\_\_\_} = \frac{1}{2}\left(m\text{\_\_\_\_} + m\overset{\frown}{BG} - m\overset{\frown}{BG}\right)$
   $= \frac{1}{2}\left(m\text{\_\_\_\_} + m\overset{\frown}{BG} - m\text{\_\_\_\_}\right) = \frac{1}{2}\left(m\overset{\frown}{GBF} - m\text{\_\_\_\_}\right)$

7. $m\angle JKF = m\angle BAF = \frac{1}{2}m\text{\_\_\_\_} = \frac{1}{2}\left(m\text{\_\_\_\_} + m\overset{\frown}{JB} - m\overset{\frown}{JB}\right)$
   $= \frac{1}{2}\left(m\text{\_\_\_\_} + m\overset{\frown}{JB} - m\text{\_\_\_\_}\right) = \frac{1}{2}\left(m\overset{\frown}{JF} - m\text{\_\_\_\_}\right)$

8. $m\angle JLM = m\angle NMQ = \frac{1}{2}m\text{\_\_\_\_} = \frac{1}{2}\left(m\text{\_\_\_\_} + m\overset{\frown}{JN} - m\overset{\frown}{JN}\right)$
   $= \frac{1}{2}\left(m\text{\_\_\_\_} + m\overset{\frown}{JN} - m\text{\_\_\_\_}\right) = \frac{1}{2}\left(m\overset{\frown}{JNM} - m\text{\_\_\_\_}\right)$

9. Again, express the boldface statements in general terms.

The statements made in exercise 9 generate the theorems with regard to measurement of the various angles related to the intercepted arcs of the circle. Students should find it a rewarding experience to develop the relationships, rather than be

111

told the relationships by a teacher or a textbook, and then merely prove they are true.

The correct responses to the preceding exercises are

1. Corresponding angles of parallel lines   2. $\overarc{BF}$ 3. $\overarc{AM}, \overarc{MF}$
4. $\overarc{NF}, \overarc{NF}, \overarc{NM}$ 5. $\overarc{NF}, \overarc{NF}$ 6. $\overarc{BF}, \overarc{BF}, \overarc{BF}, \overarc{HA}, \overarc{HA}$
7. $\overarc{BF}, \overarc{BF}, \overarc{BF}, \overarc{JA}, \overarc{JA}$ 8. $\overarc{NM}, \overarc{NM}, \overarc{NM}, \overarc{JM}, \overarc{JM}$

Introducing and Motivating the Measure of an Angle Formed by Two Chords*

Objective: To motivate the need to relate the measure of the angle formed by two chords intersecting in a circle to the measures of the intercepted arcs

Materials: Chalkboard or Geometer's Sketchpad

Procedure: Some problems appear to be rather difficult even though they are very easy to state and understand. The difficulty may be either that the solver is misled along a path that may not be fruitful or that a common relationship is overlooked. Such is the case with this problem. Once solved, students should have a fresh outlook on problems of this nature. Consider the following figure:

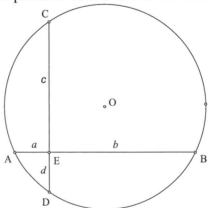

---

* This idea comes circuitously from Professor Melvin Hochster, University of Michigan.

112

For circle O, $\overline{AB} \perp \overline{CD}$. Find the diameter of the circle in terms of a, b, c, and d.

It is natural to seek to use the Pythagorean theorem, because perpendicularity was given. Similarity may also come into play. However, these approaches usually leave the diameter out of the discussion. This can lead to frustration. Here the relationship between $\angle CEB$ and arcs $\overset{\frown}{CB}$ and $\overset{\frown}{AD}$ ought to be considered. Once the relationship that $m\angle CEB = \frac{1}{2}(m\overset{\frown}{CB} + m\overset{\frown}{AD})$ is established, it is clear that $m\overset{\frown}{CB} + m\overset{\frown}{AD} = 180°$.

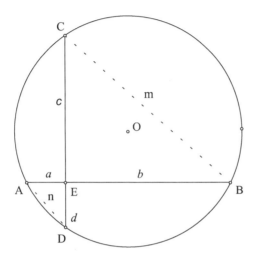

Consider the two right triangles: $\triangle CEB$ and $\triangle AED$ and apply the Pythagorean theorem to each one. Then $m^2 = c^2 + b^2$ and $n^2 = a^2 + d^2$.

Let us do something a bit unusual now. We move arcs $\overset{\frown}{CB}$ and $\overset{\frown}{AD}$ along the circle so that they share a common endpoint, A and C.

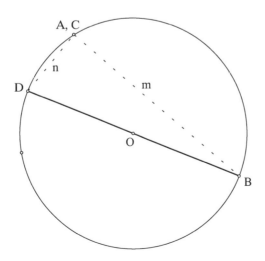

Whereas $m\overset{\frown}{CB} + m\overset{\frown}{AD} = 180°$, $\overline{DB}$ must be a diameter of circle O, and because $\angle DAB$ is inscribed in a semicircle, $\angle DAB$ is a right angle. Therefore, diameter $BD = \sqrt{m^2 + n^2}$, which from the preceding information equals $\sqrt{(c^2 + b^2) + (a^2 + d^2)} = \sqrt{a^2 + b^2 + c^2 + d^2}$.

Therefore, a simply stated problem has a surprise solution that critically depends on angle measurement with a circle, specifically, the angle formed by two chords intersecting in a circle.

GEOMETRY IDEA 16

Using the Property of the Opposite Angles of an Inscribed Quadrilateral

Objective: To provide a surprising application of the relationship of the opposite angles of an inscribed quadrilateral

Materials: Geometer's Sketchpad or other geometric construction tools

Procedure: We teach about the opposite angles of an inscribed quadrilateral and often give some perfunctory exercises. This key relationship about a very important family of quadrilaterals can be presented in a more interesting way by showing a most surprising relationship that can be easily explained by knowing some basics about this quadrilateral.

Perhaps the best known theorem about the opposite angles of an inscribed quadrilateral is that they are supplementary. This is easily proved by realizing that each of a pair of opposite angles of an inscribed quadrilateral has a measure one-half that of the measure of the intercepted arc of the circle. Whereas the sum of the measures of those two arcs is 360°, the sum of the measures of the angles is $\frac{1}{2}(360°) = 180°$. Hence they are supplementary.

Consider the following inscribed quadrilateral $ABCD$. We construct the bisectors of the four angles and note the points at which they intersect the circle as P, Q, R, and S.

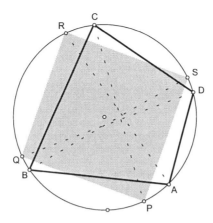

Quadrilateral *PQRS* appears to be a rectangle. Why? This is where the property of opposite angles being supplementary comes into play:

$$m\angle BAR = \frac{1}{2}m\angle BAD \quad \text{and} \quad m\angle BCP = \frac{1}{2}m\angle BCD$$

Therefore,

$$m\angle BAR + m\angle BCP = \frac{1}{2}(m\angle BAD + m\angle BCD)$$

However, $m\angle BAD + m\angle BCD = 180°$; thus,

$$m\angle BAR + m\angle BCP = \frac{1}{2}(180°) = 90°$$

Consider the intercepted arcs of each of these two angles: $m\overset{\frown}{BR} = 2m\angle BAR$ and $m\overset{\frown}{BP} = 2m\angle BCP$. Therefore, $m\overset{\frown}{BR} + m\overset{\frown}{BP} = 2(90°) = 180°$. With $m\overset{\frown}{RBP} = 180°$, we know that $m\angle RSP = 90°$ and $m\angle RQP = 90°$. A similar argument can be made to show that $\angle QRS$ and $\angle QPS$ are also right angles. Thus we have a rectangle. It may be interesting for students to consider the circumstances under which the rectangle will be a square. In any case, this very visual relationship makes very nice use of this often neglected or glossed-over theorem about the opposite angles of an inscribed quadrilateral.

Introducing the Concept of Slope

Objective: To understand and define slope

Materials: Graph paper and a straightedge, or Geometer's Sketchpad

Procedure: Have students imagine that they are walking along the inclined line from left to right. Ask them which of the following lines would be easiest to walk along.

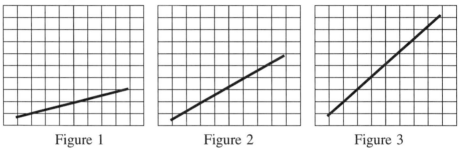

| Figure 1 | Figure 2 | Figure 3 |

In Figure 1, we rise 2 units for a horizontal distance of 8 units. This is not very steep and ought not to be too difficult to walk. In Figure 2, we rise 5 units for a distance of 8 units horizontally. This is a bit more difficult to walk, because it is steeper than the previous case. Even steeper is the walk in Figure 3, where we rise 8 units for a horizontal distance of 8 units. This is even steeper. Were we to assign a measure of steepness to the "walk" along the line from left to right, Figure 1 would be the smallest of the three steepnesses, and Figure 3 would be the greatest. How would the greatest steepness look? The steepness is greatest in Figure 4.

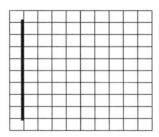

Figure 4

We assign a number to each of these measures of steepness. The greater the number, the steeper the walk. This number (or measure) is called the slope. It refers to the ratio of the "rise" to the "run." That is, the slope is defined as the ratio of the *vertical change* ($\triangle y$) to the *horizontal change* ($\triangle x$).

We write this for the xy plane as

$$\text{slope} = \frac{\Delta y}{\Delta x}$$

In Figure 4, the vertical line appears to be infinitely steep, so no slope is defined for it. Notice that the change in the horizontal direction is 0, and we know that $\frac{\Delta y}{0}$ is undefined.

The horizontal line in Figure 5 shows no steepness and therefore, the slope is 0. Here there is no rise, so $\Delta y = 0$ and the slope $\frac{\Delta y}{\Delta x} = 0$.

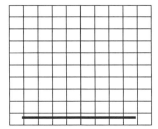

Figure 5

Consider what happens when the horizontal line tips the other way. This time, in Figure 6, there is a drop of 2 units for a horizontal distance of 8 units. The walk along the line appears to be downhill. This drop can be considered negative. The steepness, or slope, here is defined as *the ratio of the "drop" or "negative rise" to the distance traveled* in that time. So in Figure 6, the slope is $\frac{\Delta y}{\Delta x} = \frac{-2}{8} = -\frac{1}{4}$.

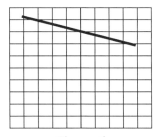

Figure 6

When the drop increases as in Figure 7, then the steepness becomes more negative. Here there is a drop of 7 units or a rise of −7 units. The negative steepness is greater than in Figure 6. The slope is now more negative, because $\frac{\Delta y}{\Delta x} = \frac{-7}{8} = -\frac{7}{8} < -\frac{1}{4}$.

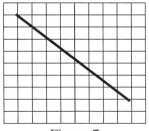

Figure 7

By introducing students to the measure of the steepness of a hill, both positive and negative (i.e., uphill and downhill), the concept of slope begins with the intuitive and makes sense throughout further study.

Introducing Concurrency Through Paper Folding

Objective: To realize the concept of concurrency by direct experimentation

Materials: Several sheets of paper

Procedure: The three most basic concurrency relationships that students encounter in the study of geometry concern altitudes, angle bisectors, and medians. Students should cut a conveniently sized acute scalene triangle from a piece of paper.

To find the concurrency of the *altitudes* of a triangle, students should fold vertex A onto $\overline{AB}$ so that vertex C is on the crease (see Figure 1).

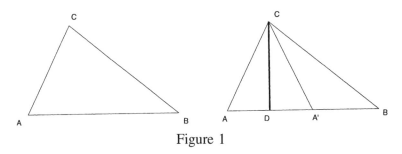

Figure 1

This procedure is then repeated for each of the vertices. When all three altitudes have been created by a crease, students will notice that the creases (i.e., the altitudes) contain a common point, the point of concurrency.

To find the concurrency of the *angle bisectors* of a triangle, students should fold side $\overline{AC}$ onto side $\overline{CB}$. The crease $\overline{CE}$ is the bisector of $\angle ACB$ (see Figure 2).

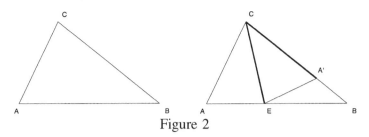

Figure 2

This procedure is then repeated for each of the vertices. When all three angle bisectors have been created by creases, students will notice that the creases (i.e., angle bisectors) contain a common point, the point of concurrency.

To find the concurrency of the *medians* of a triangle students should fold vertex A onto vertex B. This results in the perpendicular bisector of $\overline{AB}$. Mark the intersection with $\overline{AB}$ as M. Point M is the midpoint of $\overline{AB}$. Then make a crease by making a fold containing points C and M. This is a median of the triangle (see Figure 3).

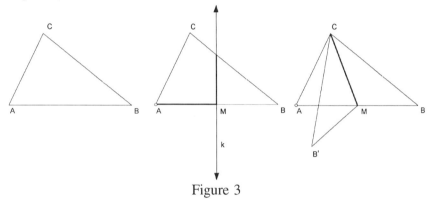

Figure 3

This procedure is then repeated for each of the vertices. When all three medians have been created by creases, students will notice that the creases (i.e., medians) contain a common point, the point of concurrency.

Students should be cautioned that although these paper-folding exercises strongly suggest that the three altitudes, angle bisectors, and medians are concurrent, it, by no means, constitutes a strict mathematical proof of these relationships. Consider some more of these paper-folding exercises.

Students should also notice that the *perpendicular bisectors* (see line k in the center triangle of Figure 3) of the sides are concurrent. This point of concurrency is the center of the circumscribed circle of $\triangle ABC$. This third activity gives us two concurrencies.

Similar activities can be conducted to show that the bisectors of two exterior angles and the bisector of the remaining interior angle of a triangle are concurrent. (Using a nonisosceles triangle is preferred, because it encourages student generalizations.)

Introducing the Centroid of a Triangle

Objective: To have students discover some relationships that involve the centroid of a triangle

Materials: Cardboard, pencil, a drinking straw, string, paper clips, and a large nail

Procedure: Students should consider the properties of the centroid of a triangle (i.e., the intersection point of the three medians). The usual procedure is to tell them that it is the balance point of the triangle. In this activity, students not only discover that the centroid is the balance point of a triangle, but they also discover that the three triangles formed by joining the centroid to each vertex of the original triangle are equal in area.

Students should work in groups of three or four. Begin by having each group carefully cut out a scalene, acute-angled triangle from the cardboard. (This will enable more generalizations than a symmetric triangle, such as an isosceles triangle.) There are no other restrictions on the kind of triangle they wish to use. Using rulers, have them locate the centroid by drawing line segments from each vertex to the midpoint of the side opposite. After locating this point, ask the students to try to balance their triangle on the point of a pencil. They should discover that the triangle balances when the point of the pencil is exactly on the centroid.

Next, ask them to carefully cut out the three triangles formed by the lines from the centroid to each vertex and the sides of the original triangle. Have the groups use the straw, the nail, string and paper clips to make a balance scale, and attempt to balance their three triangles in pairs. They should conclude that the weights of all three triangular regions are the same, regardless of the fact that they are not congruent. Furthermore, because the thickness dimension of each triangle is the same (because they were cut from the same piece of cardboard), the areas must be equal. Thus, they have demonstrated that the centroid is the balance point for the original triangle and the triangles formed by joining the centroid to each vertex are equal in area.

Student groups should now repeat this experiment with triangles of any size or shape. They should attempt to form a general hypothesis regarding the centroid of any triangle, namely that triangles AGC, BGC, and ABG are all equal in area.

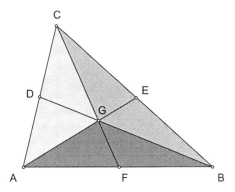

There are other properties of the centroid that can be discovered by experimentation. Such introductions to geometric figures can be very enlightening when students discover them independently (sometimes with helpful hints from you, the teacher). For example, they can discover that the medians trisect each other at the centroid. This can be very nicely done with the Geometer's Sketchpad program.

GEOMETRY IDEA **20**

Introducing the Centroid of a Triangle
Via a Property

Objective: To provide a motivating problem that leads to the trisection property of the centroid

Materials: Chalkboard or Geometer's Sketchpad program

Procedure: To introduce the property that the medians of a triangle trisect each other (at a point called the centroid), it might be nice to challenge students with the question, "From which point in a triangle can segments be drawn to the vertices to partition the area of the triangle into three equal areas?" (see Figure 1).

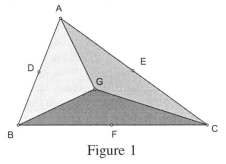

Figure 1

Students will probably experiment with different points to determine the one that has the required property. This sort of blind guess and check usually proves to be fruitless.

Begin the presentation by considering the triangle ABC with its medians drawn as shown in Figure 2.

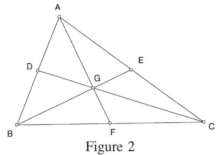

Figure 2

Remind students that when two triangles share the same altitude, their areas are in the ratio of their base lengths. Thus,

$$\text{Area } \triangle ACD = \text{Area } \triangle BCD \quad \text{or} \quad \text{Area } \triangle ACD = \frac{1}{2} \text{Area } \triangle ABC$$

We have

$$\text{Area } \triangle ACD = \text{Area } \triangle BCD$$

and similarly

$$\text{Area } \triangle AGD = \text{Area } \triangle BGD$$

but

$$\text{Area } \triangle ACG = \text{Area } \triangle ACD - \text{Area } \triangle AGD$$

and

$$\text{Area } \triangle BCG = \text{Area } \triangle BCD - \text{Area } \triangle BGD$$

By subtraction

$$\text{Area } \triangle ACG = \text{Area } \triangle BCG$$

In a similar way

$$\text{Area } \triangle ABG = \text{Area } \triangle ACG = \text{Area } \triangle BCG = \frac{1}{3} \text{Area } \triangle ABC$$

We get, for instance,

$$\text{Area } \triangle AGD = \frac{1}{2} \text{Area } \triangle ABG = \frac{1}{2} \text{Area } \triangle ACG$$

122

Therefore, because the triangles *AGD* and *ACG* have the same altitude (from *A* to $\overline{DC}$), $DG = \frac{1}{2}CG$; put another way, $GD = \frac{1}{3}CD$. This establishes the trisection property of the centroid of a triangle, that is, the centroid is a trisection point of each of the three medians.

GEOMETRY IDEA **21**

Introducing Regular Polygons

Objective: To provide some intuitive feeling for the symmetry of a regular polygon

Materials: Pieces of string and some long strips of paper of uniform width

Procedure: Regular polygons are familiar to most students because they are the most prevalent figures in our environment. Introducing these figures through some clever paper folding provides a new level of appreciation that should motivate much of the further study planned.

Begin by having the students tie the knots shown in Figures 1–4. The students should leave each knot loose so that it can be analyzed and copied later.

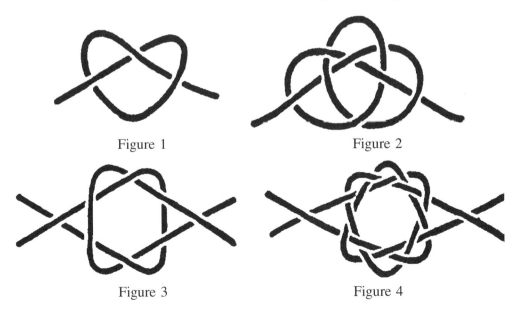

Figure 1

Figure 2

Figure 3

Figure 4

Begin with the knot shown in Figure 1. This knot should be copied with a strip of paper, pulled taut and pressed flat. The resulting regular pentagon should now be obvious (Figure 5). When held up to the light, the diagonals (forming a regular pentagram) are visible.

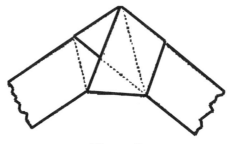

Figure 5

All regular polygons with an odd number of sides can be constructed by paper folding in this way. The knot shown in Figure 2 produces a regular heptagon (Figure 6).

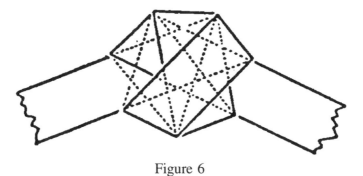

Figure 6

Regular polygons with an even number of sides are produced by two strips of paper following the model of the analogue with two pieces of string. The construction for a regular hexagon is shown in Figure 3. It requires two strips of paper (Figure 7).

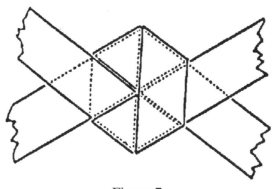

Figure 7

The construction of the regular octagon is a bit more difficult. The model knot is shown in Figure 4. However, the paper folding would be much easier if one strip were first folded as shown in the bottom left diagram in Figure 8 and then interlinked with a second one of the same kind to form the octagon shown in the upper right diagram of Figure 8.

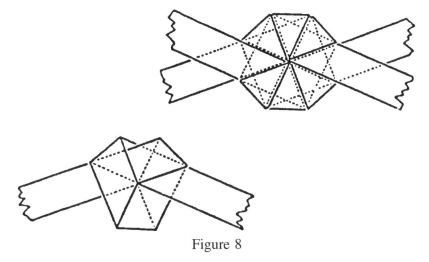

Figure 8

This rather unusual opening to the study of regular polygons can broaden the experiential basis for students of geometry to the point where their thinking produces some rather interesting results.

GEOMETRY IDEA 22

Introducing π

Objective: To give students an intuitive understanding of π going back to its roots

Materials: Chalkboard and a tall cylindrical glass

Procedure: There are many ways to introduce the concept of π. One can give a sense of its usefulness by conducting the following "experiment."

Select a tall and narrow cylindrical drinking glass that "appears" to have a longer height than its circumference. (The typical tall narrow drinking glass fits this requirement.) Ask a friend if the circumference is greater than or less than the height. Now ask the friend how we might test this conjecture (aside from using a piece of string). Recall that the formula for the circumference of a circle is $C = \pi d$ (π times the diameter). You may recall that $\pi = 3.14$ is the usual approximation, but we'll be even more crude and use $\pi = 3$. Thus the circumference will be 3 times the diameter, which can be easily "measured" with a stick or a pencil and then marked off 3 times along the height of the glass. Usually you will find that the circumference is longer than the height of the tall glass, even though it does not appear to be so. This little optical trick is useful to demonstrate the value of π.

Students always relish the notion that a hidden code can reveal long lost secrets. Such is the case with the common interpretation of the value of π in the Bible. There are two places in the Bible where the same sentence appears, identical in every way except for one word, which is spelled differently in the two citations. These passages refer to the description of a pool or fountain in King Solomon's temple. They are found in 1 Kings 7:23 and 2 Chronicles 4:2, and read as follows:

> And he made the molten sea of ten cubits from brim to brim, round in compass, and the height thereof was five cubits; and a line of thirty cubits did compass it round about.

The circular structure described here is said to have a circumference of 30 cubits and a diameter of 10 cubits. (A cubit is the length from a person's fingertip to elbow.) From this account, we notice that the Bible has $\pi = \frac{30}{10} = 3$.

This is obviously a very primitive approximation of π. A late 18th century rabbi, Elijah of Vilna (today: Vilnius, the capital of Lithuania), one of the great modern biblical scholars, who earned the title "Gaon of Vilna" (meaning brilliance of Vilna), came up with a remarkable discovery—one that makes most history of mathematics books faulty if they say that the Bible approximated the value of π as 3. Elijah of Vilna noticed that the Hebrew word for "line measure" was written differently in each of the two Biblical passages.

In 1 Kings 7:23, it was written as קוה, whereas in 2 Chronicles 4:2 it was written as קו. Elijah applied the biblical analysis technique called gematria, where the Hebrew letters are given their appropriate numerical values according to their sequence in the Hebrew alphabet, to the two spellings of the word for "line measure" and made the following determination: The letter values are ק $= 100$, ו $= 6$, and ה $= 5$. Therefore, the spelling for "line measure" in 1 Kings 7:23 is קוה $= 5 + 6 + 100 = 111$, whereas in 2 Chronicles 4:2, the spelling קו $= 6 + 100 = 106$. He then took the ratio of these two values, $\frac{111}{106} = 1.0472$ (to four decimal places), which he considered the necessary correction factor, because when it is multiplied by the 3 stated in the Bible as the approximation for π, we get 3.1416, which is π correct to four decimal places. Such accuracy is quite astonishing for ancient times. To support this notion, have students use the string to measure the circumference and diameter of several circular objects and find their quotient. They will most likely not get near this four-place accuracy.

The history of the development of the value of π is rich with interesting anecdotes, which can be used to help introduce the concept in an interesting way. One such demonstration, which actually shows how the early values of π were obtained, follows.

It is clear that the length of the quarter arc of the circle is shorter than the length of a side of the larger square and longer than the side of the smaller square. (Notice that the sum of the lengths shown as bold line segments equals the length of a side of the larger square.)

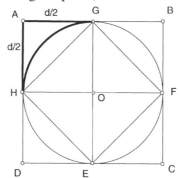

The length of the arc $\overset{\frown}{HG}$ is between $AH + AG$ and HG. If $AG = \frac{d}{2}$, then for right $\triangle HAG$,

$$\left(\frac{d}{2}\right)^2 + \left(\frac{d}{2}\right)^2 = (HG)^2, \qquad HG = \frac{d}{\sqrt{2}}$$

The length of the quarter arc $\overset{\frown}{HG}$ is between d and $\frac{d}{\sqrt{2}}$. The circumference of the entire circle is, therefore, between the perimeter of the larger and smaller squares, or between $4d$ and $\frac{4d}{\sqrt{2}}$, that is, between 4 and 2.8284, for a circle with unit diameter. For such a circle, the circumference would have length π, so $4 > \pi > 2.8284$. Had we taken a hexagon rather than a square, we would have found $3 < \pi < 2\sqrt{3}$, or $3 < \pi < 3.4641$.

Archimedes used regular polygons with even more sides. He used regular polygons with 96 sides and found that $3\frac{10}{71} < \pi < 3\frac{1}{7}$, which, in decimal form, is $3.1408 < \pi < 3.1429$. With increasing number of sides, the approximation of π gets more accurate.

The Area of a Circle

Objective: To develop the formula for the area of a circle

Materials: A piece of cardboard, a protractor, and a pair of scissors

Procedure: Begin by drawing a convenient size circle on the piece of cardboard. Divide the circle into 16 equal arcs. This may be done by marking off consecutive arcs of 22.5° or by consecutively dividing the circle into two parts, then four parts, then bisecting each of these quarter arcs, and so on.

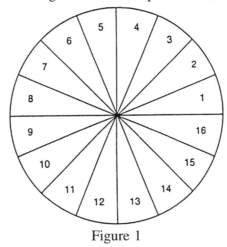

Figure 1

These sectors (Figure 1) are then cut apart and placed in the manner shown in Figure 2.

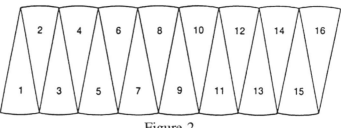

Figure 2

This placement suggests that we have a figure that approximates a parallelogram. That is, were the circle cut into more sectors, the figure would look even more like a true parallelogram. Let us assume it is a parallelogram. In this case, the base would have length $\frac{1}{2}C$, where $C = 2\pi r$ (r is the radius). The area of the parallelogram is equal to the product of its base and altitude (which here is r). Therefore, the area of the parallelogram $= (\frac{1}{2}C)r = \frac{1}{2}(2\pi r)(r) = \pi r^2$, which is the commonly known formula for the area of a circle.

Comparing Areas of Similar Polygons

Objective: To show some interesting results from using the relationship of the areas of similar polygons

Materials: A chalkboard or Geometer's Sketchpad

Procedure: Using an intuitive discussion on the comparison of linear measures and area measures, guide the students to recognizing that the comparison of two similar figures (not just triangles) is based on the ratio of similitude. This is the ratio of any two corresponding linear parts. The extension is that the areas of two similar figures, measured in square units, should then be related by the square of the ratio of similitude or the square of the ratio of any two corresponding linear parts.

Clearly understanding this fact (with or without proof) allows for some nice applications that demonstrate its "power." Consider the following triangle ABC, with right angle at C, and where $\overline{CD} \perp \overline{AB}$ at D.

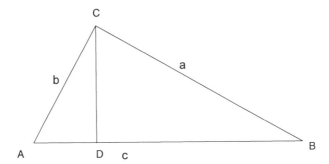

We can easily prove that the three triangles are similar, that is, $\triangle CDB \sim \triangle ADC \sim \triangle ACB$.

One set of corresponding sides is a, b, and c. Thus the ratio of the areas of these three similar right triangles is Area $\triangle CDB$: Area $\triangle ADC$: Area $\triangle ACB =$ $a^2 : b^2 : c^2$.

This can be stated another way: there is a value k, such that Area $\triangle CDB = ka^2$, Area $\triangle ADC = kb^2$, and Area $\triangle ACB = kc^2$.

Since Area $\triangle CDB +$ Area $\triangle ADC =$ Area $\triangle ACB$, it follows that $ka^2 + kb^2 = kc^2$ or $a^2 + b = c^2$, which is the Pythagorean theorem. A further extension of the Pythagorean theorem can be deduced, if we consider a right triangle with similar polygons drawn on each side. To keep the discussion general, we may also use semicircles, which are certainly similar.

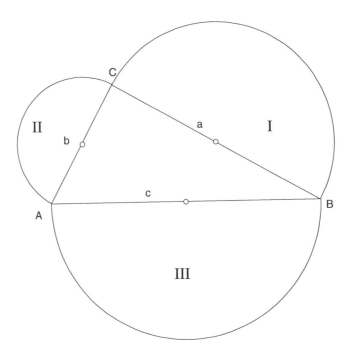

Since the areas of the three semicircles are in the ratio of $a^2 : b^2 : c^2$, we can write their respective areas as Area I $= ka^2$, Area II $= kb^2$, and Area III $= kc^2$ for some number k. By the Pythagorean theorem, we know that for right triangle ABC, $a^2 + b = c^2$. We can conclude that $ka^2 + kb^2 = kc^2$, which tells us that Area I + Area II = Area III. There are other similar interesting extensions of the Pythagorean theorem that can be used for student enrichment.

$\boxed{\textbf{GEOMETRY IDEA 25}}$

Relating Circles

Materials: Geometer's Sketchpad or chalkboard and compasses

Objective: To provide a basis for the comparison of the areas and the circumferences of circles

Procedure: An appreciation of the linear measures of circles as compared to their areas is an important factor in understanding the properties of circles. Recall that the ratio of the areas of two circles (or, for that matter, any two similar polygons) is the square of the ratio of any two corresponding linear parts (such as circumferences, radii, or diameters).

Suppose you have four equal pieces of string. Form a circle with the first one. Cut the second piece of string into two equal parts and form two congruent circles. Cut the third piece of string into three equal pieces and form three congruent circles. In a similar way, form four congruent circles from the fourth piece of string. These circles are shown in Figures 1–4.

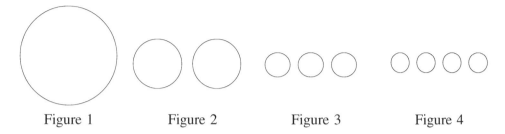

Figure 1   Figure 2   Figure 3   Figure 4

The question is, "How do the areas formed by the circles compare from figure to figure?" That is, how does the total area of the four small circles in Figure 4 compare to the area of the circle in Figure 1? How does the total area of the three small circles in Figure 3 compare to the area of the circle in Figure 1? How does the total area of the two small circles in Figure 2 compare to the area of the circle in Figure 1? These questions lead to some interesting and perhaps motivating results.

Whereas the ratio of the circumference of one of the smaller circles of Figure 2 to that of the large circle (Figure 1) is $1:2$, the ratio of the areas is $1:4$. Thus the area of one of the smaller circles of Figure 2 is $\frac{1}{4}$ the area of the large circle (Figure 1). Therefore, although the sum of the circumferences of the two circles of Figure 2 equals the circumference of the circle of Figure 1, the sum of the areas is $\frac{1}{2}$ the area of the large circle.

Similarly, the circumference of one of the circles of Figure 3 is $\frac{1}{3}$ the circumference of the circle of Figure 1 (because the sum of the circumferences of the three equal smaller circles is equal to the circumference of the large circle of Figure 1). Whereas one of these three equal smaller circles has an area of $\frac{1^2}{3^2} = \frac{1}{9}$ the area of the larger circle, the sum of the areas of the three smaller circles of Figure 3 is $\frac{1}{3}$ the area of the large circle.

We follow this scheme to establish that the sum of the areas of the four small circles in Figure 4 is $\frac{1}{4}$ the area of the large circle (Figure 1). This leads to some interesting generalizations, such as the fact that the number of equal circles whose circumference sum is equal to the circumference of the largest circle is inversely proportional to the fraction of the area represented by the sum of the smaller circles to the area of the larger circle. This procedure allows students to realize that comparison of the areas of circles can be somewhat surprising. Caution should be exercised!

Invariants in Geometry

Objective: To demonstrate what invariants are and how they behave

Materials: Geometer's Sketchpad

Procedure: When students prove a theorem in geometry, they generally do it as an exercise and do not think beyond the conclusion of the proof. When they prove that the diagonals of a parallelogram bisect each other, they ought to realize that this is true for all parallelograms. It is an invariant condition for all parallelograms. They may wish to draw several differently shaped parallelograms and notice that in all cases the diagonals bisect each other. This concept of invariants can be made more dramatic by using the Geometer's Sketchpad and drawing the figure under study (as is the parallelogram here), and then distorting it while noticing that the invariant aspect remains the same.

It is even more impressive to take less well-known theorems and use them as models of invariants. Consider the following theorem: *The quadrilateral formed by joining the midpoints of the sides of a given quadrilateral is always a parallelogram.** We draw this figure with Geometer's Sketchpad:

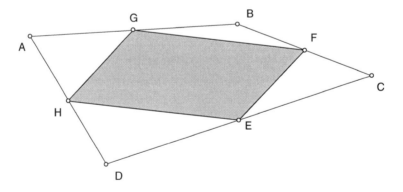

Notice that the shaded quadrilateral is a parallelogram. With Geometer's Sketchpad, we can distort this figure into several differently shaped quadrilaterals *ABCD*:

---

* This was used earlier in another context in Geometry Idea 10.

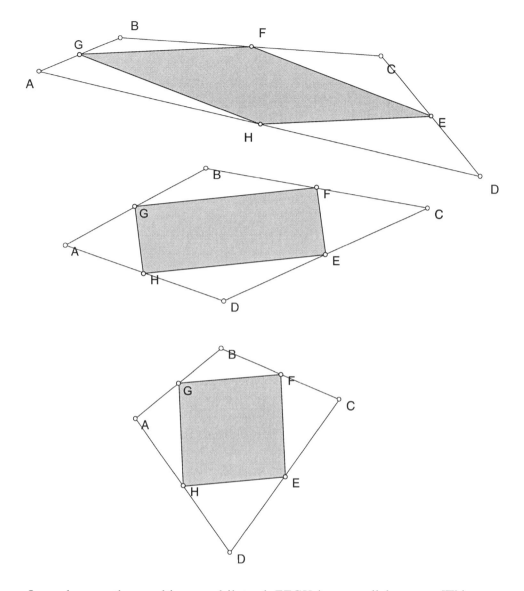

In each case, the resulting quadrilateral *EFGH* is a parallelogram. [This can be easily proved by drawing one diagonal of quadrilateral *ABCD*. The two opposite sides of the inner quadrilateral are parallel to this diagonal and are each half the length of the diagonal (because the sides are also the midlines of two triangles that share the diagonal as a common side).] Using this scheme, we can experiment and then determine the conditions under which the parallelogram is a square, a rectangle, or a rhombus.

Similar exercises to exhibit invariants can be done with concurrency relationships, such as drawing the three altitudes of a triangle and showing that the three altitudes are concurrent for all triangle shapes. This can also be done with medians, angle bisectors, perpendicular bisectors of the sides of a triangle, and so forth.

133

A very lovely, although rather difficult to prove, illustration of invariants is known as Morley's theorem.* Here we draw the trisectors of the angles of a given triangle and note that the intersection points of the adjacent trisectors, X, Y, and Z, form an equilateral triangle. This holds true for any shape change of the original triangle ABC. See the figures below. These have been drawn and "stretched" on Geometers Sketchpad.

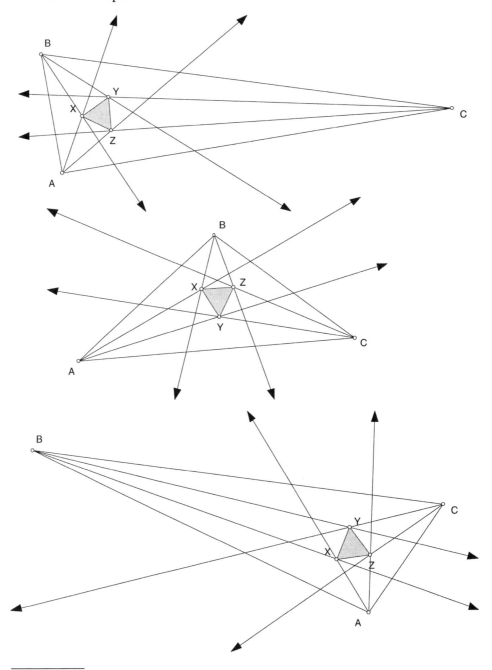

* For some proofs of Morley's theorem, see A. S. Posamentier and C. T. Salkind, *Challenging Problems in Geometry*, pp. 158–161 (Dover, New York, 1996).

There are many other illustrations of this invariant concept in geometry, and the Geometer's Sketchpad is a fine tool with which to experiment and discover (or verify) relationships.

GEOMETRY IDEA **27**

Avoiding Mistakes in Geometric Proofs

Objective: To demonstrate some common mistakes in geometric proofs

Materials: Chalkboard and Geometer's Sketchpad (optional)

Procedure: Geometry students studying proofs that use auxiliary line segments often question the need to rigorously establish the existence and properties of these segments. Students also develop a dependence on a diagram without analyzing its correctness. This unit introduces two fallacious proofs so that students can better grasp the need to justify the uniqueness, the positions, and the properties of auxiliary segments.

Present your students with the following "proof". They will recognize that it contains a fallacy. Ask them to try to determine where the error occurs.

Given: $ABCD$ is a rectangle
$\overline{FA} \cong \overline{BA}$
R is the midpoint of $\overline{BC}$
N is the midpoint of $\overline{CF}$

Prove: A right angle is equal in measure to an obtuse angle ($\angle CDA \cong \angle FAD$)

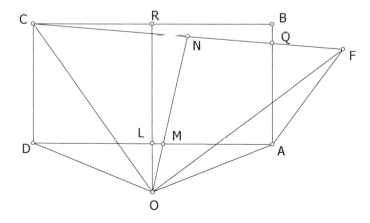

135

"Proof": Draw $\overrightarrow{RL}$ perpendicular to $\overline{CB}$ and draw $\overrightarrow{NM}$ perpendicular to $\overline{CF}$. Then $\overrightarrow{RL}$ and $\overrightarrow{NM}$ intersect at point O. If they didn't intersect, $\overline{RL}$ and $\overline{MN}$ would be parallel and this would mean $\overline{CB}$ is parallel to $\overline{CF}$ which is impossible, since it contradicts the hypothesis.

Draw $\overline{DO}$, $\overline{CO}$, $\overline{FO}$, and $\overline{AO}$. Because $\overline{RO}$ is the perpendicular bisector of $\overline{CB}$ and $\overline{DA}$, $\overline{DO} \cong \overline{AO}$, because $\overline{NO}$ is the perpendicular bisector of $\overline{CF}$, $\overline{CO} \cong \overline{FO}$, and because $\overline{FA} \cong \overline{BA}$ and $\overline{BA} \cong \overline{CD}$, we have $\overline{FA} \cong \overline{CD}$. This enables us to establish $\triangle CDO \cong \triangle FAO$ [side–side–side (SSS)], so that $\angle ODC \cong \angle OAF$. Because $\overline{OD} \cong \overline{OA}$, we have $\angle ODA \cong \angle OAD$. Now, $m\angle ODC - m\angle ODA = m\angle OAF - m\angle OAD$ or $m\angle CDA = m\angle FAD$.

If students inspect the proof and find nothing wrong with it, ask them to use a ruler and a pair of compasses to reconstruct the diagram. The correct diagram looks like this:

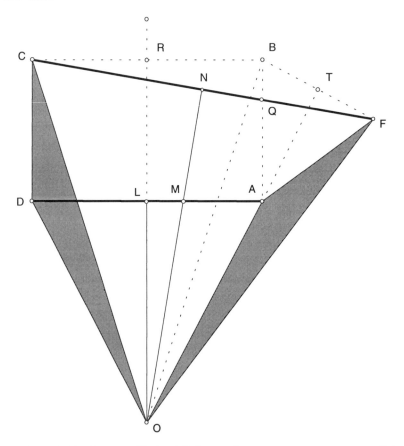

Construction of this figure will shed light on the correct arrangement of the various parts. At point A we erect a perpendicular, then set $AB = CD$ and complete the rectangle $ABCD$. For this rectangle, the perpendicular bisector of $\overline{AD}$ is also the perpendicular bisector of $\overline{BC}$. Therefore, $OC = OB$, $OC = OF$, and then $OB = OF$. Because both points A and O are equidistant from the endpoints of

$\overline{BF}$, $\overleftrightarrow{AO}$ must be the perpendicular bisector of $\overline{BF}$. $\triangle CDO$ is transformed into $\triangle BAO$ (through a reflection in $\overleftrightarrow{OLR}$) and $\triangle BAO$ is transformed into $\triangle FAO$ (through a reflection in $\overleftrightarrow{OAT}$). $\triangle CDO$ is transformed into $\triangle FAO$ by a rotation about O through $\angle DOA$, which has the same measure as $\angle BAF$, that is, the difference between the original obtuse and right angles.

Although the triangles are congruent, our ability to subtract the specific angles no longer exists. Thus, the difficulty with this proof lies in its dependence on an incorrectly drawn diagram.

A second illustration helps secure the notion being highlighted here. Present students with the following proof that any point in the interior of a circle is also on the circle.

Given: Circle O with radius r
Let A be any point in the interior of the circle distinct from O

Prove: A is on the circle

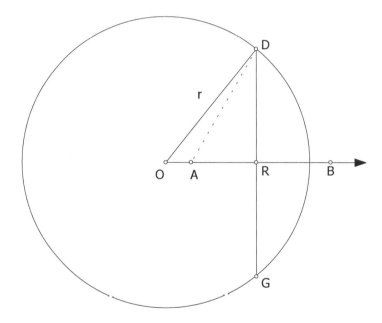

"*Proof*": Let B be on the extension of $\overline{OA}$ through A such that $OA \cdot OB = r^2$. (Clearly OB is greater than r, because OA is less than r.) Let the perpendicular bisector of $\overline{AB}$ meet the circle in points D and G, where R is the midpoint of $\overline{AB}$.

We now have

$$OA = OR - RA \quad \text{and} \quad OB = OR + RB = OR + RA$$

$$\therefore r^2 = (OR - RA)(OR + RA)$$
$$= OR^2 - RA^2$$
$$= (r^2 - DR^2) - (AD^2 - DR^2) \quad \text{(by the Pythagorean theorem)}$$
$$= r^2 - AD^2$$

Therefore, $AD^2 = 0$, and A coincides with D and lies on the circle.

The fallacy in this proof lies in the fact that we drew an auxiliary line ($\overleftrightarrow{DRG}$) with *two* conditions—that $\overline{DRG}$ is the perpendicular bisector of $\overline{AB}$ and that it intersects the circle. Actually, all points on the perpendicular bisector of $\overline{AB}$ lie in the exterior of the circle and, therefore, cannot intersect the circle:

$$r^2 = OA(OB)$$
$$= OA(OA + AB) \tag{1}$$
$$= OA^2 + (OA)(AB)$$

Now the proof assumes

$$OA + \frac{AB}{2} < r$$
$$2(OA) + AB < 2r \tag{2}$$
$$4(OA)^2 + 4(OA)(AB) + AB^2 < 4r^2$$

From Equation 1, $r^2 = OA^2 + (OA)(AB)$, so by substituting into Equation 2, we get $4r^2 + AB^2 < 4r^2$, $AB^2 < 0$, which is impossible.

This proof emphasizes the care we must take to use only one condition when drawing auxiliary sets. Additional illustrations of geometric fallacies may be helpful to exhibit other properties that are not to be taken for granted.

GEOMETRY IDEA **28**

Systematic Order in Successive Geometric Moves—Patterns!

Objective: To show how a series of successive moves leads to a common series

Materials: Chalkboard, toothpicks, paper and pencil

Procedure: Use toothpicks to set up the following arrangements. What is the minimum number of toothpicks to be removed in each of the following figures ($n \times n$ squares) so that no square remains? This question leads to some experimentation and ought to be carried out beyond the 3×3 square. We show what happens with the few samples presented in the diagrams.

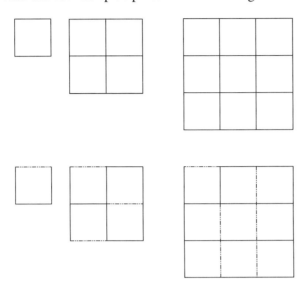

The pattern that evolves from the systematic removal of toothpicks is shown in the table

n (where n is the number of small squares in a row)	1	2	3	4	$\cdots$	n
Minimum number of toothpicks removed	1	3	6	10	$\cdots$	$\frac{n(n+1)}{2}$

In each case, the number of removed toothpicks is equal to the successive partial summands of the series of natural numbers $1 + 2 + 3 + 4 + 5 + \cdots$.

Students should appreciate this attractive sequence for the minimum number of removed toothpicks. It happens to be called the sequence of triangular numbers, because dots of these numbers can be placed in the form of equilateral triangles:

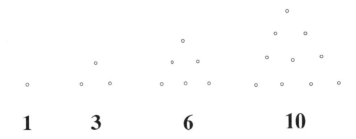

1   3   6   10

Another systematic buildup can be done by placing toothpicks on a table so that no three toothpicks have a common intersection point and the number of intersection points is maximized.

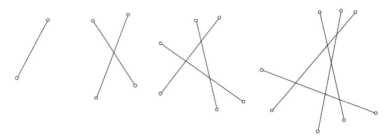

Logging the successive addition of toothpicks yields the table

Number of toothpicks	1	2	3	4	5	6	$\cdots$	n
Number of intersection points	0	1	$1+2$	$1+2+3$	$1+2+3+4$	$1+2+3+4+5$	$\cdots$	$\frac{(n-1)n}{2}$

We can use points on a line segment as another example. Consider the number of segments determined by increased numbers of points on line segment AB.

	No. of points between A and B	No. of segments	
$A \circ\!\!-\!\! \circ B$	0	1	$=1$
$A \circ\!\!-\!\!-\!\! \underset{C}{\circ}\!\!-\!\!-\!\!-\!\!-\!\!-\!\!-\!\!-\!\!-\!\!-\!\!-\!\!-\!\! \circ B$	1	$1+2$	$=3$
$A \circ\!\!-\!\!-\!\! \underset{C}{\circ}\!\!-\!\!-\!\! \underset{D}{\circ}\!\!-\!\!-\!\!-\!\!-\!\! \circ B$	2	$1+2+3$	$=6$
$A \circ\!\!-\!\!-\!\! \underset{C}{\circ}\!\!-\!\!-\!\! \underset{D}{\circ}\!\!-\!\! \underset{E}{\circ}\!\!-\!\!-\!\! \circ B$	3	$1+2+3+4$	$=10$
$A \circ\!\!-\!\! \underset{C}{\circ}\!\!-\!\! \underset{D}{\circ}\!\!-\!\! \underset{E}{\circ}\!\!-\!\! \underset{F}{\circ}\!\!-\!\! \circ B$	4	$1+2+3+4+5$	$=15$
$A \circ\!\!-\!\! \underset{C}{\circ}\!\!-\!\! \underset{D}{\circ}\!\!-\!\! \underset{E}{\circ}\!\!-\!\! \underset{F}{\circ}\!\!-\!\! \underset{G}{\circ}\!\!-\!\! \circ B$	5	$1+2+3+4+5+6=21$	

Again the series of triangular numbers appears. Stress that the systematic geometric buildup yields consistent mathematical relationships.

We can even use the Pascal triangle to find the sum of the series of the first n natural numbers:

							1							
						1		1						
					1		2		1					
				1		3		3		1				
			1		4		6		4		1			
		1		5		10		10		5		1		
	1		6		15		20		15		6		1	
1		7		21		35		35		21		7		1

The sum of the first n natural numbers is the number below (and not in the same diagonal) the last number in the series. That is, the sum of the first five natural numbers is 15 (shown shaded), located below the 5. The same procedure can be used to sum the triangular numbers.

We also see a nice pattern with the partial sums of the first n natural numbers:

1 (mod 2)	1
$1 + 2$ (mod 3)	0
$1 + 2 + 3$ (mod 4)	2
$1 + 2 + 3 + 4$ (mod 5)	0
$1 + 2 + 3 + 4 + 5$ (mod 6)	3
$1 + 2 + 3 + 4 + 5 + 6$ (mod7)	0
$\vdots$	$\vdots$

	If n is odd, the sum is $\frac{n+1}{2}$ (mod $(n + 1)$)
$1 + 2 + 3 + 4 + 5 + 6 + 7 + \cdots + n$ (mod $(n + 1)$)	If n is even, the sum is 0 (mod $(n + 1)$)

There are many more of these geometric or arithmetic systematic buildups that can lead to the series of natural numbers. It is important for students to see these patterns so that their appreciation for the order of things in mathematics becomes clear and intuitive.

GEOMETRY IDEA 29

Introducing the Construction of a Regular Pentagon

Objective: To demonstrate a construction that looks correct, but isn't, and determine why it isn't

Materials: Chalkboard, straightedge, compasses, and, if possible, Geometer's Sketchpad

Procedure: Perhaps the most important artist Germany has contributed to Western culture is Albrecht Dürer. In mathematical circles, we may have encountered his work in the form of his famous engraving, "Melancholia" (1514), which depicts a sad angel among many mathematical tools and a magic square in the background. It is this magic square that has made the engraving so well known to mathematicians. However, a much forgotten Dürer work (done in 1525) is a geometric construction (using a straightedge and compasses) of a regular pentagon that he assumed was correct, but is not. Its deviation from a perfect regular pentagon in minuscule, but that cannot be ignored. A nice way to lead into the construction (the correct and accepted one, that is) is to show Dürer's work and explore why it is not correct. Incidentally, until recently, engineering books still provided Dürer's method as a method for constructing a regular pentagon. We provide it here.

Refer to the accompanying diagram. Beginning with a segment *AB*, five circles of radius *AB* are constructed as follows:

1. Circles with centers at *A* and *B* are drawn and intersect at *Q* and *N*.
2. Then the circle with center *Q* is drawn to intersect circles *A* and *B* at points *R* and *S*, respectively.
3. $\overline{QN}$ intersects circle *Q* at *P*.
4. $\overline{SP}$ and $\overline{RP}$ intersect circles *A* and *B* at points *E* and *C*, respectively.
5. Draw the circles with centers at *E* and *C* with radius *AB* to intersect at *D*.
6. The polygon *ABCDE* is (supposedly) a regular pentagon.

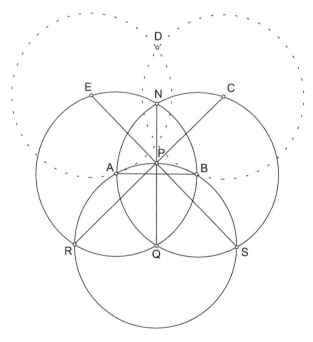

(It's not as complicated as it looks!)

Join the points in order to get the pentagon *ABCDE*:

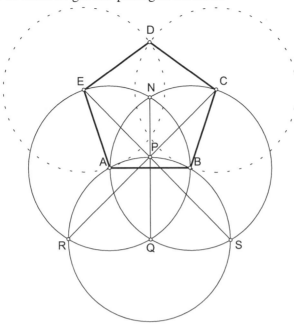

Although the pentagon "looks" regular, $m\angle ABC$ is about $\frac{22}{60}$ of a degree too large. That is, for *ABCDE* to be a regular pentagon, the measure of each angle must be 108°. Instead, we show that $m\angle ABC \approx 108.3661202°$.

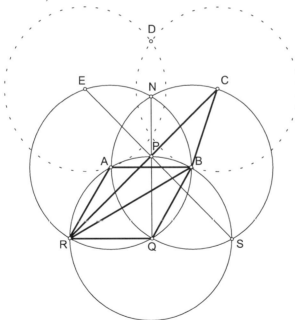

In rhombus $ABQR$, $\angle ARQ = 60°$, and $BR = AB\sqrt{3}$, because $\overline{BR}$ is actually twice the length of an altitude of equilateral $\triangle ARQ$. Whereas $\triangle PRQ$ is an isosceles right triangle, $m\angle PRQ = 45°$, and then $m\angle BRC = 15°$.

We apply the law of sines to $\triangle BCR$:

$$\frac{BR}{\sin \angle BCR} = \frac{BC}{\sin \angle BRC}$$

That is,

$$\frac{AB\sqrt{3}}{\sin \angle BCR} = \frac{AB}{\sin 15°} \quad \text{or} \quad \sin \angle BCR = \sqrt{3} \sin 15°$$

Therefore, $m\angle BCR \approx 26.63387984$. In $\triangle BCR$,

$$m\angle RBC = 180° - m\angle BRC - m\angle BCR \approx 180° - 15° - 26.63387984°$$
$$\approx 138.3661202°$$

Thus, because $m\angle ABR = 30°$,

$$m\angle ABC = m\angle RBC - m\angle ABR \approx 138.3661202° - 30° \approx 108.3661202°$$

not 108°, as it should for it to be a regular pentagon!

This rather simple construction may be a bit complicated to explain, but for many students, it is well worth the time investment. The pentagon looks right, but isn't! Much can be said about this phenomenon.

Some students may want to experiment to see if this construction really fits the foregoing construction discussion. Here Geometer's Sketchpad can be very useful, because it enables angle measurement. The following script outlines the construction, followed by the actual constructed figure. Notice how accurate our prediction (or the Geometer's Sketchpad measurement) was!

Given: Point A and point B

Steps:

1. Let $[c1]$ = circle with center at point B passing through point A.
2. Let $[c2]$ = circle with center at point A passing through point B.
3. Let Q = intersection of circle $[c2]$ and circle $[c1]$.
4. Let $[c3]$ = circle with center at point Q passing through point B.
5. Let N = intersection of circle $[c1]$ and circle $[c2]$.
6. Let $[j]$ = segment between point N and point Q.
7. Let S = intersection of circle $[c1]$ and circle $[c3]$.
8. Let P = intersection of circle $[c3]$ and segment $[j]$.
9. Let $[k]$ = ray between point S and point P.
10. Let R = intersection of circle $[c2]$ and circle $[c3]$.
11. Let $[l]$ = ray between point R and point P.
12. Let $[m]$ = segment between point A and point B.
13. Let E = intersection of circle $[c2]$ and ray $[k]$.

14. Let [c4] = circle centered at point E with radius length [m].
15. Let C = intersection of circle [c1] and ray [l].
16. Let [c5] = circle centered at point C with radius length [m].
17. Let [n] = segment between point A and point E.
18. Let D = intersection of circle [c4] and circle [c5].
19. Let [o] = segment between point E and point D.
20. Let [p] = segment between point D and point C.
21. Let [q] = segment between point C and point B.
22. Let [p1] = polygon interior with vertices A, B, C, D, and E.

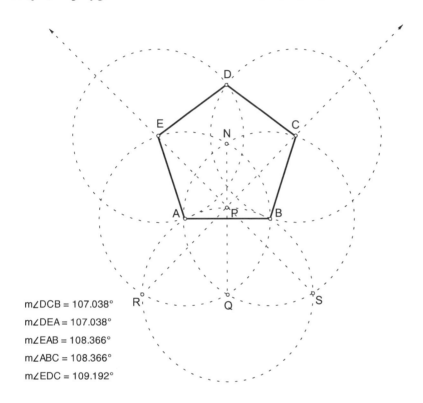

m∠DCB = 107.038°
m∠DEA = 107.038°
m∠EAB = 108.366°
m∠ABC = 108.366°
m∠EDC = 109.192°

For entertainment students might be interested in another such "almost-regular" polygon. Dürer also developed ingenious methods for constructing a heptagon and a nonagon, each of which was almost regular. Consider Dürer's construction of the almost-regular nonagon.

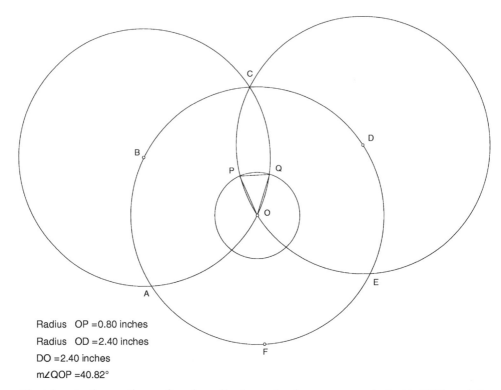

Radius OP =0.80 inches

Radius OD =2.40 inches

DO =2.40 inches

m∠QOP =40.82°

First locate the vertices of an inscribed regular hexagon on circle O. With points B and D as centers, construct circles with radius OD to intersect circle O at point C. Draw a concentric circle with radius $\frac{1}{3}$ of the radius of the original circle O and intersecting circles D and B at points P and Q, respectively. Since in isosceles $\triangle POQ$, $\angle POQ \approx 40°$, $\overline{PQ}$ is the side of an almost-nonagon, which would be inscribed in the smaller circle. That is, one could *almost* mark off the chords of length PQ nine times consecutively on the smaller circle to form a nonagon. You can see from the above figure that since $\angle QOP \approx 40.82°$ nine adjacent congruent angles of this measure will be greater than 360°. We know, of course that both a regular heptagon and a regular nonagon cannot be constructed with the usual Euclidean tools (unmarked straightedge and a pair of compasses).

Trigonometry Ideas

Derivation of the Law of Sines. I

Objective: To derive the law of sines

Materials: Chalkboard or screen on which to draw the diagram

Procedure: Suppose you are planning a lesson to introduce the law of sines. You would like to develop or derive the law and you would like to have ample time to apply it to "practical" examples as well as the drill that typically follows the introduction of the law. To fit this "package" into a normal 50 minute lesson, you either can relegate a more serious inspection of the derivation to a homework assignment and simply introduce the law of sines and its applications to the triangle, or you may search for a concise derivation of the law of sines such as follows.

Consider the triangle ABC with median $\overline{AM}$:

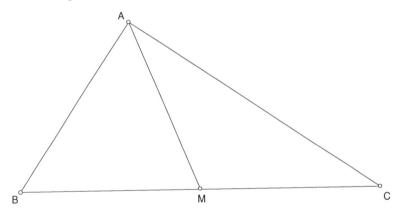

The area of $\triangle ABM = \frac{1}{2}(AB)(BM)\sin B$
and the area of $\triangle ACM = \frac{1}{2}(AC)(CM)\sin C$.

Because the areas of these two triangles are equal and $BM = CM$, it follows that $AB \sin B = AC \sin C$.

This gives us the law of sines:

$$\frac{AB}{\sin C} = \frac{AC}{\sin B}$$

With this simple proof, or derivation, of the law of sines, the time that remains for applications is maximized!

Derivation of the Law of Sines. II

Objective: To derive the law of sines

Materials: Chalkboard or screen on which to draw the diagram

Procedure: Suppose you are planning a lesson to introduce the law of sines. You would like to develop or derive the law and you would like to have ample time to apply it to "practical" examples as well as the drill that typically follows the introduction of the law. To fit this "package" into a normal 50 minute lesson, you either can relegate a more serious inspection of the derivation to a homework assignment and simply introduce the law of sines and its applications to the triangle, or you may search for a concise derivation of the law of sines such as follows.

Consider the circumcircle of $\triangle ABC$ with diameter $\overline{AD}$. We then have two right triangles, $\triangle ABD$ and $\triangle ACD$, because they are each inscribed in a semicircle.

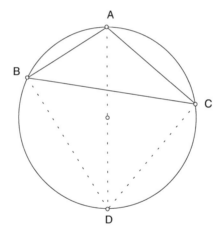

In $\triangle ACD$,

$$\sin \angle ADC = \frac{AC}{AD}$$

$$\text{diameter } AD = \frac{AC}{\sin \angle ADC}$$

Because $\angle ADC$ and $\angle ABC$ both have a measure of $\frac{1}{2}\overset{\frown}{AC}$, $\angle ADC \cong \angle ABC$. Therefore,

$$\text{diameter } AD = \frac{AC}{\sin \angle ABC}$$

150

Similarly,

$$\text{diameter } AD = \frac{AB}{\sin \angle ADB} = \frac{AB}{\sin \angle ACB}$$

Therefore,

$$\frac{AC}{\sin \angle ABC} = \frac{AB}{\sin \angle ACB}$$

which can then be followed in a similar way to the third part of the law of sines. This very concise proof allows you ample time to do a complete lesson on a topic that might otherwise require more than one lesson to introduce.

Derivation of the Law of Sines. III

Objective: To derive the law of sines

Materials: Chalkboard or screen on which to draw the diagram

Procedure: Suppose you are planning a lesson to introduce the law of sines. You would like to develop or derive the law and you would like to have ample time to apply it to "practical" examples as well as the drill that typically follows the introduction of the law. To fit this "package" into a normal 50 minute lesson, you either can relegate a more serious inspection of the derivation to a homework assignment and simply introduce the law of sines and its applications to the triangle, or you may search for a concise derivation of the law of sines such as follows.

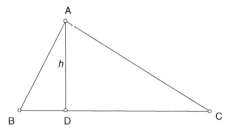

A simple derivation follows directly from $\triangle ABC$ with altitude h.

$$\sin \angle ABC = \frac{h}{AB} \qquad \sin \angle ACB = \frac{h}{AC} \qquad \frac{\sin \angle ABC}{\sin \angle ACB} = \frac{\frac{h}{AB}}{\frac{h}{AC}} = \frac{AC}{AB}$$

151

Therefore,

$$\frac{AC}{\sin \angle ABC} = \frac{AB}{\sin \angle ACB}$$

which can then be followed in a similar way to the third part of the law of sines. This very concise proof allows you ample time to do a complete lesson on a topic that might otherwise require more than one lesson to introduce.

Introductory Excursion to Enable an Alternate Approach to Trigonometry Relationships*

Objective: To introduce Ptolemy's theorem for use in introducing trigonometric concepts

Materials: Chalkboard or Geometer's Sketchpad program

Procedure: This approach to presenting trigonometric relationships is more geometric and may be easier for students to understand. It is appropriate for use in traditional trigonometry classes or in pre-calculus classes.

Begin by presenting the quadrilateral, which may be inscribed in a circle, called a "cyclic quadrilateral." Of course, not all quadrilaterals are cyclic. In the following diagram, quadrilateral *ABCD* is inscribed in circle *O*.

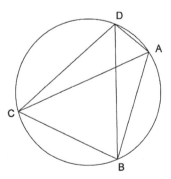

Recall the following theorems about cyclic quadrilaterals:

---

* This unit is necessary for Trigonometry Ideas 5 and 6.

In a cyclic quadrilateral, (a) the opposite angles are supplementary and (b) the angle between a side and a diagonal is congruent to the angle between the opposite side and the other diagonal.

One of the most useful theorems with regard to cyclic quadrilaterals is known as Ptolemy's theorem. This theorem is the basis for the development of trigonometric relationships shown in the next two units.

Ptolemy's Theorem: In a cyclic quadrilateral, the product of the lengths of the diagonals is equal to the sum of the products of the lengths of the opposite sides.

In the accompanying diagram, $ab + cd = ef$.

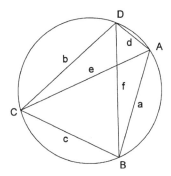

(*Note*: The converse of Ptolemy's theorem is also true. It provides a method to prove that a quadrilateral is cyclic.)

The following proof of Ptolemy's theorem is one of many.*

Case I: Diagonal $\overline{CA}$ bisects $\angle DCB$.

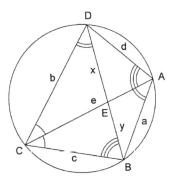

Let $x = DE$ and $y = EB$. Also, $\angle CDB \cong \angle BAC$, $\triangle DCE \sim \triangle ACB$, which implies $\frac{x}{b} = \frac{a}{e}$ and gives $ab = xe$. Since $\angle CDB \cong \angle CAB$, $\triangle BCE \sim \triangle ACD$, which implies $\frac{y}{c} = \frac{d}{e}$ and gives $cd = ye$. Add the two equations: $ab + cd = xe + ye = (x + y)e$. Hence, if we let $f = x + y$, then $ab + cd = fe$.

---

* For additional proofs of Ptolemy's theorem, see *Excursions in Advanced Euclidean Geometry* by A. S. Posamentier (Addison-Wesley, Reading, MA, 1984) or *Challenging Problems in Geometry* by A. S. Posamentier and C. T. Salkind (Dover, New York, 1996).

Case II: Diagonal $\overline{CA}$ *does not bisect* $\angle DCB$.

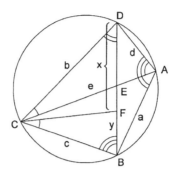

Assume $m\angle BCE > m\angle ACD$. Draw segment $\overline{CF}$ with F on chord $\overline{DB}$, so that $m\angle BCF = m\angle DCE$. Let $x = DF$ and $y = FB$. Since $\angle CDB \cong \angle CAB$, $\triangle DCF \sim \triangle ACB$, which implies $\frac{b}{x} = \frac{e}{a}$ and results in $ab = ex$. Since $\angle CBD \cong \angle CAD$, $\triangle BCF \sim \triangle ACD$, which implies $\frac{y}{c} = \frac{d}{e}$ and results in $cd = ey$. Add the two equations: $ab + cd = ex + ey = e(x + y)$. Hence, if we let $f = x + y$, then $ab + cd = fe$.

TRIGONOMETRY IDEA 5

Using Ptolemy's Theorem to Develop Trigonometric Identities for Sums and Differences of Angles

Objective: To use Ptolemy's theorem to prove basic trigonometric identities involving sums and differences of angles

Materials: Chalkboard or Geometer's Sketchpad program

Procedure: We can use circles with unit diameters and Ptolemy's theorem to prove basic trigonometric identities that involve sums and differences of angles. The key to these proofs is drawing an appropriate diagram. In some cases, more than one diagram will yield the appropriate trigonometric identity.

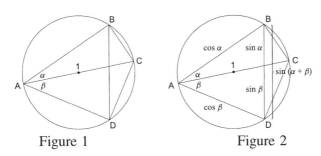

Figure 1   Figure 2

In Figure 1, a cyclic quadrilateral is drawn with $\overline{AC}$ as a diameter of length 1. $\triangle ABC$ and $\triangle ADC$ are right triangles, which enables us to label the lengths of the sides opposite $\angle \alpha$ and $\angle \beta$ as $\sin \alpha$ and $\sin \beta$, respectively (see Trigonometry Idea 9). The adjacent legs have lengths $\cos \alpha$ and $\cos \beta$. The side $(\overline{BD})$ opposite $\angle BAD$ has length equal to $\sin \angle BAD$. Recognizing that $m \angle BAD = \alpha + \beta$, we can write $BD = \sin(\alpha + \beta)$.*

Now using Ptolemy's theorem for cyclic quadrilateral $ABCD$, we get

$$\sin \alpha \cdot \cos \beta + \cos \alpha \cdot \sin \beta = \sin(\alpha + \beta) \cdot 1$$

which is the "addition identity," $\mathbf{sin(\alpha + \beta) = sin\,\alpha \cdot cos\,\beta + cos\,\alpha \cdot sin\,\beta}$.

In a similar way, we can consider the following applications of Ptolemy's theorem to derive other important theorems of trigonometry. In each case, diameter $\overline{AB}$ has a length of 1.

Application 1. *Derivation of the theorem for* $\sin(\alpha - \beta)$.

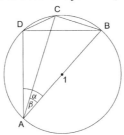

Because $m \angle DAC = \alpha - \beta$, $DC = \sin(\alpha - \beta)$. For β in right $\triangle ACB$, $CB = \sin \beta$, and $AC = \cos \beta$. For α in right $\triangle ADB$, $DB = \sin \alpha$, and $AD = \cos \alpha$.

---

* This may not be obvious at first. Consider for a moment the following figure, where the circle has diameter length 1.

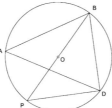

Since $\triangle PBD$ is a right triangle, the sine ratio gives us: $\sin \angle BPD = \frac{BD}{PB} = \frac{BD}{1} = BD$. But since $\angle BAD \cong \angle BPD$, we can conclude that $BD = \sin \angle BAD$.

Using Ptolemy's theorem, we get

$$AD \cdot CB + AB \cdot DC = AC \cdot DB$$

$$\cos\alpha \cdot \sin\beta + 1 \cdot \sin(\alpha - \beta) = \cos\beta \cdot \sin\alpha$$

Therefore,

$$\mathbf{\sin(\alpha - \beta) = \sin\alpha \cdot \cos\beta - \cos\alpha \cdot \sin\beta}$$

Application 2. *Derivation of the theorem for* $\cos(\alpha + \beta)$.

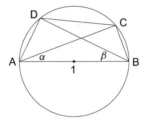

For α in right $\triangle ACB$, $CB = \sin\alpha$, and $AC = \cos\alpha$. For β in right $\triangle ADB$, $AD = \sin\beta$ and $DB = \cos\beta$. We find DC by finding $\sin\angle DBC$. In right triangle ABC,

$$m\angle ABC = 90 - \alpha$$
$$m\angle DBC = m\angle ABC - \beta = 90 - \alpha - \beta = 90 - (\alpha + \beta)$$

$$DC = \sin\angle DBC = \sin(90 - (\alpha + \beta))$$
$$= \sin 90 \cdot \cos(\alpha + \beta) - \cos 90 \cdot \sin(\alpha + \beta)$$

Using Ptolemy's theorem, we get

$$AD \cdot CB + AB \cdot DC = AC \cdot DB$$

$$\sin\beta \cdot \sin\alpha + 1 \cdot \cos(\alpha + \beta) = \cos\alpha \cdot \cos\beta$$

Thus,

$$\mathbf{\cos(\alpha + \beta) = \cos\alpha \cdot \cos\beta - \sin\alpha \cdot \sin\beta}$$

Application 3. *Alternate derivation of the theorem for* $\cos(\alpha + \beta)$.

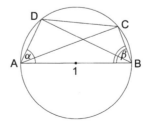

156

For α in right $\triangle ADB$, $DB = \sin\alpha$ and $AD = \cos\alpha$. For β in right $\triangle ACB$, $AC = \sin\beta$ and $CB = \cos\beta$. We find the length of $\overline{DC}$ by finding $\sin\angle DBC$. In right triangle ADB,

$$m\angle ABD = 90 - \alpha$$
$$m\angle DBC = \beta - m\angle ABD = \beta - (90 - \alpha) = (\alpha + \beta) - 90$$

$$DC = \sin\angle DBC = \sin((\alpha + \beta) - 90)$$
$$= \sin(\alpha + \beta) \cdot \cos 90 - \cos(\alpha + \beta) \cdot \sin 90$$
$$= 0 - \cos(\alpha + \beta) = -\cos(\alpha + \beta)$$

(Point out that although DC "looks" negative, $(\alpha + \beta)$ is obtuse and, therefore, has a negative cosine. $-\cos(\alpha + \beta)$ is therefore positive.)

Using Ptolemy's theorem, we get

$$AD \cdot CB + AB \cdot DC = AC \cdot DB$$

$$\cos\alpha \cdot \cos\beta + 1 \cdot (-\cos(\alpha + \beta)) = \sin\beta \cdot \sin\alpha$$

Thus,

$$\mathbf{\cos(\alpha + \beta) = \cos\alpha \cdot \cos\beta - \sin\alpha \cdot \sin\beta}$$

Application 4. *Derivation of the theorem for $\cos(\alpha - \beta)$.*

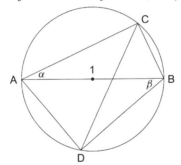

For α in right $\triangle ACB$, $CB = \sin\alpha$ and $AC = \cos\alpha$. For β in right $\triangle ADB$, $AD = \sin\beta$ and $DB = \cos\beta$. We find the length of $\overline{DC}$ by finding $\sin\angle DBC$. In right triangle ACB,

$$m\angle ABC = 90 - \alpha$$
$$m\angle DBC = \beta + m\angle ABC = \beta + (90 - \alpha) = 90 - (\alpha - \beta)$$
$$DC = \sin\angle DBC = \sin(90 - (\alpha - \beta)) = \cos(\alpha - \beta)$$

Using Ptolemy's theorem, we get

$$AD \cdot CB + AC \cdot DB = AB \cdot DC$$

$$\sin\beta \cdot \sin\alpha + \cos\alpha \cdot \cos\beta = 1 \cdot \cos(\alpha - \beta)$$

157

Thus,

$$\cos(\alpha - \beta) = \cos\alpha \cdot \cos\beta + \sin\alpha \cdot \sin\beta$$

Other trigonometric relationships can be developed in a similar way.

TRIGONOMETRY IDEA 6

Introducing the Law of Cosines. I
(Using Ptolemy's Theorem)

Objective: To derive the law of cosines using Ptolemy's theorem

Materials: Chalkboard or Geometer's Sketchpad program

Procedure: The derivation of the law of cosines is done using two cases. In both cases, we are given $\triangle ABC$ and its circumcircle. To simplify the derivations, we use the case of a circle with diameter of length 1.

Case I: The center of the circle is inside $\triangle ABC$. ($\triangle ABC$ is acute.)

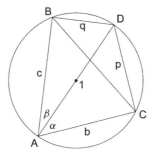

Consider diameter $\overline{AD}$. Draw $\overline{BD}$ and $\overline{DC}$. Let $CD = p$ and $DB = q$.

1. $p = \sin\alpha$ and $q = \sin\beta$; $b = \cos\alpha$ and $c = \cos\beta$.
2. Using Ptolemy's theorem with quadrilateral $ACDB$ gives $a = bq + cp$.
3. We find a^2 by squaring both sides of step 2: $a^2 = b^2q^2 + c^2p^2 + 2bcpq$.
4. Because $\triangle ABD$ and $\triangle ACD$ are right triangles, we use the Pythagorean theorem to generate replacements for p^2 and q^2: $b^2 + p^2 = 1$ and $c^2 + q^2 = 1$. Hence, $p^2 = 1 - b^2$ and $q^2 = 1 - c^2$.

5. Substituting the last two results in step 3 yields

$$a^2 = b^2(1 - c^2) + c^2(1 - b^2) + 2bcpq$$
$$= b^2 - b^2c^2 + c^2 - b^2c^2 + 2bcpq$$
$$= b^2 + c^2 - 2b^2c^2 + 2bcpq$$
$$= b^2 + c^2 - 2bc(bc - pq)$$

6. Now substituting step 1 into step 5 yields

$$a^2 = b^2 + c^2 - 2bc(\cos\alpha\cos\beta - \sin\alpha\sin\beta)$$
$$= b^2 + c^2 - 2bc \cdot \cos(\alpha + \beta)$$
$$= b^2 + c^2 - 2bc \cdot \cos A$$

which is the law of cosines.

Case II: *The center of the circle is outside* $\triangle ABC$. ($\angle ABC$ *is obtuse.*)

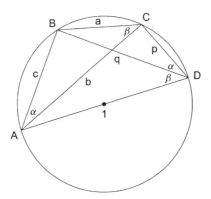

Consider diameter $\overline{AD}$. Draw $\overline{BD}$ and $\overline{DC}$. Let $CD = p$ and $DB = q$, as in Case I. Note that $m\angle CDB = m\angle CAB = \alpha$; $m\angle BDA = m\angle BCA = \beta$.

1. Using right $\triangle ADC$, we have $b = \sin(\alpha + \beta)$ and $p = \cos(\alpha + \beta)$.
2. Using right $\triangle ABD$, $c = \sin\beta$ and $q = \cos\beta$.
3. Using Ptolemy's theorem with quadrilateral $ABCD$ gives $a + cp = bq$, which can be written as $a = bq - cp$.
4. As before, we square both sides of the equation in step 3:

$$a^2 = b^2q^2 + c^2p^2 - 2bcpq$$

5. Because $\triangle ABD$ and $\triangle ACD$ are right triangles, we use the Pythagorean theorem to replace p^2 and q^2 as $b^2 + p^2 = 1$ and $c^2 + q^2 = 1$. These can be written as $p^2 = 1 - b^2$ and $q^2 = 1 - c^2$.

6. Substituting the last two results into step 4 yields

$$a^2 = b^2(1 - c^2) + c^2(1 - b^2) - 2bcpq$$
$$= b^2 - b^2c^2 + c^2 - b^2c^2 - 2bcpq$$
$$= b^2 + c^2 - 2b^2c^2 - 2bcpq$$
$$= b^2 + c^2 - 2bc(bc + pq)$$

7. Now substituting step 1 and step 2 into step 6 yields

$$a^2 = b^2 + c^2 - 2bc(\sin(\alpha + \beta) \cdot \sin\beta + \cos(\alpha + \beta) \cdot \cos\beta)$$
$$= b^2 + c^2 - 2bc \cdot \cos(\alpha + \beta - \beta)$$
$$= b^2 + c^2 - 2bc \cdot \cos\alpha$$

Because we were using α for $m\angle A$ in the accompanying diagram, we have

$$a^2 = b^2 + c^2 - 2bc \cdot \cos A$$

which is the law of cosines.

Again Ptolemy's theorem provides an alternative to the derivation of a trigono-metric theorem, a useful endeavor for students to better appreciate mathematics as more than just a series of rules to be followed.

TRIGONOMETRY IDEA 7

Introducing the Law of Cosines. II

Objective: To present an alternative introduction to the law of cosines

Materials: Chalkboard or Geometer's Sketchpad program

Procedure: The law of cosines can be introduced by showing a triangle whose parts need to be found and where the law of sines (assuming it has already been introduced) is not sufficient to do the job. This might also be done through a problem that results in such a triangle requiring a solution. Once this need has been determined, the following derivation can be used to establish the law of cosines relationship.

Begin by considering triangle ABC.

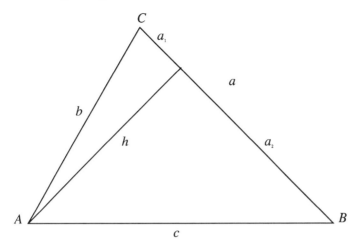

Draw perpendicular h from $\angle A$ to side a. Then

$$a = a_1 + a_2 \quad \text{or} \quad a_2 = a - a_1 \tag{1}$$

$$\cos C = \frac{a_1}{b} \qquad a_1 = b \cos C \tag{2}$$

$$\sin C = \frac{h}{b} \qquad h = b \sin C \tag{3}$$

$$c^2 = a_2^2 + h^2 = (a - a_1)^2 + h^2 = a^2 - 2aa_1 + a_1^2 + h^2 \tag{4}$$

From Equations 2 and 3,

$$c^2 = a^2 - 2ab \cos C + b^2 \cos^2 C + b^2 \sin^2 C$$
$$= a^2 - 2ab \cos C + b^2(\cos^2 C + \sin^2 C)$$
$$= a^2 - 2ab \cos C + b^2$$

The law of cosines has now been established and can be used to solve triangles.

TRIGONOMETRY IDEA 8

Introducing the Law of Cosines. III

Objective: To present an alternative introduction to the law of cosines

Materials: Chalkboard or Geometer's Sketchpad program

Procedure: The law of cosines can be introduced by showing a triangle whose parts need to be found and where the law of sines (assuming it has already been introduced) is not sufficient to do the job. This might also be done through a problem that results in such a triangle requiring a solution. Once this need has been determined, the following derivation can be used to establish the law of cosines relationship.

Begin by considering triangle ABC.

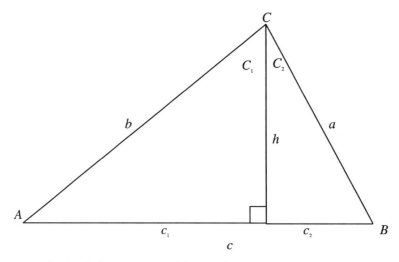

Draw perpendicular h from $\angle C$ to side c. Then

$$C_1 + C_2 = C \qquad c_1 + c_2 = c$$

$$\sin C_1 = \frac{c_1}{b} \qquad \sin C_2 = \frac{c_2}{a}$$

$$\cos C_1 = \frac{h}{b} \qquad \cos C_2 = \frac{h}{a}$$

$$\cos C = \cos(C_1 + C_2) = \cos C_1 \cos C_2 - \sin C_1 \sin C_2 = \frac{h^2}{ab} - \frac{c_1 c_2}{ab}$$

$$\cos C = \frac{1}{ab}(h^2 - c_1 c_2), \qquad h^2 - c_1 c_2 = ab \cos C$$

$$c_1^2 = b^2 - h^2, \qquad c_2^2 = a^2 - h^2$$

$$c^2 = (c_1 + c_2)^2 = c_1^2 + 2c_1 c_2 + c_2^2 = (b^2 - h^2) + 2c_1 c_2 + (a^2 - h^2)$$
$$= b^2 - 2h^2 + 2c_1 c_2 + a^2 = a^2 - 2(h^2 - c_1 c_2) + b^2$$
$$= a^2 - 2ab \cos C + b^2$$

This is the law of cosines and it may be applied to solving a triangle, that is, determining missing sides or angles of given triangles.

Alternate Approach to Introducing Trigonometric Identities

Objective: To use circles with unit diameters to prove basic trigonometric identities

Materials: Chalkboard or Geometer's Sketchpad program

Procedure: The use of circles with unit diameters to prove basic trigonometric identities is quite unusual and interesting. The only difficulty from a mathematical point of view is that the proofs are valid only for *limited* values of θ. However, in many trigonometry classes, the traditional proofs that are used are also valid only for limited values of θ.

To simplify our work in trigonometry, we use circles of unit diameter. In the accompanying diagram, we see that

$$\sin \theta = BC \qquad \cos \theta = AC$$

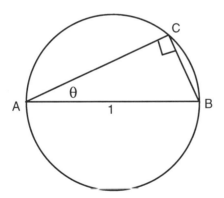

We summarize these statements as follows: In a circle with unit diameter, if an inscribed angle has a diameter as one of its sides and the chord opposite the angle is drawn to complete a right triangle, then

1. The length of the *side opposite* the angle is the sine of the angle
2. The length of the *other side* of the angle is the cosine of the angle

Because the special case where an angle inscribed in a circle has a diameter as one of its sides is rather limiting, consider the case such as $\angle CAB$ in the figure

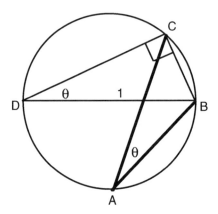

Through B and the center of the circle, construct a diameter $\overline{BD}$. Because this circle has a unit diameter, $DB = 1$. Draw chord $\overline{DC}$.

The following observations can be made about the diagram:

1. $\triangle DCB$ must be a right triangle because it is inscribed in a semicircle.
2. $\angle D \cong \angle A$ because both angles are inscribed in the same arc.
3. $CB = \sin\theta$ in triangle CBD.

We can now conclude that for *any* angle inscribed in a circle with unit diameter, the length of the *side opposite* this angle is the sine of the angle.

The foregoing results may seem trivial, but can be useful to prove some basic trigonometric facts.

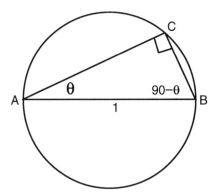

At this point let your students find the length of $\overline{CB}$ in the accompanying figure. If the focus is on $\angle A$, $CB = \sin\theta$. If the focus is on $\angle B$, $CB = \cos(90 - \theta)$. Therefore,

$$\sin\theta = \cos(90 - \theta)$$

Similarly, from AC,

$$\sin(90 - \theta) = \cos\theta$$

Consider the following applications. In each case, the diagram may be used to derive an important relationship of trigonometry. (Each circle has a unit diameter.)

1.

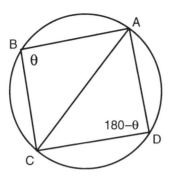

$$\sin\theta = \sin(180 - \theta)$$

2.

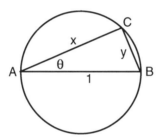

$\overline{AB}$ is diameter of the circle:

$$\sin^2\theta + \cos^2\theta = 1$$

3.

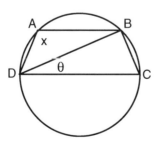

Given $\overline{AB} \parallel \overline{CD}$, where $\overline{CD}$ is a diameter of the circle, because $m\angle C = 90 - \theta$ and $m\angle A = 180 - m\angle C$,

$$x = 90 + \theta \quad \text{and} \quad \cos\theta = \sin(90 + \theta)$$

165

Converting to Sines and Cosines

Objective: To demonstrate how converting to sine and cosine can make a difficult problem simple

Materials: Chalkboard

Procedure: Students are often advised to change trigonometric functions to sine and cosine equivalents. This practice is particularly helpful when proving identities. However, there are times when this conversion can make a seemingly difficult or almost insurmountable problem trivial. Consider the following problem:

Find the rational value of

$$\tan 10° \cdot \tan 20° \cdot \tan 30° \cdot \tan 40° \cdot \tan 50° \cdot \tan 60° \cdot \tan 70° \cdot \tan 80°$$

Begin by converting each of these tangent functions to their equivalents in terms of sine and cosine:

$$\frac{\sin 10° \cdot \sin 20° \cdot \sin 30° \cdot \sin 40° \cdot \sin 50° \cdot \sin 60° \cdot \sin 70° \cdot \sin 80°}{\cos 10° \cdot \cos 20° \cdot \cos 30° \cdot \cos 40° \cdot \cos 50° \cdot \cos 60° \cdot \cos 70° \cdot \cos 80°}$$

Apply the relationship that $\sin \theta = \cos(90° - \theta)$ to each term in the numerator to get

$$\frac{\cos 80° \cdot \cos 70° \cdot \cos 60° \cdot \cos 50° \cdot \cos 40° \cdot \cos 30° \cdot \cos 20° \cdot \cos 10°}{\cos 10° \cdot \cos 20° \cdot \cos 30° \cdot \cos 40° \cdot \cos 50° \cdot \cos 60° \cdot \cos 70° \cdot \cos 80°} = 1$$

since numerator and denominator are equal.

An alternative way to solve this problem is to use the relationship $\tan \theta = \cot(90° - \theta)$. Converting the last four terms of the original expression we get

$$\tan 10° \cdot \tan 20° \cdot \tan 30° \cdot \tan 40° \cdot \cot 40° \cdot \cot 30° \cdot \cot 20° \cdot \cot 10°$$

which, by pairing, gives us

$$(\tan 10° \cdot \cot 10°)(\tan 20° \cdot \cot 20°)(\tan 30° \cdot \cot 30°)(\tan 40° \cdot \cot 40°)$$
$$= 1 \cdot 1 \cdot 1 \cdot 1 = 1$$

This rather short exercise demonstrates the value of being able to convert trigonometric functions to their equivalents.

Using the Double Angle Formula
for the Sine Function

Objective: To show a clever example where the double angle relationship for sines is essential

Materials: Chalkboard

Procedure: Without much introduction, present the following problem for solution:

Find the rational value of $\cos 20° \cdot \cos 40° \cdot \cos 80°$

Key to this simplification is the relationship that $\sin 2\theta = 2\sin\theta \cdot \cos\theta$. Begin by multiplying the given expression by 1 in the form of $\frac{2\sin 20°}{2\sin 20°}$ to get

$$\frac{2\sin 20°}{2\sin 20°} \cdot \cos 20° \cos 40° \cdot \cos 80°$$

$$= \frac{(2\sin 20° \cdot \cos 20°) \cdot \cos 40° \cdot \cos 80°}{2\sin 20°}$$

$$(\text{because} \quad 2\sin 20° \cos 20° = \sin 40°)$$

$$= \frac{2}{2} \cdot \frac{(\sin 40°) \cdot \cos 40° \cdot \cos 80°}{2\sin 20°} = \frac{(2\sin 40° \cdot \cos 40°) \cdot \cos 80°}{2 \cdot 2 \cdot \sin 20°}$$

$$= \frac{(\sin 80°) \cdot \cos 80°}{2 \cdot 2 \cdot \sin 20°} = \frac{2}{2} \cdot \frac{\sin 80° \cdot \cos 80°}{2 \cdot 2 \cdot \sin 20°} = \frac{\sin 160°}{2 \cdot 2 \cdot 2 \cdot \sin 20°}$$

$$= \frac{\sin 20°}{8 \cdot \sin 20°} = \frac{1}{8}$$

The rather overwhelming task at the outset is made fairly simple by the use of the double angle formula for the sine function. Such examples give some "real" value to learning these relationships.

Making the Angle Sum Function Meaningful

Objective: To show a rather clever application of $\sin(A + B)$ to make it meaningful

Materials: Chalkboard and Geometer's Sketchpad

Procedure: Begin by using the Geometer's Sketchpad to draw three right triangles with sides of lengths

$$3, \ 4, \ 5 \qquad 8, \ 15, \ 17 \qquad 36, \ 77, \ 85$$

In each case, the size of the triangle is not important, just the shape. That is, the relationship among the sides of each triangle must be as indicated.

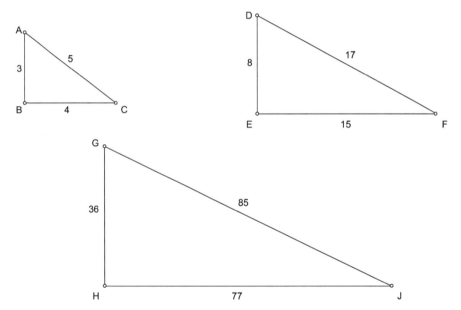

The task at hand is to find the sum of the measures of the smallest angles of each of these right triangles. Because the smallest angle of a triangle is opposite the smallest side, we seek to find the sum of $m\angle C$, $m\angle F$, and $m\angle J$.

From $\triangle ABC$ we get the trigonometric ratios

$$\sin C = \frac{3}{5} \qquad \cos C = \frac{4}{5}$$

Similarly, from $\triangle DEF$,

$$\sin F = \frac{8}{17} \qquad \cos F = \frac{15}{17}$$

Now,

$$\sin(C + F) = \sin C \cdot \cos F + \cos C \cdot \sin F = \frac{3}{5} \cdot \frac{15}{17} + \frac{4}{5} \cdot \frac{8}{17} = \frac{77}{85}$$

We notice from the third triangle that

$$\cos J = \frac{77}{85} = \sin(90 - J)$$

Because both values are equal to $\frac{77}{85}$, $\sin(C + F) = \sin(90 - J)$. We conclude that

$$m\angle C + m\angle F = 90 - m\angle J \quad \text{or} \quad m\angle C + m\angle F + m\angle J = 90$$

which was the value to be found.

We can "verify" this result with the Geometer's Sketchpad. Here are the measures of the angles:

$$m\angle ACB \approx 37° \qquad m\angle DFE \approx 28° \qquad m\angle GJH \approx 25°$$

This problem points out a nice use of the angle sum function.

| TRIGONOMETRY IDEA **13** |

Responding to the Angle-Trisection Question

Objective: To provide an explanation of the impossibility of the angle trisection using a straightedge and compasses

Materials: Chalkboard

Procedure: A commonly asked question to which teachers are asked to respond is how can an angle be trisected using Euclidean tools (a straightedge and compasses). Teachers are quick to make the point that, although a general angle cannot be trisected with Euclidean tools, specific angles can be so trisected. For example, a 90° angle can be trisected, as can a 135° angle, but a 120° angle cannot be trisected with these tools. Of course, students should be told that this doesn't mean that a general angle cannot be trisected; rather, it means that other tools are necessary to do the job.

The question of trisection of a general angle has belabored mathematicians for many years. It has the distinction of being one of the three famous problems of antiquity. It is no longer a problem today, because it has been solved. That is, we now can prove that the trisection of a general angle is impossible with Euclidean tools. How can you best demonstrate this to students? We offer one such demonstration here.

A proposed geometric construction is possible with a straightedge and compasses alone if and only if the numbers that algebraically define the required geometric elements can be derived from those that define the given elements by a finite number of rational operations and extractions of square root. This may be called the criterion of constructibility.

The trisection problem requires the existence of a method that will trisect any angle.

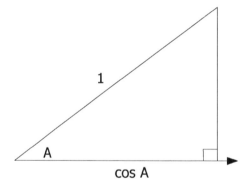

From a given angle A, we construct a segment with length equal to $\cos A$. If we take an arbitrary unit-length segment as the hypotenuse, $\cos A$ is the length of the segment cut off on the other side of $\angle A$ by the perpendicular from the opposite end of the hypotenuse. If we can trisect $\angle A$, we can also find the cosine of one-third the angle, $\cos \frac{A}{3}$. If we can show that $\cos \frac{A}{3}$ cannot be constructed, then we have shown that $\angle A$ cannot be trisected. Using proof by counterexample, we prove an angle of measure 120 cannot be trisected. We must, however, accept the identity

$$\cos A = 4\cos^3 \frac{A}{3} - 3\cos \frac{A}{3}$$

If we multiply through by 2 and replace $2\cos \frac{A}{3}$ with x, we have

$$2\cos A = x^3 - 3x$$

170

Because $\cos 120° = -\frac{1}{2}$, we have

$$x^3 - 3x + 1 = 0$$

From the criterion of constructibility, we know that constructible roots must be of the form $a + b\sqrt{c}$, where a and b are rational and c is constructible.*

First, then, we must show that $x^3 - 3x + 1 = 0$ has no rational roots. To do this, we assume that there is a rational root, $\frac{p}{q}$, where p and q have no common factor greater than 1. Substituting for $\frac{p}{q}$, we have

$$\left(\frac{p}{q}\right)^3 - 3\left(\frac{p}{q}\right) + 1 = 0$$
$$p^3 - 3pq^2 + q^3 = 0$$
$$q^3 = 3pq^2 - p^3$$
$$= p(3q^2 - p^2)$$

This means that q^3, and hence q, has the factor p. Since p and q have no common factor greater than 1 it follows that p must equal ± 1. Also, solving for p^3,

$$p^3 = 3pq^2 - q^3$$
$$= q^2(3p - q)$$

This means p and q must have a common factor, and hence $q = \pm 1$. We can conclude from this that the only rational root of $x^3 - 3x + 1 = 0$ is $r = \pm 1$. By substitution, we can show that neither $+1$ nor -1 is a root.

Next, assume $x^3 - 3x + 1 = 0$ has a constructible root $a + b\sqrt{c}$. By substitution in the equation $x^3 - 3x + 1 = 0$, we can show that if $a + b\sqrt{c}$ is a root, then its conjugate, $a - b\sqrt{c}$, is also a root.

The sum of the roots of the polynomial equation

$$x^n + a_1 x^{n-1} + a_2 x^{n-2} + \cdots + a_n = 0$$

is $r_1 + r_2 + r_3 + \cdots + r_n = -a_1$. It follows from this that the sum of the roots of $x^3 - 3x + 1 = 0$ is zero. If two roots are $a + b\sqrt{c}$ and $a - b\sqrt{c}$, with the third root r, we have

$$a + b\sqrt{c} + a - b\sqrt{c} + r = 0$$

$$r = -2a$$

However, a is rational and hence r is rational, and we have a contradiction. Hence, the angle whose measure is 120 cannot be trisected.

This nifty proof that a general angle cannot be trisected with Euclidean tools is useful when posed with the often-asked question about angle trisection.

_____
* We treat the case where c is natural.

171

Probability and Statistics Ideas

Introduction of a Sample Space

Objective: To demonstrate the need for constructing a sample space

Materials: Four red chips and four black chips for each group of students

Procedure: When students begin their study of probability, they look for formulas to resolve every situation. Rarely do they set up the sample space (i.e., the collection of all possible outcomes of a conceptual experiment) to see what is actually taking place. This activity places the students in a game situation, where their intuition works against them. Unless they actually set up the sample space, they will not be able to resolve the inequity of the game.

Begin by placing one red chip and two black chips in an envelope. Give the students the following rules for the game they are about to play:

1. They will draw two chips from the envelope, without looking.
2. If the colors of the two chips are different, the teacher scores a point. If they are the same, the student scores the point.
3. The first player to score 5 points is the winner.
4. After each draw, the chips are returned to the envelope and the envelope is shaken.

Ask the students if they think the game is fair (that is, each player has an equal chance of gaining a point). After a discussion of their answers, play the game several times until the students realize that the game is not fair. (The teacher should win the game most of the time.) Now ask them what single chip they would add to make the game fair. Most of the students will suggest adding a second red chip to the envelope. At this point, introduce the idea of setting up the sample space as follows:

Situation 1: One red chip and two black chips. The possible draws (the sample space) would be

RB_1 RB_2 $\mathbf{B_1B_2}$

Thus, the student has only 1 out of 3 chances of scoring a point, for a $\frac{1}{3}$ probability. The original game is unfair.

Situation 2: Adding one red chip, so we have two red chips and two black chips. The possible draws (the sample space) would be

R_1B_1 R_1B_2 $\mathbf{R_1R_2}$
R_2B_1 R_2B_2 $\mathbf{B_1B_2}$

Surprise! The student has only 2 out of 6 chances of scoring a point, for a $\frac{1}{3}$ probability. The game is, once again, unfair.

Situation 3: Adding another black chip to the original chips, we get one red chip and three black chips. Now the sample space consists of the six possible draws.

R_1B_1 $\quad$ R_1B_2 $\quad$ R_1B_3

B_1B_2 $\quad$ **B_1B_3** $\quad$ **B_2B_3**

This time the student has 3 out of 6 chances of scoring a point, for a $\frac{1}{2}$ probability. The game is now fair.

The use of the sample space easily reveals that the students' intuition does not yield a correct resolution of the problem, thus making the concept of a sample space "indispensable."

PROBABILITY AND STATISTICS IDEA 2

Using Sample Spaces to Solve Tricky Probability Problems

Objective: To demonstrate a probability problem that intuitively generates the wrong answer, yet with the use of sample spaces becomes simple

Materials: Chalkboard and three cardboard cards marked as follows:
$\quad$ Card 1: $\quad$ both sides VOCAL
$\quad$ Card 2: $\quad$ both sides INSTRUMENTAL
$\quad$ Card 3: $\quad$ one side VOCAL the other side INSTRUMENTAL

Procedure: Begin by presenting the following problem for solution:

A person has just three phonograph records. The first has vocal performances on both sides, the second has instrumental music on both sides, and the third has vocal performances on one side and instrumental music on the other side. This person, who is in a darkened room, puts on one of these records. What is the probability that he hears a vocal performance?

$\quad$ Denote by $v_{1,1}$: side 1 of record 1
$\quad$ Denote by $v_{2,1}$: side 2 of record 1
$\quad$ Denote by $i_{1,2}$: side 1 of record 2
$\quad$ Denote by $i_{2,2}$: side 2 of record 2

Denote by $v_{1,3}$: side 1 of record 3
Denote by $i_{2,3}$: side 2 of record 3

The sample space consists of the six possible equally likely outcomes: $v_{1,1}$, $v_{2,1}$, $i_{1,2}$, $i_{2,2}$, $v_{1,3}$, $i_{2,3}$. Precisely three of which: $v_{1,1}$, $v_{2,1}$, $v_{1,3}$ consist of vocal performances. Therefore the probability of hearing a vocal performance is $\frac{3}{6} = \frac{1}{2}$.

Now consider a somewhat more difficult problem.

> A person has just three phonograph records. The first has vocal performances on both sides, the second has instrumental music on both sides, and the third has vocal performances on one side and instrumental music on the other side. This person, who is in a darkened room, puts on one of these records and hears a vocal performance. What is the (conditional) probability that the other side of that same record is also vocal?

The usual response is $\frac{1}{2}$, with the "reasoning" that *one of the two* vocal sided records has vocal on the other side. This reasoning is wrong!

The correct reasoning is that there are six record-sides equally likely to be played. Because the person in the problem is playing a vocal side, the sample space for this is limited to the set $\{v_{1,1}, v_{2,1}, v_{1,3}\}$. Two of the three elements ($v_{1,1}, v_{2,1}$) of the sample space set represent a vocal on the other side. Therefore the probability is $\frac{2}{3}$. This easily missolved problem demonstrates the usefulness of setting up a sample space. Compare this conditional probability $\left(\frac{2}{3}\right)$ with the probability $\left(\frac{1}{2}\right)$ of the first problem above.

PROBABILITY AND STATISTICS IDEA 3

Introducing Probability Through Counting (or Probability as Relative Frequency)

Objective: To understand the basic concept of probability

Materials: Chalkboard, two paper bags, five red checkers, and seven black checkers

Procedure: There is a thinking adjustment required when a student first encounters probability. Simple illustrations like pulling an ace out of a deck of 52 cards require little imagination. However, a problem such as the following does require some probability-thinking skills. It is a good opportunity to begin to train students to think logically.

Consider the following problem: Two identical paper bags contain red and black checkers.

> Bag A contains two red and three black checkers
> Bag B contains three red and four black checkers

A bag is chosen at random and a red checker is drawn from it. What is the probability that Bag A was chosen?

Because the first even common multiple of 5 and 7 (the bags' checker capacities) is 70, we use this as the number of trials for our hypothetical experiment. Because the bag was chosen at random, we can assume that each bag was chosen 35 times.

> From Bag A, a red checker will be selected 2 out of 5 times, so for 35 trials, a red checker will be drawn 14 times.
> From Bag B, a red checker will be selected 3 out of 7 times, so for 35 trials, a red checker will be drawn 15 times.

Therefore a red checker will be drawn $14 + 15 = 29$ times, of which 14 would be from Bag A. Therefore, the probability that the red checker will be drawn from Bag A is $\frac{14}{29}$.

This exercise shows students the kind of comparison necessary to succeed with probability.

PROBABILITY AND STATISTICS IDEA 4

In Probability You Cannot Always Rely on Your Intuition

Objective: To demonstrate an unexpected answer to a probability question and to introduce the notion of complementary probabilities

Materials: Have available 10 groups of about 35 people each (these can be lists instead of "live groups")

Procedure: Begin by asking the class what they think the chances are (or the probability is) that two classmates have the same birth date (month and day only) in their class of about 30+ students. Students usually begin to think about the likelihood of two people having the same date out of a selection of 365 days (assuming no leap year). Perhaps 2 out of 365? Ask them to consider the "randomly" selected group of the first 35 presidents of the United States. They may be astonished that there are two with the same birth date: James K. Polk (November 2, 1795) and Warren G. Harding (November 2, 1865). The class will probably be surprised to learn that for a group of 35, the probability that two members will have the same birth date is greater than .8. Students may wish to try their own experiment by visiting 10 nearby classrooms to check on date matches. For groups of 30, the probability that there will be a match is greater than .7, or in 7 of these 10 rooms there ought to be a match of birth dates. What causes this incredible result?

Students should now be curious to learn how this probability is computed. Guide them as follows:

What is the probability that one selected student matches his or her own birth date? Clearly certainty, or 1.

This can be written as $\frac{365}{365}$.

> The probability that another student does *not* match, either of the first student is $\frac{365-1}{365} = \frac{364}{365}$.
>
> The probability that another student does *not* match either of the first and second students is $\frac{365-2}{365} = \frac{363}{365}$.
>
> The probability that none of 35 students have the same birth date is the product of these probabilities:

$$p = \frac{365}{365} \cdot \frac{365-1}{365} \cdot \frac{365-2}{365} \cdot \ldots \cdot \frac{365-34}{365}$$

Because either the probability (q) that two students in the group *have* the same birth date or the probability (p) that two students in the group do *not* have the same birth date is a certainty, the sum of those probabilities must be 1. Thus, $p + q = 1$.

In this case,

$$q = 1 - \frac{365}{365} \cdot \frac{365-1}{365} \cdot \frac{365-2}{365} \cdot \ldots \cdot \frac{365-33}{365} \cdot \frac{365-34}{365}$$
$$\approx .8143832388747152$$

In other words, the probability that there will be a birth date match in a randomly selected group of 35 people is somewhat greater than $\frac{8}{10}$. This is quite unexpected when we consider there were 365 dates from which to choose. Students may want to investigate the nature of the probability function. Here are a few values to serve as a guide:

Number of people in group	Probability of a birth date match
10	.1169481777110776
15	.2529013197636863
20	.4114383835805799
25	.5686997039694639
30	.7063162427192686
35	.8143832388747152
40	.891231809817949
45	.9409758994657749
50	.9703735795779884
55	.9862622888164461
60	.994122660865348
65	.9976831073124921
70	.9991595759651571

Students should notice how quickly almost certainty is reached. Were we to do this with the death dates of the first 35 presidents, we would notice that two died on March 8th (Millard Fillmore and William H. Taft) and three died on the 4th of July (Adams, Jefferson, and Monroe). Above all, this demonstration should serve as an eye-opener about relying on intuition too much.

PROBABILITY AND STATISTICS IDEA 5

When "Averages" Are Not Averages: Introducing Weighted Averages

Objective: To introduce students to the notion that not all quantities can be "averaged" without adjustment

Materials: Chalkboard and the sports section of a newspaper that gives baseball box scores

Procedure: Begin by asking students to explain what a "baseball batting average" is. Most people, especially after trying to explain this concept, begin to realize that it is not an average in the way they usually define an "average"—the arithmetic mean. It might be good to search the sports section of the local newspaper to find two baseball players who currently have the same batting average, but who have achieved their respective averages with a different number of hits. We use a hypothetical example here.

Consider two players: David and Lisa, each with a batting average of .667. David achieved his batting average by getting 20 hits for 30 at bats, whereas Lisa achieved her batting average by getting 2 hits for 3 at bats.

The next day both perform equally, getting 1 hit for 2 at bats (for a .500 batting average). We might expect that they then still have the same batting average at the end of the day. Calculate their respective averages:

> David now has $20 + 1 = 21$ hits for $30 + 2 = 32$ at bats for a $\frac{21}{32} = .656$ batting average.

> Lisa now has $2 + 1 = 3$ hits for $3 + 2 = 5$ at bats for a $\frac{3}{5} = .600$ batting average.

Surprise! They do not have equal batting averages.

Suppose we consider the next day, when Lisa performs considerably better than David does. Lisa gets 2 hits for 3 at bats, whereas David gets 1 hit for 3 at bats. We now calculate their respective averages:

> David has $21 + 1 = 22$ hits for $32 + 3 = 35$ at bats for a batting average of $\frac{22}{35} = .629$.

> Lisa has $3 + 2 = 5$ hits for $5 + 3 = 8$ at bats for a batting average of $\frac{5}{8} = .625$.

Amazingly, despite Lisa's much superior performance on this day, her batting average, which was the same as David's at the start, is still lower.

There is much to be learned from this "misuse" of the word "average," but more importantly students will get an appreciation of the notion of varying weights of items being averaged. Further consideration of this theme is found in Algebra Idea 20.

Conditional Probability in Geometry

Objective: To introduce students to conditional probability with a physical illustration to dramatize this important concept*

Materials: Chalkboard or Geometer's Sketchpad

Procedure: Pose the following question for consideration: Consider two concentric circles, where the radius of the smaller is one-half that of the larger. What is the probability that a point selected randomly in the larger circle is also in the smaller one?

The typical (and correct) answer is $\frac{1}{4}$.

We know that the area of the smaller circle is $\frac{1}{4}$ the area of the larger circle. Therefore, if a point is selected at random in the larger circle, the probability that it would be in the smaller circle as well is $\frac{1}{4}$.

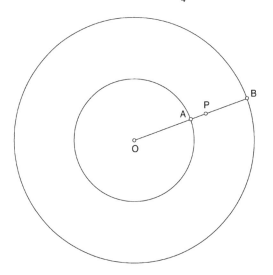

However, we could look at this question differently. The randomly selected point P must lie on some radius of the larger circle, say $\overline{OAB}$, where A is its midpoint. The probability that a point P on $\overline{OAB}$ is on $\overline{OA}$ (i.e., in the smaller circle) is $\frac{1}{2}$. Now if we do this for any other point in the larger circle, we find the probability of the point being in the smaller circle is $\frac{1}{2}$. This, of course, is not correct. Where was the error made in the second calculation?

---

* Compare Probability and Statistics Idea 2, where conditional probability was introduced in a different context.

The "error" lies in the initial definition of each of two different sample spaces. In the first case, the sample space is the entire area of the larger circle, whereas in the second case, the sample space is the set of points on $\overline{OAB}$. Clearly, when a point is selected on $\overline{OAB}$, the probability that the point will be on $\overline{OA}$ is $\frac{1}{2}$. These are two entirely different problems even though (to dramatize the issue) they appear to be the same. Conditional probability is an important concept to stress, and what better way to instill this idea than through a demonstration that shows obvious absurdities.

PROBABILITY AND STATISTICS IDEA 7

Introducing the Pascal Triangle

Objective: To show several interesting properties of the Pascal triangle before actually using it

Materials: Chalkboard and preprepared transparencies with the Pascal triangle already written

Procedure: There are probably boundless applications of the Pascal triangle. This arrangement of numbers seems to permeate most branches of mathematics, oftentimes surprisingly.

Begin by providing the Pascal triangle, showing that it is constructed by adding each pair of numbers and placing their sum below the space between them.

```
              1
            1   1
          1   2   1
        1   3   3   1
      1   4   6   4   1
    1   5  10  10   5   1
  1   6  15  20  15   6   1
1   7  21  35  35  21   7   1
1  8  28  56  70  56  28  8  1
```

By adding across the rows, we get the powers of 2: $2^0, 2^1, 2^2, 2^3, 2^4, \ldots$.

By interpreting the members of all cells in a row as digits of a number, we get powers of 11: The rows are

$$1 = 11^0,$$
$$11 = 11^1,$$
$$121 = 11^2,$$
$$1331 = 11^3,$$
$$14641 = 11^4,$$
$$15[10][10]51 = 161051 = 11^5$$

$$\vdots$$

At the point of 11^5, this scheme gets a bit tricky because the units digit is retained by the place position and the tens digit is added to the next place.

By drawing lines to indicate an "oblique" addition, the Fibonacci numbers, $1, 1, 2, 3, 5, 8, 13, 21, 34, \ldots$, are generated:

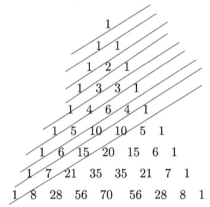

By cutting off a section of the Pascal triangle, we get row sums that represent the number of sections into which a circle is partitioned by joining an increasing number of points on a circle (see Algebra Idea 12).

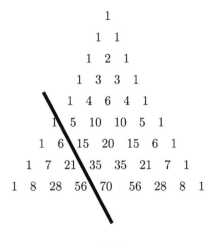

184

The numbers in the third diagonal represent the triangular numbers, 1, 3, 6, 10, 15, 21, 28, . . .:

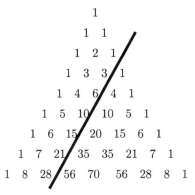

```
                    1
                  1   1
                1   2   1
              1   3   3 / 1
            1   4   6 / 4   1
          1   5  10 / 10   5   1
        1   6  15 / 20  15   6   1
      1   7  21 / 35  35  21   7   1
    1   8  28 / 56  70  56  28   8   1
```

The Pascal triangle gives the number of subsets of a given set. For example, inspecting row: if a set has five elements, then there is one subset having 5 elements. See the following chart for more examples.

Size of the subsets of a set of 5 elements	Number of subsets
5 elements	1
4 elements	5
3 elements	10
2 elements	10
1 element	5
0 elements	1

Draw a hexagon around any seven elements and the sum of these elements is twice the element directly below it. In the following Pascal triangle, the sum of the elements $(6 + 4 + 10 + 10 + 5 + 20 + 15)$ in the hexagon is 70, which is twice 35, the number directly below it.

```
                    1
                  1   1
                1   2   1
              1   3   3   1
            1   4 / 6   4 \ 1
          1   5 ⟨10  10   5⟩ 1
        1   6  15 \20  15 / 6   1
      1   7  21  35  35  21   7   1
    1   8  28  56  70  56  28   8   1
```

There are many other interesting patterns and relationships that exist in the Pascal triangle. Students will find it entertaining and rewarding to search for other patterns and relationships. Once this is explored, the Pascal triangle can be used for the coefficients of the binomial theorem and for measure of probability.

185

Comparing Means Algebraically

Objective: To provide a method for comparing the magnitude of the arithmetic, geometric, and harmonic means of two numbers

Materials: Chalkboard

Procedure: The **arithmetic mean** is one of the earliest taught concepts from the field of statistics. It is simply the sum of the items being averaged divided by the number of items. For two items a and b, it is $\frac{a+b}{2}$.

The **geometric mean** may be encountered in geometry (often seen as the mean proportional) and is the nth root of the product of the n items. For two items a and b, it is $\sqrt{ab}$.

The **harmonic mean** is not too popular, because there is not much that can be done with it. It is defined as the reciprocal of the arithmetic mean of the reciprocals of the n elements. It usually comes up as the mean of rates over the same base, and for n items is n times the product of the n items divided by the sum of products of the n items taken $(n-1)$ at a time. For two items a and b, it is $\frac{2ab}{a+b}$.

We now show how these three means can be compared in size using simple algebra. For the two numbers a and b,

$$(a-b)^2 \geqslant 0$$
$$a^2 - 2ab + b^2 \geqslant 0$$

Add $4ab$ to both sides:

$$a^2 + 2ab + b^2 \geqslant 4ab$$

Take the positive square root of both sides:

$$a+b \geqslant 2\sqrt{ab} \quad \text{or} \quad \frac{a+b}{2} \geqslant \sqrt{ab}$$

This implies that the *arithmetic mean* is greater than or equal to the *geometric mean*.

Continuing from the "add $4ab \cdots$" step,

$$a^2 + 2ab + b^2 \geqslant 4ab$$
$$(a+b)^2 \geqslant 4ab$$

186

Multiply both sides by ab:

$$ab(a+b)^2 \geqslant (4ab)(ab)$$
$$ab \geqslant \frac{4a^2b^2}{(a+b)^2}$$

Take the positive square root of both sides:

$$\sqrt{ab} \geqslant \frac{2ab}{a+b}$$

This implies that the *geometric mean* is greater than or equal to the *harmonic mean*. We can then conclude that

arithmetic mean $\geqslant$ geometric mean $\geqslant$ harmonic mean

Here we showed this three-part inequality holds true for two items. Have students consider showing that the inequality holds for 3 or more items.

PROBABILITY AND STATISTICS IDEA 9

Comparing Means Geometrically

Objective: To provide a method for comparing the magnitude of the arithmetic, geometric, and harmonic means of two numbers

Materials: Chalkboard and Geometer's Sketchpad program

Procedure: The **arithmetic mean** is one of the earliest taught concepts from the field of statistics. It is simply the sum of the items being averaged divided by the number of items. For two items a and b, it is $\frac{a+b}{2}$.

The **geometric mean** may be encountered in geometry (often seen as the mean proportional) and is the nth root of the product of the n items. For two items a and b, it is $\sqrt{ab}$.

The **harmonic mean** is not too popular, because there is not much that can be done with it. It is defined as the reciprocal of the arithmetic mean of the reciprocals of the n elements. It usually comes up as the mean of rates over the same base, and for n items is n times the product of the n items divided by the sum of products of the n items taken $(n-1)$ at a time. For two items a and b, it is $\frac{2ab}{a+b}$.

We now show how these three means may be compared in size using a geometric model.

187

Consider a semicircle, with center O and radius $\overline{RO}$. A perpendicular from R meets the diameter $\overline{AB}$ at P. From P, a perpendicular is drawn to $\overline{RO}$, meeting it at S.

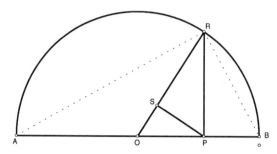

Let us begin by designating the key line segments that will be used in our mean comparison. They are $AP = a$ and $BP = b$.

We now have to find line segments in the accompanying figure that represents the various means in terms of a and b.

The arithmetic mean for a and b is RO, and is found as follows:

$$RO = \frac{1}{2}AB = \frac{1}{2}(AP + BP) = \frac{1}{2}(a + b)$$

The geometric mean for a and b is PR and is found as follows: $\triangle BPR \sim \triangle RPA$; therefore,

$$\frac{PB}{PR} = \frac{PR}{AP} \quad \text{or} \quad (PR)^2 = (AP)(PB) = ab$$

so that $PR = \sqrt{ab}$.

The harmonic mean for a and b is RS and is found as follows: $\triangle RPO \sim \triangle RSP$; therefore,

$$\frac{RO}{PR} = \frac{PR}{RS} \quad \text{or} \quad RS = \frac{(PR)^2}{RO}$$

but $(PR)^2 = ab$ and $RO = \frac{1}{2}(a + b)$, so we get

$$RS = \frac{2ab}{a + b}$$

Now for the comparisons. Consider $\triangle ROP$, where $RO > PR$. In $\triangle RSP$, $PR > RS$. Therefore, $RO > PR > RS$.

If, on the other hand, $\overline{RO} \perp \overline{AB}$, then $RO = PR = RS$. Therefore, $RO \geqslant PR \geqslant RS$. That is, the arithmetic mean is greater than or equal to the geometric mean, which is greater than or equal to the harmonic mean.

Other Topics Ideas

Asking the Right Questions

Objective: To provide illustrations where careful scrutiny of the question is necessary to obtain a correct answer

Materials: An 8×8 graph grid with 32 domino-type tiles the size of two squares on the grid

Procedure: Through certain well-thought-out questions, students' scrutiny of a mathematical problem can be significantly simplified. Consider the following problem: Given a chessboard and 32 dominos, each the exact size of two of the squares on the chessboard, can you show how 31 of these dominos can cover the chessboard, when a pair of opposite black squares have been removed?

As soon as this question is posed, students get busy trying various arrangements of square covering. This may be done with actual tiles or with a graph grid drawn on paper and then shading adjacent squares two at a time. Before long, frustration begins to set in because no one has been successful. Here the key is to go back to the question. First of all, the question does not say to do this tile covering; it asks if it can be done. However, because of the way we have been trained, the question is often misread and interpreted as "do it." A bit of clever insight helps. Ask yourself the question, "When a domino tile is placed on the chessboard, what kind of squares are covered?" A black tile and a white tile must be covered by each domino placed on the chessboard. Are there an equal number of black and white squares on the truncated chessboard? No. There are two fewer black squares than white squares. Therefore, it is impossible to cover the truncated chessboard with 31 domino tiles. Asking the right questions and inspecting the question asked are important aspects of being successful in mathematics.

191

Making Arithmetic Means Meaningful

Objective: To provide an opportunity to better understand the concept of average

Materials: Chalkboard

Procedure: There are various notions of what an average (arithmetic mean) really represents. Consider the following problem: On a mathematics examination, the average score of those passing the examination was 65, and the average score of those failing was 35. If the average score of all those taking the examination was 53, what percentage of those taking the examination passed it?

At first glance, this appears to be rather confusing. The key to a reasonable solution is to understand what is meant by an "average score." It could represent the total of scores divided by the number of scores considered. It also could mean that everyone attained that average score. We could simplify this problem by "assuming" that all the passing scores were 65 (that certainly yields an average of 65!). Likewise, we could assume that all the failing scores were 35.

If p represents the number of passing scores and q represents the number of failing scores, then $65p + 35q = 53(p + q)$, because we assume that, when looking at the total population, the examination scores were all 53 (so as to get an average score of 53).

This equation simplifies to

$$12p = 18q \quad \text{or} \quad \frac{p}{q} = \frac{3}{2}$$

Using a not too frequently used technique, we can derive the following equality from the preceding equation:

$$\frac{p}{p+q} = \frac{\frac{p}{q}}{\frac{p+q}{q}} = \frac{\frac{p}{q}}{\frac{p}{q}+1} = \frac{\frac{3}{2}}{\frac{3}{2}+1} = \frac{3}{3+2} = \frac{3}{5}$$

which then tells us that the passing scores were $\frac{3}{5}$ or 60% of the total population.

This situation is useful to help students understand that considering the average of a population through its specific equivalent, namely assigning the average score to each member, not only helps solve a rather pesky problem, but also brings more meaning to an otherwise confusing situation.

Using Place Value to Strengthen Reasoning Ability

Objective: To use the addition algorithm to practice reasoning

Materials: Chalkboard

Procedure: Applying reasoning skills to analyzing an addition algorithm situation can be very important in training mathematical thinking. Consider the following letters that represent the digits of a simple addition:

$$
\begin{array}{r}
\text{S E N D} \\
+\text{M O R E} \\
\hline
\text{M O N E Y}
\end{array}
$$

Find the digits that represent the letters to make this addition correct. Show that the solution is unique.

Most important in this activity is the analysis, and particular attention should be given to the reasoning used.

None of the letters can exceed the value 9, specifically, neither S nor M exceeds 9, so that MO < 19, which implies that M = 1, since $m \neq 0$.

SE < 99 and MO < 19, so MON < SE + MO + 1 = 119, and because no two letters can represent the same digit, the letter O must equal 0 (zero) and S = 9.

The most that can be carried over to another column is 1. Therefore, N = E + 1, because 1 is carried from N + R.

Whereas E = N − 1, adding 10 to both sides of this equation gives us E + 10 = N + 9 (E + 10 means that the sum N + R > 10). Because there is a 1 carried over from D + E and because N + R = N + 9, it follows that R = 8.

Whereas S = 9 and R = 8, it follows that D $\leqslant$ 7, N $\leqslant$ 7, and E $\leqslant$ 6. Now, D + E = Y + 10 < 14. However, if E = 6, then N = E + 1 = 7, which means D < 6, so D + E = 10 or 11, both of which are imposible. Therefore, E = 5.

Then N = 6, D = 7, and Y = 3, so that the addition looks like

$$
\begin{array}{r}
9\ 5\ 6\ 7 \\
+1\ 0\ 8\ 5 \\
\hline
1\ 0\ 6\ 5\ 2
\end{array}
$$

This rather strenuous activity should provide some important experience for use in a later study of mathematics.

Prime Numbers

Objective: To identify prime numbers

Materials: Chalkboard

Procedure: A lesson on the introduction of **prime numbers** usually begins with a formal definition: *an integer greater than* 1, *whose only divisors are one and itself.* Students then learn how to isolate the primes with the help of the sieve of Eratosthenes (named after Eratosthenes of Alexandria, 276–194 BC). To list all the primes up to n, they make a chart of all the numbers from 2 to n. Beginning with the numbers after 2, they remove all the multiples of 2. Then beginning with the numbers after 3, they remove all the multiples of 3 and continue in this manner until all multiples of primes not greater than $\sqrt{n}$, except the primes themselves, have been removed.

To list all primes less than 50, we may use the sieve of Eratosthenes as follows:

2	3	4	5	6	7	8	9	10	
11	12	13	14	15	16	17	18	19	20
21	22	23	24	25	26	27	28	29	30
31	32	33	34	35	36	37	38	39	40
41	42	43	44	45	46	47	48	49	50

First, cross out (underline) all numbers greater than 2 that are multiples of 2, that is, every second number after 2. Next cross out (underline) all numbers greater than 3 that are divisible by 3, that is, every third number after 3. Note that some numbers, the multiples of 2 and 3, are underlined twice. Next strike out (underline) all numbers greater than 5 (the first number greater than 3 that has not been previously underlined) that are divisible by 5, that is, every fifth number after 5. Note again that some numbers, the multiples of 2, 3, and 5 are underlined three times. Finally, strike out all numbers greater than 7 (the first number greater than 5 not previously underlined) that are divisible by 7, that is, every seventh number after 7. The numbers that have not been eliminated,

2   3   5   7   11   13   17   19   23   29   31   37   41   43   47

are precisely the 15 primes less than 50. Composite numbers fall through the sieve (or strainer) leaving the primes.

Once the concept of a prime has been presented, little is done with it other than to admire it. There are some very interesting things that can be done with primes.

We consider two famous conjectures, one of which was ultimately proved, and the other that remains unproved.

Gottfried Wilhelm von Leibnitz (1646–1716), the coinventor of calculus as we know it today, conjectured that $(p - 1)! + 1$ is divisible by p if and only if p is a prime. Although he believed it to be true, he never published a proof of it. The relationship became famous when Edward Waring, professor of mathematics at Cambridge University, published the "discovery" of his friend the judge, Sir John Wilson, in 1770. The proof of this relationship, however, did not appear until Joseph Louis Lagrange (1736–1813) published it in 1771. This remarkable theorem, unfittingly referred to today as Wilson's theorem, can be a fine test of a prime number. For example, if $p = 7$, then $(7 - 1)! + 1 = (1 \cdot 2 \cdot 3 \cdot 4 \cdot 5 \cdot 6) + 1 = 721$, which is divisible by 7, establishing 7 as a prime number by Wilson's theorem, whereas, if $p = 8$, then $(8 - 1)! + 1 = (1 \cdot 2 \cdot 3 \cdot 4 \cdot 5 \cdot 6 \cdot 7) + 1 = 5041$, which is not divisible by 8. Therefore, by Wilson's theorem, 8 is not a prime number.

The class may want to test for primes using Wilson's theorem. Here is a table that shows this for the first few cases.

n	$(n - 1)!$	$(n - 1)! + 1$	$[(n - 1)! + 1] \bmod n$	Type of number
2	$1! = 1$	2	0	Prime
3	$2! = 2$	3	0	Prime
4	$3! = 6$	7	3	Composite
5	$4! = 24$	25	0	Prime
6	$5! = 120$	121	1	Composite
7	$6! = 720$	721	0	Prime
8	$7! = 5,040$	5,041	1	Composite
9	$8! = 40,320$	40,321	1	Composite
10	$9! = 362,880$	362,881	1	Composite
11	$10! = 3,628,800$	3,628,801	0	Prime
12	$11! = 39,916,800$	39,916,801	1	Composite
13	$12! = 479,001,600$	479,001,601	0	Prime
14	$13! = 6,227,020,800$	6,227,020,801	1	Composite
15	$14! = 87,178,291,200$	87,178,291,201	1	Composite

To keep the presentation relatively simple, we prove one direction of Wilson's theorem for one number, $p = 17$. We consider the 16 integers less than 17: 1, 2, 3, 4, 5, 6, 7, ..., 14, 15, 16. We now take any integer less than 17, for example, and form the multiples with these numbers: 3, 6, 9, 12, 15, 18, 21, ..., 42, 45, 48. The remainders of these numbers when divided by 17 (i.e., modulus 17) are: 3, 6, 9, 12, 15, 1, 4, 7, 10, 13, 16, 2, 5, 8, 11, 14. No number appears more than once, a fact that can be proved in the general case as well. This implies that one of these remainders must be 1. Had we chosen a number other than 3 as a multiplier, another series would have resulted and there would have been a 1 (e.g., $4 \cdot 13 \equiv 1 \bmod 17$) somewhere in the series of remainders. Therefore, each of the numbers: 2, 3, 4, 5, 6, 7, 8, 9, 10, 11, 12, 13, 14, 15 could be used as a multiplier to get 1 mod 17:

$$2 \cdot 9 \equiv 1 \bmod 17$$
$$3 \cdot 6 \equiv 1 \bmod 17$$
$$4 \cdot 13 \equiv 1 \bmod 17$$
$$5 \cdot 7 \equiv 1 \bmod 17$$
$$8 \cdot 15 \equiv 1 \bmod 17$$
$$10 \cdot 12 \equiv 1 \bmod 17$$
$$11 \cdot 14 \equiv 1 \bmod 17$$

The only two numbers from the original sequence of numbers not used are 1 and 16. For these, $1 \cdot 16 \equiv -1 \bmod 17$. By multiplying these eight congruences, we get $16! \equiv -1 \bmod 17$, which is the same thing as saying that $(17 - 1)! + 1$ is divisible by 17, which is a prime according to Wilson's theorem.

A second conjecture is perhaps one of the most famous yet unproved statements. This one is correctly attributed to Christian Goldbach (1690–1764), who stated that every even number (except 2) can be expressed as the sum of two prime numbers. Here students have a second opportunity to become more familiar with prime numbers. The first several such sums are provided in the following list:

Even number	Sum of primes
4	$2 + 2$
6	$3 + 3$
8	$3 + 5$
10	$3 + 7$ or $5 + 5$
12	$5 + 7$
14	$3 + 11$ or $7 + 7$
16	$3 + 13$ or $5 + 11$
18	$5 + 13$ or $7 + 11$

From here there is a wide field for further investigation of prime numbers.

OTHER TOPICS IDEA 5

Introducing the Concept of Relativity

Objective: To enable students to appreciate the concept of "relativity" as a way to understand the essence of some problems

Materials: Chalkboard with, perhaps, some physical models to simulate the problem in this unit

Procedure: An important concept for students to understand is that of relativity. It is also a difficult concept to grasp. Expect the class to comprehend this concept at varying rates. As a matter of fact, it might be wise to present this unit and have students reflect on it at home, when they can do so at their own pace and without outside distractions.

Begin by presenting the following problem: While rowing his boat upstream, David drops a cork overboard and continues rowing for 10 more minutes. He then turns around, chasing the cork, and retrieves it when the cork has traveled 1 mile downstream. What is the rate of the stream?

The traditional method for solving this problem, a common one in algebra, is as follows. The water carries David 1 mile downstream as well as carrying the cork 1 mile downstream. We let t equal the time the cork travels downstream after the initial 10 minutes, r equal the speed of rowing in still water, and s equal the rate of the stream. Recalling that the product of rate and time equals the distance traveled, we get the distance of the cork is $t(r + s) - 10(r - s) = (10+t)s$. Therefore, $t = 10$. So the time the cork had been traveling downstream $10 + 10 = 20$ minutes, which is a rate of 3 miles per hour.

The problem can be simplified significantly by considering the notion of relativity. It does not matter whether the stream is moving and carrying David downstream, or is still. We are concerned only with the separation and coming together of David and the cork. If the stream were stationary, David would require as much time rowing to the cork as he did rowing away from the cork. That is, he would require $10 + 10 = 20$ minutes. Because the cork travels 1 mile during these 20 minutes, the stream's rate of speed is 3 miles per hour.

Again, this may not be an easy concept to grasp for some students and is best left for them to ponder in quiet. It is a concept worth understanding, because it has many useful applications in everyday life thinking processes. This is, after all, one of the purposes of learning mathematics.

OTHER TOPICS IDEA **6**

Introduction to Number Theory

Objective: To use a number oddity to show the value of number theory

Materials: Chalkboard

Procedure: There are lots of unusual number patterns and relationships that often boggle the mind. Some cannot be proved (as yet!), such as the famous Goldbach conjecture, which states that *every even number greater than* 2 *can be expressed as the sum of two prime numbers.* (See Other Topics Idea 4.) He also asserted that *every odd number can be expressed as the sum of three primes.* The latter conjecture (1742), also unproved, is not as widely known as the former.

Have students experiment with a calculator and make this conjecture on their own: One plus the sum of the squares of any three consecutive odd numbers is always divisible by 12.

The beauty and the instructional benefit of this are manifested in the simplicity of the procedure used to prove this statement. First we must establish a way to represent an odd and an even number. For any integer n, $2n$ will always be *even* and $2n + 1$, the next consecutive number must then be *odd*. We begin by letting $2n + 1$ be the middle of the three consecutive odd numbers under consideration. Then $[2n + 1] - 2 = 2n - 1$ is the next smaller odd number and $[2n + 1] + 2 = 2n + 3$ is the next larger odd number. We are now ready to represent the relationship we are seeking to prove,

$$(2n - 1)^2 + (2n + 1)^2 + (2n + 3)^2 + 1 = 12n^2 + 12n + 12$$
$$= 12\left(n^2 + n + 1\right) = 12M$$

where M merely represents some integer. (Because n is an integer, n^2 is also an integer, so the sum $n^2 + n + 1$ must also be an integer. Represent that integer as M.) We can then conclude that this sum of squares plus 1 is always divisible by 12.

This should be merely a springboard to other similar investigations into number theory.

OTHER TOPICS IDEA 7

Extracting a Square Root

Objective: To show students a relatively simple method for extracting square roots so that they get a better understanding of the notion

Materials: Chalkboard

Procedure: Clearly, anyone who wants to find the square root of a number certainly would use a calculator. However, by introducing the notion of the extraction of a square root through a manual method that relies on the notion of what a square root is, the concept will be better understood.

This method was first published in 1690 by the English mathematician Joseph Raphson (or Ralphson) in his book, *Analysis Alquationum Universalis*. Raphson attributed it to Newton and, therefore, the algorithm bears both names.

It is perhaps best to see the method used in a specific example: Suppose we wish to find $\sqrt{27}$. Obviously, the calculator would be used here. However, you might like to introduce the task by having students guess at what this value might be. Certainly it is between $\sqrt{25}$ and $\sqrt{36}$, or between 5 and 6, but closer to 5. Suppose we guess at 5.2. If this were the correct square root, then if we were to divide 27 by 5.2, we would get 5.2. However, this is not the case here, because $\sqrt{27} \neq 5.2$. We seek a closer approximation. To do that, we find $\frac{27}{5.2} = 5.191$. To get a closer approximation we find the average of 5.2 and 5.191. $\frac{5.2+5.191}{2} = 5.195$, which is a better approximation than earlier. This process continues, each time with additional decimal places, so that an allowance is made for a closer approximation. That is, $\frac{27}{5.195} = 5.1973$, continuing this process: $\frac{5.195+5.1973}{2} = 5.19615$. Again $\frac{27}{5.19615} = 5.196155$, and $\frac{5.19615+5.196155}{2} = 5.1961525$, which is a better approximation of $\sqrt{27}$. This continuous process provides insight into finding the square root of a number that is not a perfect square.

OTHER TOPICS IDEA 8

Introducing Indirect Proof

Objective: To provide an illustration of a simple indirect proof, where a direct proof would be too cumbersome if possible or feasible at all

Materials: Chalkboard as well as paper and pencil

Procedure: With the intent of providing a simple example of indirect proof to show its use in an unencumbered form, begin by presenting the following problem: Prove that if two positive numbers have a sum of 1001 then their product cannot be divisible by 1001.

As is typical of indirect proofs, we try to prove the contrapositive by assuming that the two numbers, say p and q, are such that their product, pq, is divisible by 1001. Because $1001 = 7 \cdot 11 \cdot 13$, pq must be divisible by 7. Thus, either p or q must be divisible by 7. However, $p + q = 1001$ is also divisible by 7. Therefore, if 7 divides one of the numbers, it must divide both of the numbers. This is an important concept that may need some extra attention.

In the same way, we can show that 11 and 13 must each divide both of the numbers, p and q. We now have p and q each divisible by 7, 11, and 13, or, to put it another way, p and q are both multiples of 1001. This would make it impossible for them to have a sum of 1001. Therefore, the statement is true.

The important issue in this introduction to the indirect proof is the notion of using a statement equivalent to the original one, the contrapositive of the original statement, instead of the original statement.

Keeping Differentiation Meaningful

Objective: To demonstrate what happens when differentiation is done when it is meaningless

Materials: Chalkboard

Procedure: Show the following argument* and ask for comments about its correctness:

1. $x^2 = (x)(x) = x + x + x + \cdots + x$ (a total of x addends)
2. By differentiating

    $$\frac{d(x^2)}{dx} = \frac{d(x + x + x + \cdots + x)}{dx} \quad \text{(a total of } x \text{ addends)}$$

3. $2x = 1 + 1 + 1 + \cdots + 1$ (a total of x addends)
4. $2x = x$
5. $2 = 1$

This is truly absurd! So what's wrong? A simple explanation is that in the first step, the definition of multiplication as repeated addition is valid only for integers. Therefore, the function is not continuous and differentiation is meaningless for this definition.

We can also see this fault by considering a simpler situation:

1. $x = 1 + 1 + 1 + \cdots + 1$ (a total of x addends)

---

* We are grateful to Steven Conrad for providing us with this clever demonstration, which he first published in the *Mathematics Magazine* (Mathematical Association of America, 1969).

2. By differentiating $1 = 0 + 0 + 0 + \cdots + 0$ (a total of x addends)
3. $1 = 0$

To see what is wrong, notice that the right side of step 1, as a function of x, depends only on the number of terms. In such a case, there is no theorem that says that to differentiate such a function of x it is legitimate to differentiate term by term. Similarly, in step 1 (of our original demonstration) the right side is a function of x, which depends not only on the individual summands, but also on the number of terms. Clearly, term by term differentiation is not valid because the number of terms, as well as the individual summands, is also a function of x.

OTHER TOPICS IDEA 10

Irrationality of $\sqrt{m}$

Objective: To introduce the notion of irrationality along with a clever proof using indirect reasoning

Materials: Chalkboard

Procedure: As a springboard to higher mathematics, teachers should introduce the notion of an indirect proof of something that all students "know." This indirect proof is particularly clever and can serve as an excellent beginning to mathematical thinking on a higher order than that previously required. (The proof to be given is a particularly pleasing example of Fermat's famous method of infinite descent.) The theorem to be proved states that the square root of an integer that is not a perfect square is irrational. Stated formally it is: If m is a positive integer that is not the square of an integer, then $\sqrt{m}$ is irrational.

Proof: First, note that $\sqrt{m}$ is not an integer, because

$$\text{if } \sqrt{m} = I, \quad \text{an integer} \tag{1}$$

then

$$m = I^2 \tag{2}$$

which contradicts the assumption that m is not the square of an integer. Then there exists a unique integer n that satisfies

$$n < \sqrt{m} < n + 1 \tag{3}$$

Next, it suffices to prove that α, defined by

$$\alpha = \sqrt{m} - n \qquad (4)$$

is irrational, because if $\sqrt{m}$ were rational, then α would also be rational.

Assume then that α is rational. Then there exist positive integers p and q such that

$$\alpha = \frac{p}{q} \qquad (5)$$

Furthermore, we may assume, without loss of generality, that the fraction $\frac{p}{q}$ is expressed in lowest terms, that is, p and q have no factor in common. Alternatively, without loss of generality, we may assume that in the representation $\frac{p}{q}$, q has the smallest possible value.

Finally, in view of Equations 3 and 4,

$$0 < \alpha < 1 \qquad (6)$$

and

$$0 < p < q \qquad (7)$$

Next, multiplying numerator and denominator of

$$\frac{q}{p} = \frac{1}{\alpha} = \frac{1}{\sqrt{m} - n} \qquad (8)$$

by $\sqrt{m} + n$, it follows from Equation 4 that

$$\frac{q}{p} = \frac{\sqrt{m} + n}{m - n^2} = \frac{\alpha + 2n}{m - n^2} \qquad (9)$$

Solving for α, we find

$$\alpha + 2n = \frac{(m - n^2)q}{p} \qquad (10)$$

or

$$\alpha = \frac{(m - n^2)q}{p} - 2n = \frac{(m - n^2)q - 2np}{p} = \frac{r}{p} \qquad (11)$$

where

$$r = (m - n^2)q - 2np \qquad (12)$$

Because

$$\alpha > 0 \quad \text{and} \quad p > 0 \qquad (13)$$

it follows that r is a positive integer. Hence

$$\alpha = \frac{r}{p} \qquad\qquad (14)$$

is a representation of α as a ratio of two positive integers (where previously in Equations 5, 6, and 7 it was established that for $\alpha = \frac{p}{q}, 0 < p < q$).

However this (p as denominator, where $p < q$) contradicts the assumption that $\frac{p}{q}$ is already expressed in lowest terms so that q is the smallest possible denominator that can be used in any representation of α as the ratio of two positive integers. Therefore, $\sqrt{m}$ is irrational.

It is the process as well as the result that is important as an introduction to some more sophisticated mathematical thinking.

OTHER TOPICS IDEA **11**[*]

Introduction to the Factorial Function $x!$

Objective: To define the factorial function $x!$ when x is a positive integer and to develop some of its elementary properties

Materials: Chalkboard

Procedure: The topic of factorials is usually embedded in the study of combinatorics and its application in probability. The factorial in its own right is worth some consideration as a function with some interesting applications. We provide a way in which this can be done rather simply. The factorial function $x!$ is usually first studied in connection with permutations and combinations. Recall the definitions

$$ {}_nP_r = \frac{n!}{(n-r)!} \quad \text{and} \quad {}_nC_r = \frac{n!}{(n-r)!r!} $$

Over the next five Idea units we set out to discover properties of $x!$ that are valid for nonnegative integer values of x. We conclude this introductory unit with an extension of our understandings of the properties of $x!$ for all rational values of x.

---

[*] This is the first of five units that ought to be presented together. Although this unit is independent of the others, each succeeding unit depends on its predecessors.

We begin with the traditional definition of what is meant by "x factorial," which is written $x!$.

If x is a positive integer, then $x!$ is defined by

$$x! = x(x-1)(x-2)\cdots 3 \cdot 2 \cdot 1 \tag{11.1}$$

Thus, $1! = 1$, $2! = 2$, $3! = 6$, $4! = 24$, and so forth.

The fundamental property of $x!$ is

$$(x+1)\,x! = (x+1)! \tag{11.2}$$

or, alternatively,

$$\frac{1}{x!} = \frac{x+1}{(x+1)!} \tag{11.3}$$

Proof: When x is a positive integer, Equation 11.2 implies

$$(x+1)! = (x+1)(x)(x-1)(x-2)\cdots(3)(2)(1) = (x+1)x! \tag{11.4}$$

Remark: To extend the definition of $x!$ when x is not a positive integer, we assume that the fundamental properties, Equations 11.2 and 11.3, hold for all values of x.

Therefore, we arrive at $0! = 1$.

Proof: Let $x = 0$ in Equation 11.2 to obtain

$$0! = (0+1)\,(0!) = (0+1)! = 1!$$

or

$$0! = 1 \tag{11.5}$$

If x is an integer greater than or equal to 0,

$$x! > 0 \tag{11.6}$$

This may be proved by using Equations 11.1 and 11.5.

To advance our understanding of the factorial function, we can consider another application or relationship that relates to it. If n is a positive integer,

$$\frac{1}{(-n)!} = 0 \tag{11.7}$$

The proof is by mathematical induction on the variable n.

We begin with Equation 11.3 and replace x by n to get

$$\frac{n+1}{(n+1)!} = \frac{1}{n!} \tag{11.3a}$$

Let $n = -1$. Since $0! = 1$, we get

$$\frac{1}{(-1)!} = \frac{-1 + 1}{(-1 + 1)!} = \frac{0}{0!} = \frac{0}{1} = 0. \tag{11.8}$$

Now, Equation 11.7 is true when $n = 1$.

Before proceeding with the induction, we let $n = -2$ in Equation 11.3a. In view of Equation 11.8,

$$\frac{1}{(-2)!} = \frac{-2 + 1}{(-2 + 1)!} = \frac{-1}{(-1)!} = -\left(\frac{1}{(-1)!}\right) = 0 \tag{11.9}$$

which is the case $n = 2$ in Equation 11.7.

Continuing in this way, we can justify Equation 11.7, namely $\frac{1}{(-n)!} = 0$, for every positive integer n.

However, to carry out the formal inductive proof, we assume that Equation 11.7 holds true and show that then Equation 11.7 holds true when n is replaced by $n + 1$. So we let $x = -n - 1$ in Equation 11.3:

$$\frac{1}{(-(n + 1))!} = \frac{(-n - 1) + 1}{((-n - 1) + 1)!} = \frac{-n}{(-n)!} = (-n)\frac{1}{(-n)!} = 0 \tag{11.10}$$

which is Equation 11.7 with n replaced by $n + 1$. This completes the induction proof because Equation 11.7 holds when $n = 1$ (Equation 11.8).

| OTHER TOPICS IDEA 12* |

Introduction to the Function $x^{(n)}$

Objective: To define the function $x^{(n)}$, when n is an integer and to develop some of its elementary properties

Materials: Chalkboard

---

* This unit is dependent on Other Topics Idea 11.

Procedure: Because the theme of factorials is not too commonly treated in the curriculum, we provide a series of interesting facts with the hope that it will stimulate curiosity and interest in further investigation. Here, then are some highlights.

Building on the discussion of the factorial function $x!$ in the previous unit, introduce another function $x^{(n)}$ by defining it as follows: If n is a positive integer, we define $x^{(n)}$ by means of

$$x^{(n)} = x\,(x-1)\,(x-2)\cdots(x-n+1) \tag{12.1}$$

where x is arbitrary.

The function $x^{(n)}$ is a generalization of the factorial, because if $x = n$, Equation 12.1 reduces to

$$n^{(n)} = n\,(n-1)\,(n-2)\cdots(1) = n! \tag{12.2}$$

We consider some elementary properties of $x^{(n)}$ in the following discussion.

- If x and n are positive integers, and $x > n$,

$$x^{(n)} = \frac{x!}{(x-n)!} \tag{12.3}$$

To prove this multiply the right-hand side of Equation 12.1 by $\frac{(x-n)!}{(x-n)!}$.

- If n is a positive integer,

$$(x+1)\,x^{(n)} = (x+1)^{(n+1)} \tag{12.4}$$

The proof simply employs the definition in Equation 12.1.

- If n is a positive integer,

$$x\,(x+n)^{(n)} = (x+n)^{(n+1)} \tag{12.5}$$

To prove this use the definition in Equation 12.1.

- If n is a positive integer,

$$(x-n)\,x^{(n)} = x^{(n+1)} \tag{12.6}$$

The proof involves using the definition in Equation 12.1.

- If n is a positive integer, we are led to a definition of $x^{(-n)}$ by replacing n by $-n$ in Equation 12.6. Thus for arbitrary integer n,

$$(x+n)\,x^{(-n)} = x^{(-n+1)} \tag{12.7}$$

which is defined when we replace n by $-n$ in Equation 12.6.

- Replace n by $n+1$ in Equation 12.7 to get

$$(x+n+1)\,x^{(-n-1)} = x^{(-n)} \tag{12.8}$$

206

- Let $n = 0$ in Equation 12.3 to get

$$x^{(0)} = 1 \tag{12.9}$$

for all x.
- Consider $x^{(-n)}$, where n is a positive integer.

After we state the next property, we prove it by mathematical induction. We can discover the next property by observing a pattern in much the same way we did with nonpositive integer exponents (see Algebra Idea 15). This then leads us to define $x^{(-n)}$ for positive integers n by means of

$$x^{(-n)} = \frac{1}{(x+n)^{(n)}} \tag{12.10}$$

Consider the following pattern. We start with (say)

$4^{(4)} = 4 \cdot 3 \cdot 2 \cdot 1 = 24$

Divide by 1 to get   Divide by 5 to get

$4^{(3)} = 4 \cdot 3 \cdot 2 = 24$ $4^{(-1)} = \dfrac{1}{5} = \dfrac{1}{5^{(1)}} = \dfrac{1}{(4+1)^{(1)}}$

Divide by 2 to get   Divide by 6 to get

$4^{(2)} = 4 \cdot 3 = 12$ $4^{(-2)} = \dfrac{1}{30} = \dfrac{1}{6^{(2)}} = \dfrac{1}{(4+2)^{(2)}}$

Divide by 3 to get   Divide by 7 to get

$4^{(1)} = 4$ $4^{(-3)} = \dfrac{1}{210} = \dfrac{1}{7^{(3)}} = \dfrac{1}{(4+3)^{(3)}}$

Divide by 4 to get   and, in general,

$4^{(0)} = 1$ $4^{(-n)} = \dfrac{1}{(4+n)^{(n)}}$

We are thus led to the equation,

$$x^{(-n)} = \frac{1}{(x+n)^{(n)}} = \frac{x!}{(x+n)!} \tag{12.11}$$

where n is a positive integer.

We prove this by using mathematical induction on n. Let $n = 1$ in Equation 12.7 to obtain, in view of Equation 12.9, $(x+1)\, x^{(-1)} = x^{(0)} = 1$, which is the case $n = 1$ of Equation 12.11. Assume Equation 12.11 holds true for n. It remains to show that Equation 12.11 holds true when n is replaced by $n+1$. From Equation 12.8, the induction hypothesis, and Equation 12.4 (with x replaced by $x+n$),

$$x^{(-n-1)} = \frac{x^{(-n)}}{(x+n+1)} = \frac{1}{(x+n+1)\,(x+n)^{(n)}} = \frac{1}{(x+n+1)^{(n+1)}} \tag{12.12}$$

which is the same as Equation 12.11 with n replaced by $n + 1$. This completes the induction.

The second half of Equation 12.11 follows directly from Equation 12.3 by replacing x by $x + n$.

It is instructive to note that we are also led to the definition of $x^{(-n)}$ by simply assuming that Equation 12.3, which is valid for positive integers x and n, with $x > n$, is also valid for negative integer values of n. Thus replace n by $-n$ in Equation 12.3 to obtain

$$x^{(-n)} = \frac{x!}{(x + n)!} \quad \text{for positive integers } n \tag{12.13}$$

Again replace x by $x + n$ in Equation 12.13 to obtain

$$(x + n)^{(n)} = \frac{(x + n)!}{x!} \tag{12.14}$$

Evidently Equations 12.13 and 12.14 are simply Equation 12.11, the definition of $x^{(-n)}$ for positive integer values of n.

OTHER TOPICS IDEA 13*

Introduction to the Two Binomial Theorems

Objective: To prove the standard binomial theorem the formula for $(a + b)^n$, and its variant $(a + b)^{(n)}$

Materials: Chalkboard

Procedure: The proof of the standard binomial theorem provides a good opportunity to apply the technique of mathematical induction. This can then be generalized to prove an expansion for $(a + b)^{(n)}$, for positive integers n, by induction.

We present here the proof of the usual binomial theorem for $(a + b)^n$ so that the comparison to the next proof can be made.

---

* This unit is dependent on Other Topics Ideas 11 and 12.

If $n \geqslant 0$ is an integer, then

$$
\begin{aligned}
(a+b)^n = a^n + \frac{n}{1}a^{n-1}b + \frac{n(n-1)}{1 \cdot 2}a^{n-2}b^2 \\
+ \frac{n(n-1)(n-2)}{1 \cdot 2 \cdot 3}a^{n-3}b^3 + \cdots
\end{aligned}
\tag{13.1}
$$

The proof we use involves an induction on n. Clearly, Equation 13.1 holds when $n = 0$ or 1. Assume Equation 13.1 holds. We are to show that Equation 13.1 holds when n is replaced by $n+1$. Multiply both sides of Equation 13.1 by $a+b$:

$$
(a+b)^n(a+b) = a^n(a+b) + \frac{n}{1}a^{n-1}b(a+b) + \frac{n(n-1)}{1 \cdot 2}a^{n-2}b^2(a+b)
$$

$$
+ \frac{n(n-1)(n-2)}{1 \cdot 2 \cdot 3}a^{n-3}b^3(a+b) + \cdots
\tag{13.2}
$$

$$
\begin{aligned}
(a+b)^{n+1} = a^{n+1} + \left(a^n b + \frac{n}{1}a^n b\right) + \left(\frac{n}{1}a^{n-1}b^2 + \frac{n(n-1)}{1 \cdot 2}a^{n-1}b^2\right) \\
+ \left(\frac{n(n-1)}{1 \cdot 2}a^{n-2}b^3 + \frac{n(n-1)(n-2)}{1 \cdot 2 \cdot 3}a^{n-2}b^3\right) + \cdots
\end{aligned}
\tag{13.3}
$$

$$
\begin{aligned}
(a+b)^{n+1} = a^{n+1} + \frac{(n+1)}{1}a^n b + \frac{(n+1)n}{1 \cdot 2}a^{n-1}b^2 \\
+ \frac{(n+1)n(n-1)}{1 \cdot 2 \cdot 3}a^{n-2}b^3 + \cdots
\end{aligned}
\tag{13.4}
$$

which is the same as Equation 13.1 with n replaced by $n + 1$. The induction is complete.

Now for the generalization of the binomial theorem using a factorial function: For nonnegative integer n,

$$
\begin{aligned}
(a+b)^{(n)} = a^{(n)} + \frac{n}{1}a^{(n-1)}b^{(1)} + \frac{n(n-1)}{1 \cdot 2}a^{(n-2)}b^{(2)} \\
+ \frac{n(n-1)(n-2)}{1 \cdot 2 \cdot 3}a^{(n-3)}b^{(3)} + \cdots
\end{aligned}
\tag{13.5}
$$

The series terminates if n is a nonnegative integer. The proof of this theorem may be a bit beyond the scope of a high school class. However, we present it here so that the comparison can be made to the (preceding) proof of the usual binomial theorem.

The proof we use involves an induction on n. Clearly Equation 13.5 holds when $n = 0$ or 1. Assume that Equation 13.5 holds. We are to show that Equation 13.5

holds when n is replaced by $n+1$. Multiply both sides of Equation 13.5 by $a + b - n$:

$$(a+b)^{(n)}(a+b-n)$$
$$= a^{(n)}((a-n)+b) + \frac{n}{1}a^{(n-1)}b^{(1)}((a-n+1)+(b-1))$$
$$+ \frac{n(n-1)}{1 \cdot 2}a^{(n-2)}b^{(2)}((a-n+2)+(b-2)) \tag{13.6}$$
$$+ \frac{n(n-1)(n-2)}{1 \cdot 2 \cdot 3}a^{(n-3)}b^{(3)}((a-n+3)+(b-3))$$
$$+ \frac{n(n-1)(n-2)(n-3)}{1 \cdot 2 \cdot 3 \cdot 4}a^{(n-4)}b^{(4)}((a-n+4)+(b-4)) + \cdots$$

Regrouping, but keeping the same order of terms, we get

$$(a+b)^{(n)}(a+b-n)$$
$$= a^{(n)}(a-n) + \left[a^{(n)}b + \frac{n}{1}a^{(n-1)}b^{(1)}(a-n+1)\right]$$
$$+ \left[\frac{n}{1}a^{(n-1)}b^{(1)}(b-1) + \frac{n(n-1)}{1 \cdot 2}a^{(n-2)}b^{(2)}(a-n+2)\right]$$
$$+ \left[\frac{n(n-1)}{1 \cdot 2}a^{(n-2)}b^{(2)}(b-2) + \frac{n(n-1)(n-2)}{1 \cdot 2 \cdot 3}a^{(n-3)}b^{(3)}(a-n+3)\right]$$
$$+ \left[\frac{n(n-1)(n-2)}{1 \cdot 2 \cdot 3}a^{(n-3)}b^{(3)}(b-3)\right. \tag{13.7}$$
$$\left. + \frac{n(n-1)(n-2)(n-3)}{1 \cdot 2 \cdot 3 \cdot 4}a^{(n-4)}b^{(4)}(a-n+4)\right] + \cdots$$

However, repeated application of Equation 12.6 (from Other Topics Idea 12) yields

$$
\begin{array}{ll}
(a+b)^{(n)}(a+b-n) = (a+b)^{(n+1)} & a^{(n)}(a-n) = a^{(n+1)} \\
a^{(n)}b = a^{(n)}b^{(1)} & a^{(n-1)}(a-n+1) = a^{(n)} \\
b^{(1)}(b-1) = b^{(2)} & a^{(n-2)}(a-n+2) = a^{(n-1)} \\
b^{(2)}(b-2) = b^{(3)} & a^{(n-3)}(a-n+3) = a^{(n-2)} \\
b^{(3)}(b-3) = b^{(4)} & a^{(n-4)}(a-n+4) = a^{(n-3)}
\end{array} \tag{13.8}
$$
$$\vdots \qquad\qquad\qquad\qquad \vdots$$

Substituting from Equation 13.8 into Equation 13.7, we have

$$(a+b)^{(n+1)} = a^{(n+1)} + \left(1+\frac{n}{1}\right)a^{(n)}b^{(1)} + n\left(\frac{1}{1}+\frac{n-1}{1 \cdot 2}\right)a^{(n-1)}b^{(2)}$$
$$+ n(n-1)\left(\frac{1}{1 \cdot 2}+\frac{n-2}{1 \cdot 2 \cdot 3}\right)a^{(n-2)}b^{(3)} \tag{13.9}$$
$$+ n(n-1)(n-2)\left(\frac{1}{1 \cdot 2 \cdot 3}+\frac{n-3}{1 \cdot 2 \cdot 3 \cdot 4}\right)a^{(n-3)}b^{(4)} + \cdots$$

which, upon further simplification, reduces to

$$(a+b)^{(n+1)} = a^{(n+1)} + \frac{(n+1)}{1}a^{(n)}b^{(1)} + \frac{(n+1)\,n}{1 \cdot 2}a^{(n-1)}b^{(2)}$$
$$+ \frac{(n+1)\,n\,(n-1)}{1 \cdot 2 \cdot 3}a^{(n-2)}b^{(3)} \qquad (13.10)$$
$$+ \frac{(n+1)\,n\,(n-1)\,(n-2)}{1 \cdot 2 \cdot 3 \cdot 4}a^{(n-3)}b^{(4)} + \cdots$$

which is the same as Equation 13.5 with n replaced by $n+1$, and so the induction is complete.

$$\boxed{\textbf{OTHER TOPICS IDEA } \mathbf{14}^{*}}$$

Factorial Function Revisited

Objective: To explore extensions of the factorial function to four theorems and their proofs

Materials: Chalkboard

Procedure: Consider, explain, and demonstrate the proof of each of the following theorems.

The Addition Theorem:

$$\frac{(a+b)!}{a!b!} = 1 + \frac{ab}{(1!)^2} + \frac{a\,(a-1)\,b\,(b-1)}{(2!)^2}$$
$$+ \frac{a\,(a-1)\,(a-2)\,b\,(b-1)\,(b-2)}{(3!)^2} + \cdots \qquad (14.1)$$

$$\frac{(a+b)!}{a!b!} = 1 + \frac{a^{(1)}b^{(1)}}{(1!)^2} + \frac{a^{(2)}b^{(2)}}{(2!)^2} + \frac{a^{(3)}b^{(3)}}{(3!)^2} + \cdots \qquad (14.2)$$

The series terminates if a or b is a nonnegative integer.

---

* This unit is dependent on Other Topics Ideas 11, 12, and 13. Equations extracted from these topics are referenced by double numbers, where the first number represents the Other Topics Idea unit and the number after the period refers to the specific equation.

The proof may be done as follows: Recall Equation 13.5:

$$(a+b)^{(n)} = a^{(n)} + \frac{n}{1}a^{(n-1)}b^{(1)} + \frac{n(n-1)}{1 \cdot 2}a^{(n-2)}b^{(2)}$$
$$+ \frac{n(n-1)(n-2)}{1 \cdot 2 \cdot 3}a^{(n-3)}b^{(3)} + \cdots \qquad (13.5)$$

Let $n = a$ in Equation 13.5 to get

$$(a+b)^{(a)} = a^{(a)} + \frac{a}{1!}a^{(a-1)}b^{(1)} + \frac{a(a-1)}{2!}a^{(a-2)}b^{(2)} + \cdots$$
$$+ \frac{a(a-1)(a-2)}{3!}a^{(a-3)}b^{(3)} + \cdots \qquad (14.3)$$

On the left side of Equation 14.3, we use the relationship established in Equation 12.3, with $x = a + b$. On the right side of Equation 14.3, we use Equation 12.3 term by term with $x = a$ and $n = a, a - 1, a - 2, a - 3, \ldots$:

$$\frac{(a+b)!}{b!} = a! + \frac{a^{(1)}a!}{(1!)^2}b^{(1)} + \frac{a^{(2)}a!}{(2!)^2}b^{(2)} + \cdots \qquad (14.4)$$

$$\frac{(a+b)!}{a!b!} = 1 + \frac{a^{(1)}b^{(1)}}{(1!)^2} + \frac{a^{(2)}b^{(2)}}{(2!)^2} + \frac{a^{(3)}b^{(3)}}{(3!)^2} + \cdots \qquad (14.5)$$

Duplication Theorem: If $a \geqslant 0$,

$$\frac{(2a)!}{(a!)^2} = 1 + \left(\frac{a^{(1)}}{1!}\right)^2 + \left(\frac{a^{(2)}}{2!}\right)^2 + \left(\frac{a^{(3)}}{3!}\right)^2 + \cdots \qquad (14.6)$$

$$\frac{(2a)!}{(a!)^2} = 1 + \left(\frac{a!}{1!(a-1)!}\right)^2 + \left(\frac{a!}{2!(a-2)!}\right)^2$$
$$+ \left(\frac{a!}{3!(a-3)!}\right)^2 + \cdots \qquad (14.7)$$

$$\frac{(2a)!}{(a!)^4} = \frac{1}{(a!)^2} + \frac{1}{(1!(a-1)!)^2} + \frac{1}{(2!(a-2)!)^2}$$
$$+ \frac{1}{(3!(a-3)!)^2} + \cdots \qquad (14.8)$$

These series terminate if a is a nonnegative integer.

To prove this, let $b = a$ in Equation 14.2 and apply Equation 12.3.

212

Another theorem:

$$\frac{1}{a!\,(-a)!} = 1 - \frac{a^2}{(1!)^2} + \frac{1}{(2!)^2}a\,(a-1)\,a\,(a+1)$$

$$- \frac{1}{(3!)^2}a\,(a-1)\,(a-2)\,a\,(a+1)\,(a+2) \qquad (14.9)$$

$$+ \frac{1}{(4!)^2}a\,(a-1)\,(a-2)\,(a-3)\,a\,(a+1)\,(a+2)\,(a+3) - \cdots$$

$$\frac{1}{a!\,(-a)!} = 1 - \frac{a^2}{(1!)^2} + \frac{1}{(2!)^2}a^2\,(a^2-1) - \frac{1}{(3!)^2}a^2\,(a^2-1)\,(a^2-4)$$

$$+ \frac{1}{(4!)^2}a^2\,(a^2-1)\,(a^2-4)\,(a^2-9) - \cdots \qquad (14.10)$$

This series terminates if a is an integer.

To prove this let $b = -a$ in Equation 14.2.

Yet, another theorem: If a is an integer, then

$$1 - \frac{a^2}{(1!)^2} + \frac{1}{(2!)^2}a^2\,(a^2-1) - \frac{1}{(3!)^2}a^2\,(a^2-1)\,(a^2-4)$$

$$+ \frac{1}{(4!)^2}a^2\,(a^2-1)\,(a^2-4)\,(a^2-9) + \cdots = 1 \quad \text{or} \quad 0 \qquad (14.11)$$

according as $a = 0$ or $a \neq 0$, respectively.

To prove this theorem use Equations 11.7 and 14.10.

What began as an introduction to the factorial function has been extended far beyond its normal appearance in the high school curriculum. This was done so that you (the teacher) can develop a facility for this unusual function and compare it to other familiar functions.

OTHER TOPICS IDEA **15***

Extension of the Factorial Function $r!$ to the Case Where r Is Rational

Objective: To demonstrate the possibility of defining the factorial function $r!$ for rational, nonintegral values of r

---

* This unit is dependent on Other Topics Ideas 11–14.

Materials: Chalkboard

Procedure: We explore a rather unusual application of the factorial function, that of fractions. We begin with a consideration of $(\pm\frac{1}{2})!$ and $(\pm\frac{3}{2})!$.

We define $\frac{1}{2}!$ by letting $a = \frac{1}{2}$ in Equation 14.6.

Application 1. Find the value of $\frac{1}{2}!$. Let $a = \frac{1}{2}$ in Equation 14.6. Then

$$\frac{1}{\left(\frac{1}{2}!\right)^2} = 1 + \left(\frac{1}{2}\right)^2 + \left(\frac{1 \cdot 1}{2 \cdot 4}\right)^2 + \left(\frac{1 \cdot 1 \cdot 3}{2 \cdot 4 \cdot 6}\right)^2$$
$$+ \left(\frac{1 \cdot 1 \cdot 3 \cdot 5}{2 \cdot 4 \cdot 6 \cdot 8}\right)^2 + \left(\frac{1 \cdot 1 \cdot 3 \cdot 5 \cdot 7}{2 \cdot 4 \cdot 6 \cdot 8 \cdot 10}\right)^2 + \cdots \tag{15.1}$$

The sum of 50 terms of this series yields

$$\frac{1}{\left(\frac{1}{2}!\right)^2} \approx 1.27323 \tag{15.2}$$

or

$$\frac{1}{2}! \approx 0.88623 \tag{15.3}$$

which is correct to five significant places.

To obtain a more rapidly converging series, we proceed as follows.

Application 1a. Find the value of $\frac{1}{2}!$ again. Let $a = \frac{3}{2}$ in Equation 14.6. Then, referring also to Equation 11.2,

$$\frac{6}{\left(\frac{3}{2}!\right)^2} = \frac{8}{3\left(\frac{1}{2}!\right)^2} = 1 + \left(\frac{3}{2}\right)^2 + \left(\frac{3 \cdot 1}{2 \cdot 4}\right)^2 + \left(\frac{3 \cdot 1 \cdot 1}{2 \cdot 4 \cdot 6}\right)^2 + \left(\frac{3 \cdot 1 \cdot 1 \cdot 3}{2 \cdot 4 \cdot 6 \cdot 8}\right)^2$$
$$+ \left(\frac{3 \cdot 1 \cdot 1 \cdot 3 \cdot 5}{2 \cdot 4 \cdot 6 \cdot 8 \cdot 10}\right)^2 + \left(\frac{3 \cdot 1 \cdot 1 \cdot 3 \cdot 5 \cdot 7}{2 \cdot 4 \cdot 6 \cdot 8 \cdot 10 \cdot 12}\right)^2 + \cdots \tag{15.4}$$

The sum of 20 terms of this series yields

$$\frac{8}{3\left(\frac{1}{2}!\right)^2} \approx 3.39530510$$

or

$$\frac{1}{\left(\frac{1}{2}!\right)^2} \approx 1.27323941$$

or, finally,

$$\frac{1}{2}! \approx 0.886227 \tag{15.5}$$

which is correct to six places and should be compared with Statement 15.3.

Application 1b. Find the value of $\frac{1}{2}!$ once again. Let $a = \frac{5}{2}$ in Equation 14.6. Then, again referring to Equation 11.2,

$$\frac{5!}{\left(\frac{5}{2}!\right)^2} = \frac{128}{15\left(\frac{1}{2}!\right)^2} = 1 + \left(\frac{5}{2}\right)^2 + \left(\frac{5 \cdot 3}{2 \cdot 4}\right)^2 + \left(\frac{5 \cdot 3 \cdot 1}{2 \cdot 4 \cdot 6}\right)^2$$
$$+ \left(\frac{5 \cdot 3 \cdot 1 \cdot 1}{2 \cdot 4 \cdot 6 \cdot 8}\right)^2 + \left(\frac{5 \cdot 3 \cdot 1 \cdot 1 \cdot 3}{2 \cdot 4 \cdot 6 \cdot 8 \cdot 10}\right)^2 \qquad (15.6)$$
$$+ \left(\frac{5 \cdot 3 \cdot 1 \cdot 1 \cdot 3 \cdot 5}{2 \cdot 4 \cdot 6 \cdot 8 \cdot 10 \cdot 12}\right)^2 + \left(\frac{5 \cdot 3 \cdot 1 \cdot 1 \cdot 3 \cdot 5 \cdot 7}{2 \cdot 4 \cdot 6 \cdot 8 \cdot 10 \cdot 12 \cdot 14}\right)^2 + \cdots$$

The sum of 20 terms of this series yields

$$\frac{128}{15\left(\frac{1}{2}!\right)^2} \approx 10.86497745$$

or

$$\frac{1}{\left(\frac{1}{2}!\right)^2} \approx 1.27323955$$

or, finally,

$$\frac{1}{2}! = 0.88622693 \qquad (15.7)$$

which is correct to eight significant places and should be compared with Statements 15.5 and 15.3.

Application 1c. Find the value of $\frac{1}{2}!$ one more time. Let $a = \frac{7}{2}$ in Equation 14.6. Now we have

$$\frac{7!}{\left(\frac{7}{2}!\right)^2} = \frac{7 \cdot 6 \cdot 5 \cdot 4 \cdot 3 \cdot 2}{\left(\frac{7}{2} \cdot \frac{5}{2} \cdot \frac{3}{2} \cdot \frac{1}{2}!\right)^2} = \frac{1024}{35\left(\frac{1}{2}!\right)^2}$$
$$= 1 + \left(\frac{7}{2}\right)^2 + \left(\frac{7 \cdot 5}{2 \cdot 4}\right)^2 + \left(\frac{7 \cdot 5 \cdot 3}{2 \cdot 4 \cdot 6}\right)^2 + \left(\frac{7 \cdot 5 \cdot 3 \cdot 1}{2 \cdot 4 \cdot 6 \cdot 8}\right)^2 \qquad (15.8)$$
$$+ \left(\frac{7 \cdot 5 \cdot 3 \cdot 1 \cdot 1}{2 \cdot 4 \cdot 6 \cdot 8 \cdot 10}\right)^2 + \left(\frac{7 \cdot 5 \cdot 3 \cdot 1 \cdot 1 \cdot 3}{2 \cdot 4 \cdot 6 \cdot 8 \cdot 10 \cdot 12}\right)^2 + \cdots$$

The sum of 15 terms of this series yields

$$\frac{1024}{35\left(\frac{1}{2}!\right)^2} \approx 37.25135127$$

or

$$\frac{1}{\left(\frac{1}{2}!\right)^2} \approx 1.27323955$$

or, finally,

$$\frac{1}{2}! = 0.88622693 \qquad (15.9)$$

again correct to eight significant places.

Application 2. Find the value of $\frac{3}{2}!$:

$$\frac{3}{2}! \approx 1.32934040 \qquad (15.10)$$

Proof: Employ Equations 11.2 and 15.9 to deduce

$$\frac{3}{2}! = \frac{3}{2}\left(\frac{1}{2}\right)! \approx 1.32934040$$

Application 3. Find the value of $(-\frac{1}{2})!$:

$$\left(-\frac{1}{2}\right) = 1.77245386 \qquad (15.11)$$

Proof: Employ Equations 11.2 and 15.9 to infer

$$\left(\frac{1}{2}\right)! = \frac{1}{2}\left(-\frac{1}{2}\right)!$$
$$\left(-\frac{1}{2}\right)! = 2\left(\frac{1}{2}\right)! = 1.77245386$$

Application 4. We now find the values of $(-\frac{3}{2})! \approx -3.5449077$.

Proof: From Equation 11.2, $(-\frac{1}{2})(-\frac{3}{2})! = (-\frac{1}{2})!$ and

$$\left(-\frac{3}{2}\right)! = -2\left(-\frac{1}{2}\right)! = -3.5449077 \qquad (15.12)$$

Application 5. We now find the values of $\left(\pm\frac{1}{3}\right)!$, $\left(\pm\frac{2}{3}\right)!$, $\left(\pm\frac{4}{3}\right)!$, and $\left(\pm\frac{5}{3}\right)!$ Refer to Equation 15.2:

$$\frac{(a+b)!}{a!b!} = 1 + \frac{a^{(1)}b^{(1)}}{1!^2} + \frac{a^{(2)}b^{(2)}}{2!^2} + \frac{a^{(3)}b^{(3)}}{3!^2} + \cdots \qquad (15.2)$$

216

Let $a = b = \frac{10}{3}$ in Equation 15.2, make repeated application of Equation 11.2, and define

$$A = \frac{\frac{20}{3}!}{\left(\frac{10}{3}!\right)^2} = \frac{\frac{20}{3} \cdot \frac{17}{3} \cdot \frac{14}{3} \cdot \frac{11}{3} \cdot \frac{8}{3} \cdot \frac{5}{3} \cdot \frac{2}{3}!}{\left(\frac{10}{3} \cdot \frac{7}{3} \cdot \frac{4}{3}\right)^2 \left(\frac{1}{3}!\right)^2} = 1 + \left(\frac{10}{3}\right)^2 + \left(\frac{10 \cdot 7}{3 \cdot 6}\right)^2$$

$$+ \left(\frac{10 \cdot 7 \cdot 4}{3 \cdot 6 \cdot 9}\right)^2 + \left(\frac{10 \cdot 7 \cdot 4 \cdot 1}{3 \cdot 6 \cdot 9 \cdot 12}\right)^2 + \left(\frac{10 \cdot 7 \cdot 4 \cdot 1 \cdot 2}{3 \cdot 6 \cdot 9 \cdot 12 \cdot 15}\right)^2 \quad (15.13)$$

$$+ \left(\frac{10 \cdot 7 \cdot 4 \cdot 1 \cdot 2 \cdot 5}{3 \cdot 6 \cdot 9 \cdot 12 \cdot 15 \cdot 18}\right)^2 + \left(\frac{10 \cdot 7 \cdot 4 \cdot 1 \cdot 2 \cdot 5 \cdot 8}{3 \cdot 6 \cdot 9 \cdot 12 \cdot 15 \cdot 18 \cdot 21}\right)^2 + \cdots$$

the first 16 terms of which yield A to 8 places as follows:

	Summands			Summands
$1 = 1$	1.00000000	$\left(\frac{11}{24}\right)^2 = \frac{121}{576}$		0.00000087
$\left(\frac{10}{3}\right)^2 = \frac{100}{9}$	11.11111111	$\left(\frac{14}{27}\right)^2 = \frac{196}{729}$		0.00000023
$\left(\frac{7}{6}\right)^2 = \frac{49}{36}$	15.12345679	$\left(\frac{17}{30}\right)^2 = \frac{289}{900}$		0.00000007
$\left(\frac{4}{9}\right)^2 = \frac{16}{81}$	2.98734949	$\left(\frac{20}{33}\right)^2 = \frac{400}{1089}$		0.00000003
$\left(\frac{1}{12}\right)^2 = \frac{1}{144}$	0.02074548	$\left(\frac{23}{36}\right)^2 = \frac{529}{1296}$		0.00000001
$\left(\frac{2}{15}\right)^2 = \frac{4}{225}$	0.00036881	$\left(\frac{26}{39}\right)^2 = \frac{676}{1521}$		0.000000005
$\left(\frac{5}{18}\right)^2 = \frac{25}{324}$	0.00002846	$\left(\frac{29}{42}\right)^2 = \frac{841}{1764}$		0.000000002
$\left(\frac{8}{21}\right)^2 = \frac{64}{441}$	0.00000413	$\left(\frac{32}{45}\right)^2 = \frac{1024}{2025}$		0.000000001

$$A \approx 30.24306549 \qquad A^2 \approx 914.6430102 \qquad\qquad (15.14)$$

Let $a = b = \frac{11}{3}$ in Equation 15.2, make repeated application of Equation 11.2, and define

$$B = \frac{\frac{22}{3}!}{\left(\frac{11}{3}!\right)^2} = \frac{\frac{22}{3} \cdot \frac{19}{3} \cdot \frac{16}{3} \cdot \frac{13}{3} \cdot \frac{10}{3} \cdot \frac{7}{3} \cdot \frac{4}{3} \cdot \frac{1}{3}!}{\left(\frac{11}{3} \cdot \frac{8}{3} \cdot \frac{5}{3}\right)^2 \left(\frac{2}{3}!\right)^2} = 1 + \left(\frac{11}{3}\right)^2 + \left(\frac{11 \cdot 8}{3 \cdot 6}\right)^2$$

$$+ \left(\frac{11 \cdot 8 \cdot 5}{3 \cdot 6 \cdot 9}\right)^2 + \left(\frac{11 \cdot 8 \cdot 5 \cdot 2}{3 \cdot 6 \cdot 9 \cdot 12}\right)^2 + \left(\frac{11 \cdot 8 \cdot 5 \cdot 2 \cdot 1}{3 \cdot 6 \cdot 9 \cdot 12 \cdot 15}\right)^2 \quad (15.15)$$

$$+ \left(\frac{11 \cdot 8 \cdot 5 \cdot 2 \cdot 1 \cdot 4}{3 \cdot 6 \cdot 9 \cdot 12 \cdot 15 \cdot 18}\right)^2 + \left(\frac{11 \cdot 8 \cdot 5 \cdot 2 \cdot 1 \cdot 4 \cdot 7}{3 \cdot 6 \cdot 9 \cdot 12 \cdot 15 \cdot 18 \cdot 21}\right)^2 + \cdots$$

the first 16 terms of which yield B to 8 significant places as follows:

	Summands			Summands
$1 = 1$	1.00000000	$\left(\frac{10}{24}\right)^2 = \frac{100}{576}$		0.00000087
$\left(\frac{11}{3}\right)^2 = \frac{121}{9}$	13.44444444	$\left(\frac{13}{27}\right)^2 = \frac{169}{729}$		0.00000020
$\left(\frac{8}{6}\right)^2 = \frac{64}{36}$	23.90123456	$\left(\frac{16}{30}\right)^2 = \frac{256}{900}$		0.00000006
$\left(\frac{5}{9}\right)^2 = \frac{25}{81}$	7.37692425	$\left(\frac{19}{33}\right)^2 = \frac{361}{1089}$		0.00000002
$\left(\frac{2}{12}\right)^2 = \frac{4}{144}$	0.20491456	$\left(\frac{23}{36}\right)^2 = \frac{484}{1296}$		0.00000001
$\left(\frac{1}{15}\right)^2 = \frac{1}{225}$	0.00091073	$\left(\frac{25}{39}\right)^2 = \frac{625}{1521}$		0.000000004
$\left(\frac{4}{18}\right)^2 = \frac{16}{324}$	0.00004497	$\left(\frac{28}{42}\right)^2 = \frac{784}{1764}$		0.000000002
$\left(\frac{7}{21}\right)^2 = \frac{49}{441}$	0.00000500	$\left(\frac{31}{45}\right)^2 = \frac{961}{2025}$		0.000000001

$$B \approx 45.92847968 \qquad B^2 \approx 2109.425246 \qquad\qquad (15.16)$$

Let $a = \frac{10}{3}$, $b = \frac{11}{3}$ in Equation 15.2, make repeated application of Equation 11.2, and define

$$
\begin{aligned}
C &= \frac{7!}{\frac{10}{3}! \frac{11}{3}!} \\
&= \frac{7 \cdot 6 \cdot 5 \cdot 4 \cdot 3 \cdot 2 \cdot 1}{\left(\frac{10}{3} \cdot \frac{7}{3} \cdot \frac{4}{3}\right)\left(\frac{11}{3} \cdot \frac{8}{3} \cdot \frac{5}{3}\right) \frac{1}{3}! \frac{2}{3}!} \\
&= 1 + \frac{10 \cdot 11}{3^2} + \frac{(10 \cdot 7)(11 \cdot 8)}{(3 \cdot 6)^2} + \frac{(10 \cdot 7 \cdot 4)(11 \cdot 8 \cdot 5)}{(3 \cdot 6 \cdot 9)^2} \\
&\quad + \frac{(10 \cdot 7 \cdot 4 \cdot 1)(11 \cdot 8 \cdot 5 \cdot 2)}{(3 \cdot 6 \cdot 9 \cdot 12)^2} \\
&\quad + \frac{(10 \cdot 7 \cdot 4 \cdot 1 \cdot 2)(11 \cdot 8 \cdot 5 \cdot 2 \cdot 1)}{(3 \cdot 6 \cdot 9 \cdot 12 \cdot 15)^2} \\
&\quad + \frac{(10 \cdot 7 \cdot 4 \cdot 1 \cdot 2 \cdot 5)(11 \cdot 8 \cdot 5 \cdot 2 \cdot 1 \cdot 4)}{(3 \cdot 6 \cdot 9 \cdot 12 \cdot 15 \cdot 18)^2} \\
&\quad + \frac{(10 \cdot 7 \cdot 4 \cdot 1 \cdot 2 \cdot 5 \cdot 8)(11 \cdot 8 \cdot 5 \cdot 2 \cdot 1 \cdot 4 \cdot 7)}{(3 \cdot 6 \cdot 9 \cdot 12 \cdot 15 \cdot 18 \cdot 21)^2} + \cdots
\end{aligned}
\qquad (15.17)
$$

the first 16 terms of which yield C to 8 significant places as follows:

	Summands			Summands
1	1.00000000	$11 \cdot \frac{10}{24^2} = \frac{110}{576}$		0.00000087
$10 \cdot \frac{11}{3^2} = \frac{110}{9}$	12.22222222	$14 \cdot \frac{13}{27^2} = \frac{182}{729}$		0.00000022
$7 \cdot \frac{8}{6^2} = \frac{56}{36}$	19.01234568	$17 \cdot \frac{16}{30^2} = \frac{272}{900}$		0.00000007
$4 \cdot \frac{5}{9^2} = \frac{20}{81}$	4.69440634	$20 \cdot \frac{19}{33^2} = \frac{380}{1089}$		0.00000002
$1 \cdot \frac{2}{12^2} = \frac{2}{144}$	0.06520009	$23 \cdot \frac{22}{36^2} = \frac{506}{1296}$		0.00000001
$2 \cdot \frac{1}{15^2} = \frac{2}{225}$	0.00057956	$26 \cdot \frac{25}{39^2} = \frac{650}{1521}$		0.000000004
$5 \cdot \frac{4}{18^2} = \frac{20}{324}$	0.00003578	$29 \cdot \frac{28}{42^2} = \frac{812}{1764}$		0.000000002
$8 \cdot \frac{7}{21^2} = \frac{56}{441}$	0.00000454	$32 \cdot \frac{31}{45^2} = \frac{992}{2025}$		0.000000001

$$C = 36.99479539 \tag{15.18}$$

Refer to Equations 15.13, 15.15, and 15.17 to deduce

$$A^2 B = \frac{(20 \cdot 17 \cdot 14 \cdot 11 \cdot 8 \cdot 5)^2 (22 \cdot 19 \cdot 16 \cdot 13 \cdot 10 \cdot 7 \cdot 4)}{(10 \cdot 7 \cdot 4)^4 (11 \cdot 8 \cdot 5)^2 \cdot 3} \cdot \frac{1}{\left(\frac{1}{3}!\right)^3} \tag{15.19}$$

$$A B^2 = \frac{(20 \cdot 17 \cdot 14 \cdot 11 \cdot 8 \cdot 5)(22 \cdot 19 \cdot 16 \cdot 13 \cdot 10 \cdot 7 \cdot 4)^2}{(10 \cdot 7 \cdot 4)^2 (11 \cdot 8 \cdot 5)^4} \cdot \frac{1}{\left(\frac{2}{3}!\right)^3} \tag{15.20}$$

$$AC = \frac{(20 \cdot 17 \cdot 14 \cdot 11 \cdot 8 \cdot 5)(7 \cdot 6 \cdot 5 \cdot 4 \cdot 3 \cdot 2) 3^6}{(10 \cdot 7 \cdot 4)^2 (10 \cdot 7 \cdot 4 \cdot 11 \cdot 8 \cdot 5)} \cdot \frac{1}{\left(\frac{1}{3}!\right)^3} \tag{15.21}$$

$$BC = \frac{(22 \cdot 19 \cdot 16 \cdot 13 \cdot 10 \cdot 7 \cdot 4)(7 \cdot 6 \cdot 5 \cdot 4 \cdot 3 \cdot 2) 3^6}{(11 \cdot 8 \cdot 5)^2 (10 \cdot 7 \cdot 4 \cdot 11 \cdot 8 \cdot 5)} \cdot \frac{1}{\left(\frac{2}{3}\right)^3} \tag{15.22}$$

Refer to Equation 15.19, and Statements 15.14 and 15.16 to deduce

$$A^2 B \approx 29912.87618 \left(\frac{1}{\frac{1}{3}!}\right)^3 \approx 42008.16291 \tag{15.23}$$

Refer to Equation 15.20, and Statements 15.14 and 15.16 to deduce

$$A B^2 \approx 46933.79233 \left(\frac{1}{\frac{2}{3}!}\right)^3 \approx 63795.48586 \tag{15.24}$$

Refer to Equations 15.21 and 15.18, and Statement 15.14 to deduce

$$AC \approx 796.6928572 \left(\frac{1}{\frac{1}{3}!}\right)^3 \approx 1118.836020 \tag{15.25}$$

Refer to Equations 15.22 and 15.18, and Statement 15.16 to deduce

$$BC \approx 1250.024133 \left(\frac{\frac{1}{2}!}{\frac{2}{3}}\right)^3 \approx 1699.114708 \tag{15.26}$$

From Statements 15.23–15.26 it follows that

$$\left(\frac{1}{3}!\right)^3 \approx \frac{29912.87618}{42008.16291} \approx 0.71207294 \tag{15.27}$$

$$\left(\frac{2}{3}!\right)^3 \approx \frac{46933.79233}{63795.48586} \approx 0.73569143 \tag{15.28}$$

$$\left(\frac{1}{3}!\right)^3 \approx \frac{796.6928572}{1118.836020} \approx 0.71207294 \tag{15.29}$$

$$\left(\frac{2}{3}!\right)^3 \approx \frac{1250.024133}{1699.114708} \approx 0.73569143 \tag{15.30}$$

respectively, or finally

$$\frac{1}{3}! \approx 0.89297951 \tag{15.31}$$

$$\frac{2}{3}! \approx 0.90274529 \tag{15.32}$$

It is noteworthy that Statements 15.27 and 15.29 agree to eight decimal places, and so do Statements 15.28 and 15.30.

Now that $\frac{1}{3}!$ and $\frac{2}{3}!$ have been found, repeated application of Equation 11.2,

$$(x+1)\,x! = (x+1)! \quad \text{or} \quad x! = \frac{(x+1)!}{(x+1)} \tag{11.2}$$

yields the values of $\left(-\frac{1}{3}\right)!$, $\left(-\frac{2}{3}\right)!$, $\left(\pm\frac{4}{3}\right)!$, $\left(\pm\frac{5}{3}\right)!$, ... Thus,

$$\left(-\frac{1}{3}\right)! = \frac{\frac{2}{3}!}{\frac{2}{3}} = \frac{3}{2}\,(0.90274529) \approx 1.3541179 \tag{15.33}$$

$$\left(-\frac{2}{3}\right)! = \frac{\frac{1}{3}!}{\frac{1}{3}} = 3\,(0.89297951) \approx 2.6789385 \tag{15.34}$$

$$\frac{4}{3}! = \frac{4}{3}\left(\frac{1}{3}!\right) \approx \frac{4}{3}\,(0.89297951) \approx 1.1906394 \tag{15.35}$$

$$\left(-\frac{4}{3}\right)! = \frac{\left(\frac{1}{3}\right)!}{\left(-\frac{1}{3}\right)} \approx -3\,(1.3541179) \approx -4.062354 \tag{15.36}$$

$$\frac{5}{3}! = \frac{5}{3}\left(\frac{2}{3}\right)! \approx \frac{5}{3}(0.90274529) \approx 1.5045755 \tag{15.37}$$

$$\left(-\frac{5}{3}\right)! = \frac{\left(-\frac{2}{3}\right)!}{-\frac{2}{3}} \approx -\frac{3}{2}(2.6789385) \approx -4.018408 \tag{15.38}$$

$$\vdots$$

Application 6. We now find the value of $\left(\pm\frac{1}{5}\right)!$, $\left(\pm\frac{2}{5}\right)!$, $\left(\pm\frac{3}{5}\right)!$, $\left(\pm\frac{4}{5}\right)!$. As before, we make repeated use of Equation 15.2

$$\frac{(a+b)!}{a!b!} = 1 + \frac{a^{(1)}b^{(1)}}{1!^2} + \frac{a^{(2)}b^{(2)}}{2!^2} + \frac{a^{(3)}b^{(3)}}{3!^2} + \cdots \tag{15.2}$$

We distinguish the following 11 cases.

Application 6a. Let $a = \frac{16}{5}$, $b = \frac{16}{5}$ in Statement 15.2. Then, defining d by means of,

$$d = \frac{\frac{32}{5}!}{\left(\frac{16}{5}!\right)^2} = 1 + \left(\frac{16}{5}\right)^2 + \left(\frac{16\cdot 11}{5\cdot 10}\right)^2 + \left(\frac{16\cdot 11\cdot 6}{5\cdot 10\cdot 15}\right)^2 + \cdots$$

$$\approx 25.61796082$$

we find, in view of Equation 11.2,

$$d = \frac{\frac{32}{5}\cdot\frac{27}{5}\left(\frac{22}{5}!\right)}{\left(\frac{16}{5}\right)^2\left(\frac{11}{5}!\right)^2} = \frac{\frac{32}{5}\cdot\frac{27}{5}\cdot\frac{22}{5}\cdot\frac{17}{5}\left(\frac{12}{5}!\right)}{\left(\frac{16}{5}\cdot\frac{11}{5}\right)^2\left(\frac{6}{5}!\right)^2} = \frac{\frac{32}{5}\cdot\frac{27}{5}\cdot\frac{22}{5}\cdot\frac{17}{5}\cdot\frac{12}{5}\cdot\frac{7}{5}\left(\frac{2}{5}!\right)}{\left(\frac{16}{5}\cdot\frac{11}{5}\cdot\frac{6}{5}\right)^2\left(\frac{1}{5}!\right)^2}$$

$$d = \frac{32\cdot 27\cdot 22\cdot 17\cdot 12\cdot 7}{(16\cdot 11\cdot 6)^2}\cdot\frac{\frac{2}{5}!}{\left(\frac{1}{5}!\right)^2}$$

Define d' and D by means of

$$d' = \frac{32\cdot 27\cdot 22\cdot 17\cdot 12\cdot 7}{(16\cdot 11\cdot 6)^2} \approx 24.34090910$$

and

$$D = \frac{\frac{2}{5}!}{\left(\frac{1}{5}!\right)^2}$$

Then $d = d'D$ and

$$D = \frac{\frac{2}{5}!}{\left(\frac{1}{5}!\right)^2} = \frac{d}{d'} \approx 1.05246525 \tag{15.39}$$

Application 6b. Consider $a = \frac{16}{5}$, $b = \frac{17}{5}$. Then, as in Application 6a, we find

$$e'E = e$$

where

$$e = \frac{\frac{33}{5}!}{\left(\frac{16}{5}!\right)\left(\frac{17}{5}!\right)} = 1 + \frac{\frac{16}{5} \cdot \frac{17}{5}}{1!^2} + \frac{\left(\frac{16}{5} \cdot \frac{11}{5}\right)\left(\frac{17}{5} \cdot \frac{12}{5}\right)}{2!^2} + \cdots \approx 28.93611810$$

$$e' = \frac{33 \cdot 28 \cdot 23 \cdot 18 \cdot 13 \cdot 8}{(16 \cdot 11 \cdot 6)(17 \cdot 12 \cdot 7)} \approx 26.38235294$$

$$E = \frac{\frac{3}{5}!}{\left(\frac{1}{5}!\right)\left(\frac{2}{5}!\right)} = \frac{e}{e'} \approx 1.09679823 \tag{15.40}$$

Application 6c. Consider $a = \frac{16}{5}$, $b = \frac{18}{5}$. As in Application 6a, we now find

$$f'F = f$$

where

$$f = \frac{\frac{34}{5}!}{\left(\frac{16}{5}!\right)\left(\frac{18}{5}!\right)} = 1 + \frac{\frac{16}{5} \cdot \frac{18}{5}}{1!^2} + \frac{\left(\frac{16}{5} \cdot \frac{11}{5}\right)\left(\frac{18}{5} \cdot \frac{13}{5}\right)}{2!^2} + \cdots \approx 32.53469091$$

$$f' = \frac{34 \cdot 29 \cdot 24 \cdot 19 \cdot 14 \cdot 9}{(16 \cdot 11 \cdot 6)(18 \cdot 13 \cdot 8)} \approx 28.65777973$$

$$F = \frac{\frac{4}{5}!}{\left(\frac{1}{5}!\right)\left(\frac{3}{5}!\right)} = \frac{f}{f'} \approx 1.13528303 \tag{15.41}$$

Application 6d. Consider $a = \frac{16}{5}$, $b = \frac{19}{5}$. Then

$$g'G = g$$

where

$$g = \frac{7!}{\frac{16}{5}!\frac{19}{5}!} = 1 + \frac{\frac{16}{5} \cdot \frac{19}{5}}{1!^2} + \frac{\left(\frac{16}{5} \cdot \frac{11}{5}\right)\left(\frac{19}{5} \cdot \frac{14}{5}\right)}{2!^2} + \cdots \approx 36.42598699$$

$$g' = \frac{5^6 \cdot 7 \cdot 6 \cdot 5 \cdot 4 \cdot 3 \cdot 2}{(16 \cdot 11 \cdot 6)(19 \cdot 14 \cdot 9)} \approx 31.15031898$$

$$G = \frac{1}{\left(\frac{1}{5}!\right)\left(\frac{4}{5}!\right)} = \frac{g}{g'} \approx 1.16936161 \tag{15.42}$$

Application 6e. Consider $a = \frac{17}{5}$, $b = \frac{17}{5}$:

$$h'H = h$$

where

$$h = \frac{\frac{34}{5}!}{\left(\frac{17}{5}!\right)^2} = 1 + \frac{\left(\frac{17}{5}\right)^2}{1!^2} + \frac{\left(\frac{17}{5} \cdot \frac{12}{5}\right)^2}{2!^2} + \cdots \approx 32.86843388$$

$$h' = \frac{34 \cdot 29 \cdot 24 \cdot 19 \cdot 14 \cdot 9}{(17 \cdot 12 \cdot 7)^2} \approx 27.78151261$$

$$H = \frac{\frac{4}{5}!}{\left(\frac{2}{5}!\right)^2} = \frac{h}{h'} \approx 1.18310455 \tag{15.43}$$

Application 6f. Consider $a = \frac{17}{5}$, $b = \frac{18}{5}$:

$$j'J = j$$

where

$$j = \frac{7!}{\left(\frac{17}{5}!\right)\left(\frac{18}{5}!\right)} = 1 + \frac{\frac{17}{5} \cdot \frac{18}{5}}{1!^2} + \frac{\left(\frac{17}{5} \cdot \frac{12}{5}\right)\left(\frac{18}{5} \cdot \frac{13}{5}\right)}{2!^2} + \cdots \approx 37.15880353$$

$$j' = \frac{5^6 \cdot 7 \cdot 6 \cdot 5 \cdot 4 \cdot 3 \cdot 2}{(17 \cdot 12 \cdot 7)(18 \cdot 13 \cdot 8)} \approx 29.45889895$$

$$J = \frac{1}{\left(\frac{2}{5}!\right)\left(\frac{3}{5}!\right)} = \frac{j}{j'} \approx 1.26137788 \tag{15.44}$$

Application 6g. Consider $a = \frac{17}{5}$, $b = \frac{19}{5}$:

$$k'K = k$$

where

$$k = \frac{\frac{36}{5}!}{\left(\frac{17}{5}!\right)\left(\frac{19}{5}!\right)} = 1 + \frac{\frac{17}{5} \cdot \frac{19}{5}}{1!^2} + \frac{\left(\frac{17}{5} \cdot \frac{12}{5}\right)\left(\frac{19}{5} \cdot \frac{14}{5}\right)}{2!^2} + \cdots \approx 41.82533846$$

$$k' = \frac{36 \cdot 31 \cdot 26 \cdot 21 \cdot 16 \cdot 11 \cdot 6}{5(17 \cdot 12 \cdot 7)(19 \cdot 14 \cdot 9)} \approx 37.64422822$$

$$K = \frac{\frac{1}{5}!}{\left(\frac{2}{5}!\right)\left(\frac{4}{5}!\right)} = \frac{k}{k'} \approx 1.11106909 \tag{15.45}$$

Application 6h. Consider $a = \frac{18}{5}$, $b = \frac{18}{5}$:

$$l'L = l$$

where

$$l = \frac{\frac{36}{5}!}{\left(\frac{18}{5}!\right)^2} = 1 + \frac{\left(\frac{18}{5}\right)^2}{1!^2} + \frac{\left(\frac{18}{5} \cdot \frac{13}{5}\right)^2}{2!^2} + \cdots \approx 42.23354446$$

$$l' = \frac{36 \cdot 31 \cdot 26 \cdot 21 \cdot 16 \cdot 11 \cdot 6}{5\,(18 \cdot 13 \cdot 8)^2} \approx 36.72307693$$

$$L = \frac{\frac{1}{5}!}{\left(\frac{3}{5}!\right)^2} = \frac{l}{l'} \approx 1.15005463 \tag{15.46}$$

Application 6i. Consider $a = \frac{18}{5}$, $b = \frac{19}{5}$:

$$m'M = m$$

where

$$m = \frac{\frac{37}{5}!}{\left(\frac{18}{5}!\right)\left(\frac{19}{5}!\right)} = 1 + \frac{\frac{18}{5} \cdot \frac{19}{5}}{1!^2} + \frac{\left(\frac{18}{5} \cdot \frac{13}{5}\right)\left(\frac{19}{5} \cdot \frac{14}{5}\right)}{2!^2} + \cdots \approx 47.78465423$$

$$m' = \frac{37 \cdot 32 \cdot 27 \cdot 22 \cdot 17 \cdot 12 \cdot 7}{5\,(18 \cdot 13 \cdot 8)\,(19 \cdot 14 \cdot 9)} \approx 44.81943321$$

$$M = \frac{\frac{2}{5}!}{\left(\frac{3}{5}!\right)\left(\frac{4}{5}!\right)} = \frac{m}{m'} \approx 1.06615927 \tag{15.47}$$

Application 6j. Consider $a = \frac{19}{5}$, $b = \frac{19}{5}$:

$$n'N = n$$

where

$$n = \frac{\frac{38}{5}!}{\left(\frac{19}{5}!\right)^2} = 1 + \frac{\left(\frac{19}{5}\right)^2}{1!^2} + \frac{\left(\frac{19}{5} \cdot \frac{14}{5}\right)^2}{2!^2} + \cdots \approx 54.33949985$$

$$n' = \frac{38 \cdot 33 \cdot 28 \cdot 23 \cdot 18 \cdot 13 \cdot 8}{5\,(19 \cdot 14 \cdot 9)^2} \approx 52.75588973$$

$$N = \frac{\frac{3}{5}!}{\left(\frac{4}{5}!\right)^2} = \frac{n}{n'} \approx 1.03001769 \tag{15.48}$$

Application 6k. Finally, we find the values of $\frac{1}{5}!$, $\frac{2}{5}!$, $\frac{3}{5}!$, $\frac{4}{5}!$. Refer to Equations 15.39–15.48 (and multiply as indicated) to obtain the following formulas for $\frac{1}{5}!$, $\frac{2}{5}!$, $\frac{3}{5}!$, $\frac{4}{5}!$:

$$\frac{1}{\left(\frac{1}{5}!\right)^5} = DEFG = DE^2FM = DEF^2N \tag{15.49}$$

$$\frac{1}{\left(\frac{2}{5}!\right)^5} = EHJK = EFHK^2 = E^2HKL \qquad (15.50)$$

$$\frac{1}{\left(\frac{3}{5}!\right)^5} = FJLM = FHLM^2 = F^2KLM \qquad (15.51)$$

$$\frac{1}{\left(\frac{4}{5}!\right)^5} = GKMN = EKM^2N = DK^2MN \qquad (15.52)$$

Thus each of $\frac{1}{5}!$, $\frac{2}{5}!$, $\frac{3}{5}!$, $\frac{4}{5}!$ may be calculated in three independent ways, because each of D, E, F, G, H, J, K, L, M, N is known from Equations 15.39–15.48. It is noteworthy that when the calculations are carried out by means of Equations 15.39–15.52 the three values for each of $\frac{1}{5}!$, $\frac{2}{5}!$, $\frac{3}{5}!$, $\frac{4}{5}!$ agree to eight significant places. The final results are

$$\frac{1}{5}! \approx 0.91816874$$

$$\frac{2}{5}! \approx 0.88726382$$

$$\frac{3}{5}! \approx 0.89351535$$

$$\frac{4}{5}! \approx 0.93138377$$

presumably all correct to eight decimal places. The values of $\left(-\frac{1}{5}\right)!$, $\left(-\frac{2}{5}\right)!$, $\left(-\frac{3}{5}\right)!$, and $\left(-\frac{4}{5}\right)!$ are now readily obtained by means of Equation 11.2.

We began with an introduction and, because of the unusual nature of the factorial function and its relative neglect in the high school curriculum, we offer it here as a "great idea" for enhancing the instruction of mathematics.

CORWIN
PRESS

The Corwin Press logo—a raven striding across an open book—represents the happy union of courage and learning. We are a professional-level publisher of books and journals for K–12 educators, and we are committed to creating and providing resources that embody these qualities. Corwin's motto is "Success for All Learners."